Blairsville Junior High School
Blairsville, Pennsylvania

The
Golden Book
of
Quotations

The Golden Book of Quotations

FROM THE PENGUIN DICTIONARY OF QUOTATIONS

BY J. M. AND M. J. COHEN

ADAPTED BY ANN REIT

ILLUSTRATED BY JAMES SPANFELLER

FOREWORD BY LOUIS UNTERMEYER

Golden Press ✦ New York

Editor's Note

In order to save space, some abbreviations have been used throughout this book. They are as follows:

Attr.	Attributed
c.	from the Latin *circa* meaning *about*
Cent.	Century
Chap.	Chapter
Fl.	Flourished
Ib.	from the Latin *ibidem* meaning *in the same place*. In this book it means from the same source as the entry above
No.	Number
Para.	Paragraph
Pt.	Part
Sc.	Scene
Sect.	Section
Transl.	Translated
Vol.	Volume

The Index for this book begins on page 122 where you will find detailed instructions for its use. This index includes not only every quotation in the book, but also almost any subject you might wish to look up.

LIBRARY OF CONGRESS CATALOG CARD NUMBER: 64-24088

FOREWORD

HOW many of the following phrases have you heard before?

"Know thyself"..."Don't count your chickens before they're hatched" ..."To every thing there is a season and a time to every purpose"... "Blessed are the peace-makers"..."Should auld acquaintance be forgot" ..."Curiouser and curiouser"..."Blood, toil, tears, and sweat"..."God moves in a mysterious way"..."Survival of the fittest"..."All for one, one for all"..."God bless us every one"..."Hitch your wagon to a star"... "Never leave that till tomorrow which you can do today"..."The only thing we have to fear is fear itself"..."A thing of beauty is a joy forever" ..."With malice toward none; with charity for all"..."Necessity, who is the mother of invention"..."Hope springs eternal in the human breast"... "This above all: to thine own self be true"...

You have surely heard some of these quotations. You will hear them many times again. They have become part of the language; they will become part of your own speech. They are among the finest and most profound thoughts we know.

The pages of this book are composed of such famous words and hundreds of others like them.

Where did they originate? They came from many lands and many languages, as you can see from turning these pages. Some were expressed by the ancient Greeks; some by the prophets of the Old Testament and the New Testament saints; others by such English poets as Shakespeare and Pope and Keats, by statesmen like Lincoln and Roosevelt and Churchill, by philosophers and tellers of fables.

This, then, is a book of golden thoughts. Moreover, they are thoughts which are usable as well as memorable. It is a book for valuable references, but it is also a book for browsing, for constant surprises. You will find you have said many of these lines at various times, perhaps without knowing their sources, and you will say them again and again without realizing they are quotations. They will fit into your talk. Although they are words and ideas which other minds have shaped, they will seem to be your own thoughts, your own way of speaking. All of us need them; we cannot do without them. You, too, will make them yours.

Louis Untermeyer

Louis Untermeyer

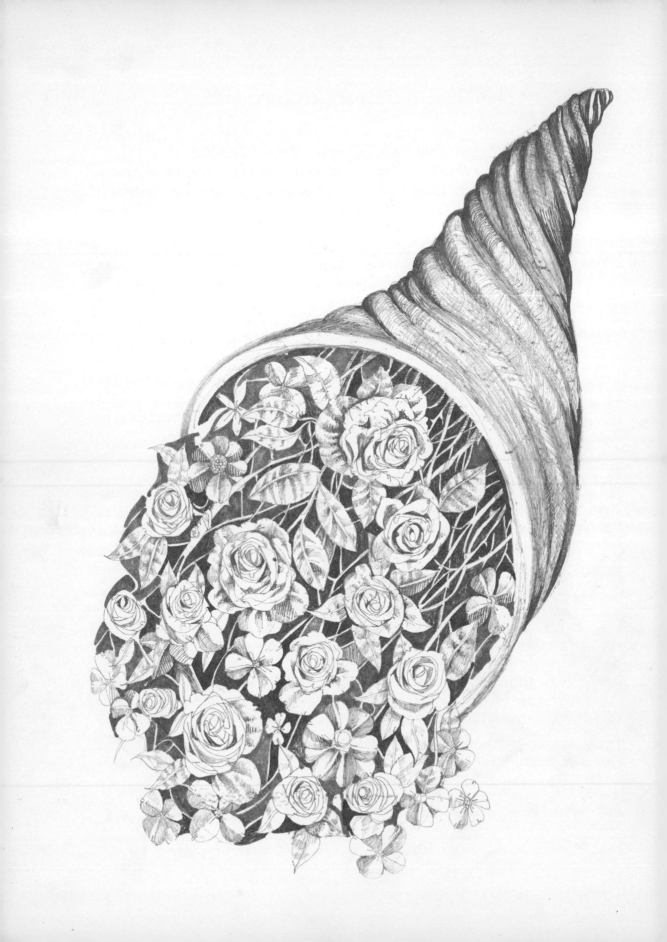

JOHN ACTON 1834–1902

Power tends to corrupt, and absolute power corrupts absolutely. Great men are always bad men.
(*Historical Essays and Studies*, Appendix)

FRANKLIN PIERCE ADAMS
1881–1960

The rich man has his motor car,
His country and his town estate.
He smokes a fifty-cent cigar
And jeers at Fate. (*The Rich Man*)

Yet though my lamp burns low and dim,
Though I must slave for livelihood—
Think you that I would change with him?
You bet I would! (*Ib.*)

HENRY ADAMS 1838–1918

For two hundred years, every Adams, from father to son, had lived within sight of State Street, and sometimes had lived in it, yet none had ever taken kindly to the town, or been taken kindly by it. (*The Education of Henry Adams*, Chap. 1)

JOHN ADAMS 1735–1826

The second day of July, 1776, will be the most memorable epoch in the history of America. I am apt to believe that it will be celebrated by succeeding generations as the great anniversary festival. (Letter to Mrs. Adams, July 3, 1776)

I pray Heaven to bestow the best of blessings on this House and all that shall hereafter inhabit it. May none but honest and wise men ever rule under this roof. (By John Adams, who was the first tenant of the White House; later inscribed in State Dining Room by Franklin D. Roosevelt)

SAMUEL ADAMS 1722–1803

A nation of shopkeepers are very seldom so disinterested. (Speech said to have been made at Philadelphia, 1776)

GEORGE ADE 1866–1944

Anybody can win, unless there happens to be a second entry. (*Dictionary of Humorous Quotations*)

The music teacher came twice each week to bridge the awful gap between Dorothy and Chopin. (*Ib.*)

Draw your salary before Spending it. (*Forty Modern Fables*, "The People's Choice")

JOSEPH ADDISON 1672–1719

From hence, let fierce contending nations
    know
What dire effects from civil discord flow.
(*Cato*, Act V. Sc. iv)

Music, the greatest good that mortals know,
And all of heaven we have below. (*Song for St. Cecelia's Day*)

In all thy humours, whether grave or mellow,
Thou'rt such a touchy, testy, pleasant fellow;
Hast so much wit, and mirth, and spleen
    about thee,

There is no living with thee nor without thee. (*The Spectator*)

Sunday clears away the rust of the whole week. (*Ib.*)

A woman seldom asks advice before she has bought her wedding clothes. (*Ib.*)

MAX ADELER   1847–1915

We have lost our little Hanner in a very painful manner. (*Little Hanner*)

Willie had a purple monkey climbing on a
    yellow stick,
And when he sucked the paint all off, it
    made him deathly sick.
(*The Purple Monkey*)

AESOP   *fl. c.* 550 B.C.

Beware that you do not lose the substance by grasping at the shadow. (*Fables*, "The Dog and the Shadow")

I am sure the grapes are sour. (*Ib.* "The Fox and the Grapes")

Thinking to get at once all the gold that the goose could give, he killed it, and opened it only to find—nothing. (*Ib.* "The Goose with the Golden Eggs")

The gods help them that help themselves. (*Ib.* "Hercules and the Waggoner")

It is not only fine feathers that make fine birds. (*Ib.* "The Jay and the Peacock")

While I see many hoof-marks going in, I see none coming out. (*Ib.* "The Lion, the Fox, and the Beasts")

I will have nothing to do with a man who can blow hot and cold with the same breath. (*Ib.* "The Man and the Satyr")

Don't count your chickens before they are hatched. (*Ib.* "The Milkmaid and Her Pail")

The boy cried "Wolf, wolf!" and the villagers came out to help him. (*Fables*, "The Shepherd's Boy")

Only cowards insult dying majesty. (*Ib.* "The Sick Lion")

The lamb that belonged to the sheep whose skin the wolf was wearing began to follow the wolf in sheep's clothing. (*Ib.* "The Wolf in Sheep's Clothing")

ALEXANDER THE GREAT   356–323 B.C.

I am dying with the help of too many physicians. (Quoted in *Treasury of Humorous Quotations*)

ABBÉ D'ALLAINVAL   1700–1753

L'embarras des Richesses.—An Embarrassment of Riches. (Title of play)

WILLIAM ALLEN   1806–1879

Fifty-four forty, or fight. (Campaign cry of James K. Polk)

WILLIAM ALLINGHAM   1828–1889

Up the airy mountain,
Down the rushy glen,
We daren't go a-hunting,
For fear of little men. (*The Fairies*)

Four ducks on a pond,
A grass-bank beyond,
A blue sky of spring,
White clouds on the wing:
What a little thing
To remember for years—
To remember with tears! (*A Memory*)

ST. AMBROSE   337–397

When in Rome, live as the Romans do; when elsewhere, live as they live elsewhere. (Advice to St. Augustine, quoted by Jeremy Taylor)

HANS CHRISTIAN ANDERSEN
1805–1875

"But the Emperor has nothing at all on!" said a little child. (*The Emperor's New Clothes*)

The Ugly Duckling. (Title of story)

ANONYMOUS

Poems

Sumer is icumen in.
Lhude sing cuccu!
Groweth sed and bloweth med
And springth the wude nu. (*Sumer is Icumen In*. 13 Cent.)

If all the world were paper,
And all the sea were ink,
And all the trees were bread and cheese,
What should we do for drink? (*If All the World Were Paper*. 17 Cent.)

In his chamber, weak and dying,
While the Norman Baron lay,
Loud, without, his men were crying,
"Shorter hours and better pay." (*A Strike among the Poets*. 19 Cent.)

Rhymes, Catches, and Epigrams

He that fights and runs away
May live to fight another day. (*Musarum Deliciae*. 17 Cent.)

Here we come gathering nuts in May,
Nuts in May,
On a cold and frosty morning. (*Here We Come Gathering Nuts in May*)

I slept and dreamed that life was beauty;
I woke and found that life was duty. (*Duty. 19 Cent.*)

Little Willie from his mirror
Licked the mercury right off,
Thinking, in his childish error,
It would cure the whooping cough.
At the funeral his mother
Smartly said to Mrs. Brown:
" 'Twas a chilly day for Willie
When the mercury went down." (*Willie's Epitaph*)

Lizzie Borden took an axe
And gave her mother forty whacks;
When she saw what she had done,
She gave her father forty-one! (*On an American trial of the 1890s*)

The noble Duke of York,
He had ten thousand men,
He marched them up to the top of the hill,
And he marched them down again.
And when they were up, they were up,
And when they were down, they were down,
And when they were only half way up,
They were neither up nor down. (*The Noble Duke of York. 18 Cent.*)

Now I lay me down to sleep;
I pray the Lord my soul to keep.
If I should die before I wake,
I pray the Lord my soul to take. (*Prayer. 18 Cent.*)

There was a young lady of Riga,
Who rode with a smile on a tiger;
They returned from the ride
With the lady inside,
And the smile on the face of the tiger. (*Limerick*)

Thirty days hath September,
April, June, and November;
All the rest have thirty-one,

Excepting February alone,
And that has twenty-eight days clear
And twenty-nine in each leap-year. (*Stevens MS. [c. 1555]*)

Greek

Know thyself. (*Written in the temple at Delphi*)

Nothing to excess. (*Written in the temple at Delphi, according to Plato's Protagoras*)

Latin

Hail Caesar, those about to die salute you. (*Gladiators' salute on entering the arena*)

Let us live then and be glad
While young life's before us. (*Medieval students' song*)

French

They shall not pass. (Watchword during defense of Verdun, 1916)

Liberté! Égalité! Fraternité!—Liberty! Equality! Fraternity! (Phrase used in the French Revolution, but actually earlier in origin)

The king is dead, long live the king. (Phrase used by the heralds to proclaim the death of one French king and the coming to the throne of his successor. First used in 1461)

SUSAN B. ANTHONY   1820–1906

Modern invention has banished the spinning-wheel, and the same law of progress makes the woman of to-day a different woman from her grandmother.

APPIUS CAECUS   4 Cent. B.C.

Each man the architect of his own fate. (Quoted by Sallust, *De Civitate*, I. 2)

ARCHIMEDES   287–212 B.C.

Eureka!—I have found it! (On making a discovery)

Give me a firm spot on which to stand, and I will move the earth. (On the lever)

LUDOVICO ARIOSTO   1474–1533

Nature made him, and then broke the mold. (*Orlando Furioso*, Canto X. Stanza 84)

ARISTOTLE   384–322 B.C.

Poetry is more philosophical and of higher value than history. (*Poetics*, Chap. 9)

Man is by nature a political animal. (*Politics*, Book I)

Even when laws have been written down, they ought not always to remain unaltered. (*Ib.* Book II)

JOHN ARMSTRONG   1709–1779

Distrust yourself, and sleep before you fight. 'Tis not too late tomorrow to be brave. (*The Art of Preserving Health*, Book IV. Line 457)

MATTHEW ARNOLD   1822–1888

And we forget because we must
And not because we will. (*Absence*)

And we are here as on a darkling plain
Swept with confused alarms of struggle and flight,
Where ignorant armies clash by night. (*Dover Beach*)

Where the great whales come sailing by,
Sail and sail, with unshut eye. (*The Forsaken Merman*)

Let the long contention cease!
Geese are swans, and swans are geese. (*The Last Word*)

SAMUEL J. ARNOLD   1774–1852

For England, home, and beauty. (*The Death of Nelson*)

WYSTAN HUGH AUDEN   1907–

A professor is one who talks in someone else's sleep. (Quoted in *Treasury of Humorous Quotations*)

Law, say the gardeners, is the sun,
Law is the one
All gardeners obey
Tomorrow, yesterday, today. (*Law, Say the Gardeners, Is the Sun*)

ST. AUGUSTINE   354–430

Thou hast created us for Thyself, and our heart is not quiet until it rests in Thee. (*Confessions*, Book I)

Hear the other side. (*De Duabus Animabus*, XIV. 2)

MARCUS AURELIUS ANTONINUS
121–180

And thou wilt give thyself relief, if thou doest every act of thy life as if it were the last. (*Meditations*, Book II. Para. 5)

Time is like a river made up of the events which happen, and its current is strong; no sooner does anything appear than it is swept away, and another comes in its place, and will be swept away too. (*Ib.* Book IV. Para. 43)

Nothing happens to any man that he is not formed by nature to bear. (*Ib.* Book V. Para. 18)

Remember that to change your mind and follow him who sets you right is to be none the less free than you were before. (*Ib.* Book VIII. Para. 16)

JANE AUSTEN 1775–1817

One half of the world cannot understand the pleasures of the other. (*Emma*, Chap. 9)

Human nature is so well disposed towards those who are in interesting situations, that a young person, who either marries or dies, is sure to be kindly spoken of. (*Ib.* Chap. 22)

It is a truth universally acknowledged, that a single man in possession of a good fortune, must be in want of a wife. (*Pride and Prejudice*, Chap. 1)

She was a woman of mean understanding, little information, and uncertain temper. (*Ib.*)

One cannot be always laughing at a man without now and then stumbling on something witty. (*Ib.* Chap. 40)

FRANCIS BACON 1561–1626

They are ill discoverers that think there is no land, when they can see nothing but sea. (*The Advancement of Learning*, Book II)

Hope is a good breakfast, but it is a bad supper. (*Apothegms*, No. 36)

What is truth? said jesting Pilate; and would not stay for an answer. (*Essays*, "Of Truth")

It is not the lie that passeth through the mind, but the lie that sinketh in and settleth in it, that doth the hurt. (*Ib.*)

A man that studieth revenge keeps his own wounds green. (*Ib.* "Of Revenge")

He was reputed one of the wise men that made answer to the question, when a man should marry? "A young man not yet, an elder man not at all." (*Ib.* "Of Marriage and Single Life")

Set it down to thyself, as well to create good precedents as to follow them. (*Ib.* "Of Great Place")

If the hill will not come to Mahomet, Mahomet will go to the hill. (*Ib.*)

In charity there is no excess. (*Ib.* "Of Goodness and Goodness of Nature")

If a man be gracious and courteous to strangers, it shows he is a citizen of the world. (*Ib.*)

The remedy is worse than the disease. (*Ib.* "Of Seditions and Trouble")

Certainly it is the nature of extreme self-lovers, as they will set an house on fire, and it were but to roast their eggs. (*Ib.* "Of Wisdom for a Man's Self")

He that will not apply new remedies must expect new evils; for time is the greatest innovator. (*Ib.* "Of Innovations")

Some books are to be tasted, others to be swallowed, and some few to be chewed and digested. (*Ib.* "Of Studies")

I have taken all knowledge to be my province. (Letter to Lord Burleigh, 1592)

EDWARD BANGS *fl.* 1775

Yankee Doodle, keep it up,
Yankee Doodle dandy;
Mind the music and the step,
And with the girls be handy.

Yankee Doodle came to town,
Riding on a pony;
Stuck a feather in his cap
And called it Macaroni.
(Yankee Doodle)

REV. RICHARD BARHAM   1788–1845

They were a little less than "kin," and rather more than "kind." (*Nell Cook*)

She drank prussic acid without any water, And died like a Duke-and-a-Duchess's daughter! (*The Tragedy*)

SABINE BARING-GOULD   1834–1924

Now the day is over, Night is drawing nigh, Shadows of the evening Steal across the sky. (Hymn)

Birds and beasts and flowers Soon will be asleep. (*Ib.*)

Onward, Christian soldiers, Marching as to war, With the Cross of Jesus Going on before. (Hymn)

PHINEAS T. BARNUM   1810–1891

There's a sucker born every minute. (Attr.)

SIR JAMES BARRIE   1860–1937

When the first baby laughed for the first time, the laugh broke into a thousand pieces and they all went skipping about, and that was the beginning of fairies. (*Peter Pan*, Act I)

Every time a child says "I don't believe in fairies," there's a little fairy somewhere that falls down dead. (*Ib.*)

But the gladness of her gladness And the sadness of her sadness Are as nothing, Charles, To the badness of her badness when she's bad. (*Rosalind*)

BERNARD BARUCH   1870–

We are in the midst of a cold war that is getting warmer. (Before Senate Committee, 1948)

KATHARINE LEE BATES   1859–1929

America! America! God shed his grace on thee And crown thy good with brotherhood From sea to shining sea! (*America the Beautiful*)

FRANCIS BEAUMONT   1584–1616
and JOHN FLETCHER   1579–1625

You are no better than you should be. (*The Coxcomb*, Act IV. Sc. iii)

As men Do walk a mile, women should talk an hour, After supper. 'Tis their exercise. (*Philaster*, Act II. Sc. iv)

THE VENERABLE BEDE   673–735

When we compare the present life of man with that time of which we have no knowledge, it seems to me like the swift flight of a lone sparrow through the banqueting-hall where you sit in the winter months. . . . This sparrow flies swiftly in through one door of the hall, and out through another. . . . Similarly, man appears on earth for a little while, but we know nothing of what went on before this life, and what follows. (*History of the English Church and People*, Book 2. Chap. 13)

BERNARD BEE   1823–1861

There is Jackson standing like a stone wall. (At first battle of Bull Run, 1861)

HENRY WARD BEECHER   1813–1887

Flowers have an expression of countenance as much as men or animals. Some seem to smile; some have a sad expression; some are pensive and diffident; others again are plain, honest and upright, like the broad-faced sunflower and the hollyhock. (*Star Papers*, "A Discourse of Flowers," Pt. II. No. 21)

Nothing marks the increasing wealth of our times and the growth of the public mind toward refinement, more than the demand for books. (*Star Papers*, "Book-Stores, Books," Pt. II. No. 21)

MAX BEERBOHM 1872–1956

I believe the twenty-four hour day has come to stay. (*A Christmas Garland*, "Perkins and Mankind")

Most women are not so young as they are painted. (*A Defence of Cosmetics*)

Strange, when you come to think of it, that of all the countless folk who have lived before our time on this planet not one is known in history or in legend as having died of laughter.
(*And Even Now*, "Laughter")

APHRA BEHN 1640–1689

Faith, sir, we are here, today, and gone tomorrow. (*The Lucky Chance*, Act IV)

Variety is the soul of pleasure. (*The Rover*, Pt. 2. Act I)

Come away; poverty's catching. (*Ib.*)

Money speaks sense in a language all nations understand. (*Ib.* Pt. 2. Act III)

ALEXANDER GRAHAM BELL 1847–1922

Mr. Watson, come here; I want you. (First sentence spoken over the telephone, March 10, 1876)

HILAIRE BELLOC 1870–1953

I shoot the Hippopotamus
With bullets made of platinum
Because if I use leaden ones
His hide is sure to flatten 'em. (*Bad Child's Book of Beasts*, "The Hippopotamus")

The chief defect of Henry King
Was chewing little bits of string. (*Cautionary Tales*, "Henry King")

Matilda told such dreadful lies,
It made one gasp and stretch one's eyes;
Her aunt, who, from her earliest youth,
Had kept a strict regard for truth,
Attempted to believe Matilda:
The effort very nearly killed her.
(*Ib.* "Matilda")

A trick that everyone abhors
In little girls is slamming doors.
(*Ib.* "Rebecca")

When I am dead, I hope it may be said:
"His sins were scarlet, but his books were
   read." (*Epigrams*, "On His Books")

ROBERT BENCHLEY 1889–1945

The biggest obstacle to professional writing today is the necessity for changing a typewriter ribbon. (*Chips Off the Old Benchley*, "Learn to Write")

A dog teaches a boy fidelity, perseverance, and to turn around three times before lying down. (*Your Boy and His Dog*)

Drawing on my fine command of language, I said nothing. (*Dictionary of Humorous Quotations*)

Daniel Boone

STEPHEN VINCENT BENÉT   1898–1943

If two New Hampshiremen aren't a match for the devil, we might as well give the country back to the Indians. *(13 O'Clock, The Devil and Daniel Webster)*

Lincoln, six feet one in his stocking feet,
The lank man, knotty and tough as a
   hickory rail,
Whose hands were always too big for white-
   kid gloves,
Whose wit was a coonskin sack of dry, tall
   tales,
Whose weathered face was homely as a
   plowed field. *(John Brown's Body, Book 2)*

When Daniel Boone goes by at night
The phantom deer arise
And all lost, wild America
Is burning in their eyes. *(Daniel Boone, 1797–1889)*

WILLIAM ROSE BENÉT   1886–1950

Jesse James was a two-gun man,
   (Roll on, Missouri!)
Strong-arm chief of an outlaw clan,
   (From Kansas to Illinois!)
He twirled an old Colt forty-five;
   (Roll on, Missouri!)
They never took Jesse James alive.
   (Roll, Missouri, roll!) *(Jesse James)*

ARNOLD BENNETT   1867–1931

"Ye can call it influenza if ye like," said Mrs. Machin. "There was no influenza in my young days. We called a cold a cold." *(The Card, Chap. 8)*

Pessimism, when you get used to it, is just as agreeable as optimism. *(Things That Have Interested Me, "The Slump in Pessimism")*

Journalists say a thing that they know isn't true, in the hope that if they keep on saying it long enough it *will* be true. *(The Title, II)*

HENRY HOLCOMB BENNETT   1863–1924

  Hats off!
Along the street there comes
A blare of bugles, a ruffle of drums,
A flash of color beneath the sky:
  Hats off!
The flag is passing by! *(The Flag Goes By)*

JEREMY BENTHAM   1748–1832

The greatest happiness of the greatest number is the foundation of morals and legislation. *(The Commonplace Book)*

EDMUND CLERIHEW BENTLEY
1875–1956

Geography is about maps,
But Biography is about chaps. *(Biography for Beginners)*

Sir Christopher Wren
Said, "I am going to dine with some men,
If anybody calls
Say I am designing St Paul's." *(Ib. "Sir Christopher Wren")*

UGO BETTI   1892–1953

Everyone has, inside himself . . . what shall I call it? A piece of good news! Everyone is . . . a very great, very important character! *(The Burnt Flower-Bed, Act III)*

JACOB BEULER   19 Cent.

If I had a donkey wot wouldn't go,
D'ye think I'd wollop him? no, no, no. (Song [c. 1822])

WILLIAM, LORD BEVERIDGE   1879–

The object of government in peace and in war is not the glory of rulers or of races, but the happiness of the common man. *(Social Insurance)*

THE BIBLE

OLD TESTAMENT

Genesis

In the beginning God created the heaven and the earth.

And the earth was without form, and void; and darkness was upon the face of the deep. (1:1)

And God said, Let there be light: and there was light. (1:3)

So God created man in his own image, in the image of God created he him; male and female created he them. (1:27)

For dust thou art, and unto dust shalt thou return. (3:19)

Am I my brother's keeper? (4:9)

Dwelt in the land of Nod, on the east of Eden. (4:16)

There were giants in the earth in those days. (6:4)

Esau selleth his birthright for a mess of pottage. (25. Chapter heading in *Genevan Bible*)

Ye shall eat the fat of the land. (45:18)

Exodus

Behold, the bush burned with fire, and the bush was not consumed. (3:2)

A land flowing with milk and honey. (3:8)

Eye for eye, tooth for tooth, hand for hand, foot for foot. (21:24; also *Deuteronomy* 19:21)

Thou shalt love thy neighbour as thyself. (19:18; also *St. Matthew*, 19:19)

Numbers

The Lord bless thee, and keep thee.

The Lord make his face shine upon thee, and be gracious unto thee. (6:24)

Deuteronomy

Man doth not live by bread only, but by every word that proceedeth out of the mouth of the Lord doth man live. (8:3; also *St. Matthew*, 4:4 and *St. Luke*, 4:4 [with "alone" for "only"])

He kept him as the apple of his eye. (32:10)

As thy days, so shall thy strength be. (33:25)

Ruth

Whither thou goest, I will go; and where thou lodgest, I will lodge: thy people shall be my people, and thy God my God. (1:16)

1 Samuel

The Lord hath sought him a man after his own heart. (13:14)

Saul hath slain his thousands, and David his ten thousands. (18:7)

2 Samuel

How are the mighty fallen in the midst of the battle! (1:25)

Would God I had died for thee, O Absalom, my son, my son! (18:33)

Job

Man is born unto trouble, as the sparks fly upward. (5:7)

I am escaped with the skin of my teeth. (19:20)

Psalms

Out of the mouth of babes and sucklings hast thou ordained strength. (8:2)

Thou hast made him a little lower than the angels. (8:5)

Up, Lord, and let not man have the upper hand. (9:19, *Book of Common Prayer* version)

Let the words of my mouth, and the meditation of my heart, be acceptable in thy sight, O Lord. (19:14)

My God, my God, why hast thou forsaken me? (22:1; also *St. Matthew*, 27:46 and *St. Mark*, 15:34)

The Lord is my shepherd; I shall not want.
   He maketh me to lie down in green pastures: he leadeth me beside the still waters. (23:1)

Yea, though I walk through the valley of the shadow of death, I will fear no evil: for thou art with me; thy rod and thy staff they comfort me. (23:4)

The earth is the Lord's, and the fulness thereof; the world, and they that dwell therein. (24:1)

God is our refuge and strength, a very present help in trouble. (46:1)

O that I had wings like a dove! for then would I fly away, and be at rest. (55:6)

They were even hard at death's door. (107: 18, *Book of Common Prayer* version)

They that go down to the sea in ships, that do business in great waters.
   These see the works of the Lord, and his wonders in the deep. (107:23)

He raiseth up the poor out of the dust, and lifteth the needy out of the dunghill. (113:7)

The mountains skipped like rams, and the little hills like lambs. (114:4)

Thy word is a lamp unto my feet, and a light unto my path. (119:105)

I will lift up mine eyes unto the hills from whence cometh my help. (121:1)

Out of the depths have I cried unto thee, O Lord. (130:1)

Proverbs

Hope deferred maketh the heart sick. (13:12)

The way of trangressors is hard. (13:15)

He that spareth his rod hateth his son. (13:24)

A merry heart maketh a cheerful countenance. (15:13)

Better is a dinner of herbs where love is, than a stalled ox and hatred therewith. (15:17)

Pride goeth before destruction, and an haughty spirit before a fall. (16:18)

Even a child is known by his doings. (20:11)

A good name is rather to be chosen than great riches. (22:1)

Train up a child in the way he should go: and when he is old, he will not depart from it. (22:6)

The slothful man saith, There is a lion in the way; a lion is in the streets. (26:13)

Ecclesiastes

To every thing there is a season, and a time to every purpose under the heaven.
   A time to be born, and a time to die; a time to plant, and a time to pluck up that which is planted. (3:1)

The race is not to the swift, nor the battle to the strong. (9:11)

Cast thy bread upon the waters: for thou shalt find it after many days. (11:1)

Song of Solomon

Rise up, my love, my fair one, and come away.
   For, lo, the winter is past, the rain is over and gone;
   The flowers appear on the earth; the time of the singing of birds is come, and the voice of the turtle is heard in our land. (2:10)

Take us the foxes, the little foxes, that spoil the vines. (2:15)

Isaiah

They shall beat their swords into plowshares, and their spears into pruning-hooks: nation shall not lift up sword against nation, neither shall they learn war any more. (2:4; also *Micah,* 4:3 ["a sword" for "sword"])

The wolf also shall dwell with the lamb, and the leopard shall lie down with the kid; and the calf and the young lion and the fatling together; and a little child shall lead them. (11:6)

Jeremiah

Can the Ethiopian change his skin, or the leopard his spots? (13:23)

Ezekiel

The fathers have eaten sour grapes, and the children's teeth are set on edge. (18:2)

Joel

Multitudes in the valley of decision. (3:14)

Micah

What doth the Lord require of thee, but to do justly, and to love mercy, and to walk humbly with thy God? (6:8)

New Testament

St. Matthew

O generation of vipers, who hath warned you to flee from the wrath to come? (3:7)

Blessed are the poor in spirit: for theirs is the kingdom of heaven. (5:3)

Blessed are the pure in heart: for they shall see God.
    Blessed are the peacemakers: for they shall be called the children of God. (5:8)

Ye are the salt of the earth: but if the salt hath lost his savour, wherewith shall it be salted? (5:13)

Resist not evil: but whosoever shall smite thee on thy right cheek, turn to him the other also. (5:39)

Let not thy left hand know what thy right hand doeth. (6:3)

Give us this day our daily bread. (6:11)

No man can serve two masters. (6:24)

Consider the lilies of the field, how they grow; they toil not, neither do they spin:
    And yet I say unto you, that even Solomon in all his glory was not arrayed like one of these. (6:28)

Take therefore no thought for the morrow: for the morrow shall take thought for the things of itself. Sufficient unto the day is the evil thereof. (6:34)

Neither cast ye your pearls before swine. (7:6)

Beware of false prophets, which come to you in sheep's clothing, but inwardly they are ravening wolves. (7:15)

I came not to send peace, but a sword. (10:34)

Come unto me, all ye that labour and are heavy laden, and I will give you rest. (11:28)

A prophet is not without honour, save in his own country. (13:57)

Thou art Peter, and upon this rock I will build my church; and the gates of hell shall not prevail against it. (16:18)

Get thee behind me, Satan. (16:23)

If ye have faith as a grain of mustard seed, ye shall say unto this mountain, Remove hence to yonder place; and it shall remove. (17:20)

If thine eye offend thee, pluck it out. (18:9)

What therefore God hath joined together, let not man put asunder. (19:6)

Thou shalt love thy neighbour as thyself. (19:19)

It is easier for a camel to go through the eye of a needle, than for a rich man to enter into the kingdom of God. (19:24)

With God all things are possible. (19:26)

Out of the mouths of babes and sucklings thou hast perfected praise. (21:16)

Render therefore unto Caesar the things which are Caesar's; and unto God the things that are God's. (22:21)

Let this cup pass from me. (26:39)

Watch and pray, that ye enter not into temptation: the spirit indeed is willing, but the flesh is weak. (26:41)

My God, my God, why hast thou forsaken me? (27:46)

St. Mark

And if a house be divided against itself, that house cannot stand. (3:25)

Suffer the little children to come unto me, and forbid them not: for of such is the kingdom of heaven. (10:14)

St. Luke

Because there was no room for them in the inn. (2:7)

Glory to God in the highest, and on earth peace, good will toward men. (2:14)

Physician, heal thyself. (4:23)

He that is not with me is against me. (11:23)

Father, forgive them; for they know not what they do. (23:34)

He that is without sin among you, let him first cast a stone at her. (8:7)

The truth shall make you free. (8:32)

I am the resurrection, and the life. (11:25)

In my Father's house are many mansions. (14:2)

Act of The Apostles

It is more blessed to give than to receive. (20:35)

Romans

The wages of sin is death. (6:23)

1 Corinthians

Though I speak with the tongues of men and of angels, and have not charity, I am become as sounding brass, or a tinkling cymbal. (13:1)

And now abideth faith, hope, charity, these three; but the greatest of these is charity. (13:13)

In a moment, in the twinkling of an eye, at the last trump. (15:52)

O death, where is thy sting? O grave, where is thy victory? (15:55)

Timothy

Not greedy of filthy lucre. (3:3)

For we brought nothing into this world, and it is certain we can carry nothing out. (6:7)

The love of money is the root of all evil. (6:10)

Revelation of St. John

These are they which came out of great tribulation, and have washed their robes, and made them white in the blood of the Lamb. (7:14)

When he had opened the seventh seal, there was silence in heaven about the space of half an hour. (8:1)

A place called in the Hebrew tongue Armageddon. (16:16)

I am Alpha and Omega, the beginning and the end, the first and the last. (22:13)

AMBROSE BIERCE 1842–1914?

Barometer, n. An ingenious instrument which indicates what kind of weather we are having. (*The Devil's Dictionary*)

Coward, n. One who in a perilous emergency thinks with his legs. (*Ib.*)

Ocean, n. A body of water occupying about two-thirds of a world made for man—who has no gills. (*Ib.*)

To be positive. To be mistaken at the top of one's voice. (*Ib.*)

SIR WILLIAM BLACKSTONE 1723–1780

It is better that ten guilty persons escape than one innocent suffer. (*Commentary on the Laws of England*, Book IV. 27)

WILLIAM BLAKE 1757–1827

A robin redbreast in a cage
Puts all Heaven in a rage.
(*Auguries of Innocence*)

He who shall hurt the little wren
Shall never be beloved by men. (*Ib.*)

A truth that's told with bad intent
Beats all the lies you can invent. (*Ib.*)

If the Sun and Moon should doubt,
They'd immediately go out. (*Ib.*)

When Sir Joshua Reynolds died
All Nature was degraded;
The King dropped a tear in the Queen's ear,
And all his pictures faded. (*On Art and Artists*)

I was angry with my friend:
I told my wrath, my wrath did end.
I was angry with my foe:
I told it not, my wrath did grow. (*Songs of Experience*, "A Poison Tree")

Tiger! Tiger! burning bright
In the forests of the night,
What immortal hand or eye
Could frame thy fearful symmetry? (*Ib.* "The Tiger")

Little Lamb, who made thee?
Dost thou know who made thee?
Gave thee life, and bid thee feed,
By the stream and o'er the mead;
Gave thee clothing of delight,
Softest clothing, woolly, bright;
Gave thee such a tender voice,
Making all the vales rejoice? (*Songs of Innocence*, "The Lamb")

A fool sees not the same tree that a wise man sees. (*The Marriage of Heaven and Hell*, "Proverbs of Hell")

PHILIP BLISS 1838–1876

Hold the fort, for I am coming (*Ho, My Comrades, See the Signal*)

JOHN WILKES BOOTH 1838–1865

Sic semper tyrannis! The South is avenged! (Spoken after he shot Lincoln, Apr. 14, 1865. The translation of the Latin is "Thus always to tyrants.")

JOHN COLLINS BOSSIDY 1860–1928

And this is good old Boston,
The home of the bean and the cod,
Where the Lowells talk to the Cabots,
And the Cabots talk only to God. (Toast proposed at Harvard dinner, 1910)

FRANCIS BOURDILLON 1852–1921

The night has a thousand eyes,
And the day but one;
Yet the light of the bright world dies
With the dying sun. (*Light*)

LORD BOWEN 1835–1894

The rain it raineth on the just
And also on the unjust fella:
But chiefly on the just, because
The unjust steals the just's umbrella.
(Quoted in Walter Sichel, *Sands of Time*)

OMAR N. BRADLEY 1893–

For however arduous the task of a commander, he cannot face the men who shall live or die by his orders without sensing how much easier is his task than the one he has set them to perform. (*A Soldier's Story*)

ANTHELME BRILLAT-SAVARIN
1755–1826

Tell me what you eat, and I will tell you what you are. (*Physiologie du Goût*)

RUPERT BROOKE 1887–1915

If I should die, think only this of me:
That there's some corner of a foreign field
That is for ever England. There shall be
In that rich earth a richer dust concealed.
(*The Soldier*)

LORD BROUGHAM 1778–1868

Education makes a people easy to lead, but difficult to drive; easy to govern but impossible to enslave. (Attr.)

The great Unwashed. (Attr.)

JOHN BROWN 1800–1859

In the first place I deny everything but what I have all along admitted—the design on my part to free the slaves. I intended certainly to have made a clean thing of that matter, as I did last winter when I went into Missouri and there took slaves without the snapping of a gun on either side, moved them through the country, and finally left them in Canada. I designed to have done the same thing again, on a larger scale. (Speech to the Court at Harpers Ferry)

I am yet too young to understand that God is any respecter of persons. I believe that to have interfered as I have done—as I have always freely admitted I have done—in behalf of His despised poor, was not wrong but right. (*Ib.*)

THOMAS BROWN 1663–1704

I do not love thee, Doctor Fell,
The reason why I cannot tell;
But this alone I know full well,
I do not love thee, Doctor Fell. (Transl. of Martial, *Epigram*, Book I. No. 33)

SIR THOMAS BROWNE 1605–1682

For my part, I have ever believed, and do now know, that there are witches. (*Religio Medici*, Pt. I. Sect. 30)

There is no road or ready way to virtue. (*Ib.* Pt. I. Sect. 54)

Charity begins at home, is the voice of the world. (*Ib.* Pt. II. Sect. 4)

ELIZABETH BARRETT BROWNING
1806–1861

If thou must love me, let it be for naught
Except for love's sake only. (*Sonnets from the Portuguese*, xiv)

God's gifts put man's best gifts to shame. (*Ib.* xxvi)

How do I love thee? Let me count the ways.
I love thee to the depth and breadth and
   height
My soul can reach, when feeling out of
   sight
For the ends of Being and ideal Grace.
(*Ib.* xliii)

I love thee with a love I seemed to lose
With my lost saints—I love thee with the
   breath,
Smiles, tears, of all my life!—and, if God
   choose,
I shall but love thee better after death. (*Ib.*)

ROBERT BROWNING 1812–1889

Ah, but a man's reach should exceed his
   grasp,
Or what's a heaven for? (*Andrea del Sarto*)

We mortals cross the ocean of this world
Each in his average cabin of a life. *(Bishop Blougram's Apology)*

If you get simple beauty and nought else,
You get about the best thing God invents.
(Fra Lippo Lippi, Line 217)

Oh, to be in England,
Now that April's there. *(Home Thoughts from Abroad)*

She had
A heart—how shall I say?—too soon made glad,
Too easily impressed. *(My Last Duchess)*

Rats!
They fought the dogs and killed the cats,
And bit the babies in the cradles,
And ate the cheeses out of the vats. *(The Pied Piper of Hamlin, Stanza ii)*

The year's at the spring
And day's at the morn;
Morning's at seven;
The hillside's dew-pearled;
The lark's on the wing;
The snail's on the thorn:
God's in his heaven—All's right with the world! *(Pippa Passes, Pt. I)*

Grow old along with me!
The best is yet to be,
The last of life, for which the first was made:
Our times are in His hand
Who saith, "A whole I planned,
Youth shows but half; trust God: see all nor be afraid!" *(Rabbi Ben Ezra, Stanza i)*

WILLIAM JENNINGS BRYAN

1860–1925

You shall not press down upon the brow of labor this crown of thorns, you shall not crucify mankind upon a cross of gold. (Speech at the National Democratic Convention, 1896)

WILLIAM CULLEN BRYANT   1794–1878

All day thy wings have fanned,
At that far height, the cold, thin atmosphere,
Yet stoop not, wary to the welcome land,
Though the dark night is near.
(To a Waterfowl)

Truth crushed to earth, shall rise again.
(The Battle-Field)

ARTHUR BULLER   1874–1944

There was a young lady named Bright,
Whose speed was far faster than light;
She set out one day
In a relative way,
And returned home the previous night.
(Limerick in *Punch*, Dec. 19, 1923)

JOHN BUNYAN   1628–1688

It beareth the name of Vanity Fair, because the town where 'tis kept is lighter than vanity. *(Pilgrim's Progress, Pt. I)*

Hanging is too good for him. *(Ib.)*

He that is down needs fear no fall,
He that is low no pride. *(Ib.* Shepherd Boy's Song)

GELETT BURGESS   1866–1951

I never saw a Purple Cow,
I never hope to see one;
But I can tell you, anyhow,
I'd rather see than be one! *(The Purple Cow)*

Ah, yes! I wrote the "Purple Cow"—
I'm sorry, now, I wrote it!
But I can tell you anyhow,
I'll kill you if you quote it! *(Cinq Ans après)*

EDMUND BURKE   1729–1797

The use of force alone is but *temporary.* It may subdue for a moment; but it does not remove the necessity of subduing again: and a nation is not governed, which is perpetually to be conquered. (*Speech on Conciliation with America, Mar. 22, 1775*)

I do not know the method of drawing up an indictment against a whole people. (*Ib.*)

No passion so effectually robs the mind of all its powers of acting and reasoning as fear. (*On the Sublime and Beautiful, Pt. II. Sect. ii*)

Beauty in distress is much the most affecting beauty. (*Ib. Pt. III. Sect. ix*)

Because half a dozen grasshoppers under a fern make the field ring with their importunate chink . . . do not imagine that those who make the noise are the only inhabitants of the field. (*Reflections on the Revolution in France*)

He that wrestles with us strengthens our nerves, and sharpens our skill. Our antagonist is our helper. (*Ib.*)

When bad men combine, the good must associate; else they will fall, one by one, an unpitied sacrifice in a contemptible struggle. (*Thoughts on the Cause of the Present Discontents*)

Somebody has said, that a king may make a nobleman, but he cannot make a gentleman. (*Letter to Wm. Smith, Jan. 29, 1795*)

It is a general popular error to imagine the loudest complainers for the public to be the most anxious for its welfare. (*Observations on "The Present State of the Nation"*)

BISHOP GILBERT BURNET   1643–1715

He (Halifax) said that he had known many kicked downstairs, but he never knew any kicked upstairs before. (*Original Memoirs*)

ROBERT BURNS   1759–1796

Should auld acquaintance be forgot,
And never brought to min'? (*Auld Lang Syne*)

We'll tak a cup o' kindness yet,
For auld lang syne. (*Auld Lang Syne*)

Gin a body meet a body
Coming through the rye;
Gin a body kiss a body,
Need a body cry? (*Coming through the Rye*)

A man's a man for a' that! (*A Man's a Man for A' That*)

Auld nature swears, the lovely dears
Her noblest work she classes O;
Her prentice han' she tried on man,
An' then she made the lasses O. (*Green Grow the Rashes*)

The golden hours on angel wings
Flew o'er me and my dearie;
For dear to me as light and life
Was my sweet Highland Mary. (*Highland Mary*)

John Anderson my jo, John,
When we were first acquent,
Your locks were like the raven,
Your bonnie brow was brent. (*John Anderson My Jo*)

Man's inhumanity to man
Makes countless thousand mourn! (*Man
Was Made to Mourn*)

My heart's in the Highlands, my heart is not
   here;
My heart's in the Highlands a-chasing the
   deer. (*My Heart's in the Highlands*)

O, my Luve's like a red red rose
That's newly sprung in June:
O, my Luve's like the melodie
That's sweetly play'd in tune. (*My Luve Is
Like a Red Red Rose*)

Liberty's in every blow!
Let us do or die! (*Scots Wha Hae*)

O wad some Pow'r the giftie gie us
To see oursels as others see us! (*To a Louse*)

Wee sleekit, cow'rin', tim'rous beastie,
O what a panic's in thy breastie!
Thou need na start awa sae hasty,
Wi' bickering brattle! (*To a Mouse*)

The best laid schemes o' mice an' men
Gang aft a-gley. (*To a Mouse*)

NICHOLAS MURRAY BUTLER
1862–1947

An expert is one who knows more and more
about less and less. (Commencement Address, Columbia University)

SAMUEL BUTLER   1612–1680

For every why he had a wherefore. (*Hudi-
bras*, Pt. I. Canto i. Line 132)

He ne'er considered it, as loath
To look a gift-horse in the mouth. (*Ib*. Pt. I.
Canto i. Line 483)

I'll make the fur
Fly around the ears of the old cur. (*Ib*. Pt. I.
Canto iii. Line 277)

RICHARD BYRD 1888–1957

A man doesn't begin to attain wisdom until he recognizes that he is no longer indispensable. (Alone, "August: The Searchlight")

GEORGE GORDON, LORD BYRON
1788–1824

There is a pleasure in the pathless woods,
There is a rapture on the lonely shore,
There is society, where none intrudes,
By the deep sea, and music in its roar:
I love not man the less, but Nature more.
(Childe Harold's Pilgrimage, Canto IV. Stanza clxxviii)

Roll on, thou deep and dark blue Ocean—roll!
Ten thousand fleets sweep over thee in vain;
Man marks the earth with ruin—his control
Stops with the shore. (Ib. Stanza clxxix)

Man's love is of man's life a thing apart,
'Tis woman's whole existence. (Don Juan, Canto I. Stanza cxciv)

He was the mildest mannered man
That ever scuttled ship or cut a throat. (Ib. Canto III. Stanza xli)

The isles of Greece, the isles of Greece!
Where burning Sappho loved and sung. (Ib. Canto III. Stanza lxxxvi. 1)

But Tom's no more—and so no more of Tom. (Ib. Canto XI. Stanza xx)

The English winter—ending in July,
To recommence in August. (Ib. Canto XIII. Stanza xlii)

Society is now one polished horde,
Formed of two mighty tribes, the Bores and Bored. (Ib. Canto XIII. Stanza xcv)

Of all the horrid, hideous notes of woe,
Sadder than owl-songs or the midnight blast,
Is that portentous phrase, "I told you so."
(Ib. Canto XIV. Stanza 1)

'Tis strange—but true; for truth is always strange;
Stranger than fiction. (Don Juan, Canto XIV. Stanza ci)

She walks in beauty, like the night
Of cloudless climes and starry skies;
And all that's best of dark and bright
Meet in her aspect and her eyes. (She Walks in Beauty)

So, we'll go no more a roving
So late into the night,
Though the heart be still as loving,
And the moon be still as bright. (So, We'll Go No More A Roving)

JULIUS CAESAR 102?–44 B.C.

Gallia est omnis divisa in partes tres.—
The whole of Gaul is divided into three parts. (De Bello Gallico, Pt. I. Para. i)

Et tu, Brute?—You also, Brutus? (Alleged dying words.)

The die is cast. ([At the crossing of the Rubicon] Suetonius, History of the Twelve Caesars, "Caius Julius Caesar," Para. 32)

Veni, vidi, vici—I came, I saw, I conquered. (Ib. Book 1. Para. 37)

Caesar's wife must be above suspicion. (Traditional, based on Plutarch's Lives: Julius Caesar)

JOHN C. CALHOUN 1782–1850

With me, the liberty of the country is all in all. If this be preserved, every thing will be preserved; but if lost, all will be lost. (Speech, 1848)

THOMAS CAMPBELL 1777–1844

Star that bringest home the bee,
And settest the weary labourer free! (Song to the Evening Star)

Ye Mariners of England
That guard our native seas,
Whose flag has braved, a thousand years,
The battle and the breeze. (*Ye Mariners of England*)

THOMAS CAMPION   1567–1620

The man of life upright,
Whose guiltless heart is free
From all dishonest deeds
Or thought of vanity. (*The Man of Life Upright*)

GEORGE CANNING   1770–1827

But of all plagues, good Heaven, thy wrath
  can send,
Save me, oh, save me, from the candid
  friend! (*New Morality*)

HENRY CAREY   1693?–1743

God save our gracious king!
Long live our noble king!
God save the king! (*God Save the King*)

Of all the girls that are so smart
There's none like pretty Sally,
She is the darling of my heart,
And she lives in our alley. (*Sally in Our Alley*)

Of all the days that's in the week
I dearly love but one day—
And that's the day that comes betwixt
A Saturday and Monday. (*Ib.*)

THOMAS CARLYLE   1795–1881

History is the essence of innumerable biographies. (*Critical and Miscellaneous Essays*, "On History")

A well-written Life is almost as rare as a well-spent one. (*Ib.* "Richter")

Burke said that there were Three Estates in Parliament; but, in the Reporters' Gallery yonder, there sat a *Fourth Estate*, more important far than they all. (*Heroes and Hero-Worship*, "The Hero as Man of Letters")

For one man that can stand prosperity, there are a hundred that will stand adversity. (*Ib.*)

No man who has once heartily and wholly laughed can be altogether irreclaimably bad. (*Sartor Resartus*, Book I. Chap. 4)

"Do the duty that lies nearest thee," which thou knowest to be a duty! Thy second duty will already have become clearer. (*Ib.* Book II. Chap. 9)

BLISS CARMAN   1861–1929

There is something in the Autumn
  that is native to my blood. (*A Vagabond Song*)

There is something in October sets the gypsy
  blood astir. (*Ib.*)

ANDREW CARNEGIE   1837–1919

Surplus wealth is a sacred trust which its possessor is bound to administer in his lifetime for the good of the community. ("Wealth," *North American Review*, June 1889)

DALE CARNEGIE   1888–

How to Win Friends and Influence People. (Title of book)

JULIA CARNEY   1823–1908

Little drops of water, little grains of sand,
Make the mighty ocean, and the pleasant
  land.
So the little minutes, humble though they
  be,
Make the mighty ages of eternity. (*Little Things*)

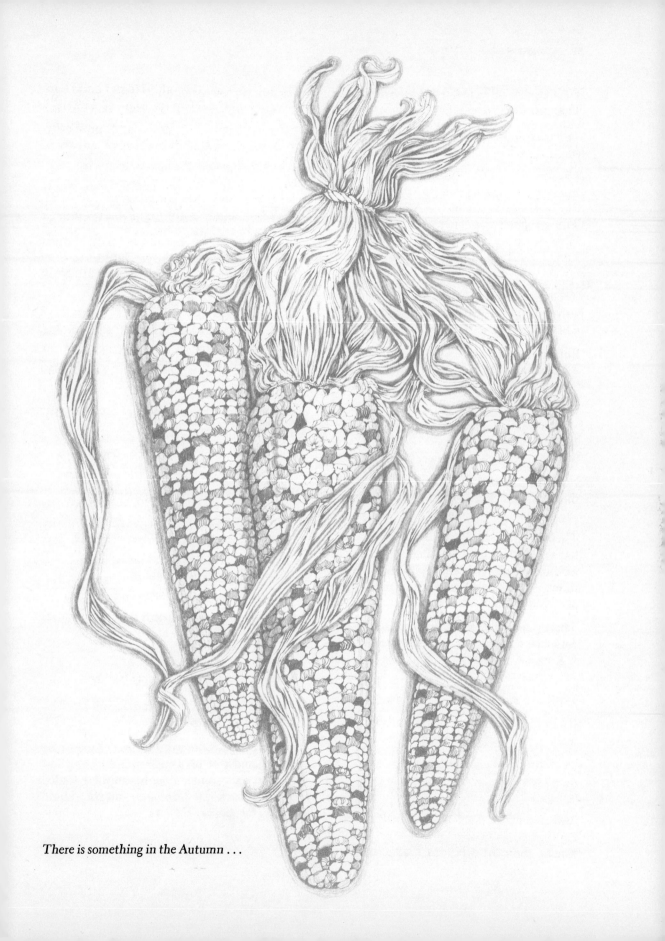

There is something in the Autumn . . .

LEWIS CARROLL (CHARLES DODGSON)

1832–1898

Curiouser and curiouser! (*Alice in Wonderland*, Chap. 2)

How doth the little crocodile
Improve his shining tail,
And pour the waters of the Nile,
On every golden scale! (*Ib.*)

"You are old, Father William," the young man said,
"And your hair has become very white;
And yet you incessantly stand on your head—
Do you think, at your age, it is right?"

"In my youth," Father William replied to his son,
"I feared it might injure the brain;
But now that I'm perfectly sure I have none,
Why, I do it again and again." (*Ib.* Chap. 5)

Do you think I can listen all day to such stuff?
Be off, or I'll kick you downstairs! (*Ib.*)

Speak roughly to your little boy,
And beat him when he sneezes:
He only does it to annoy,
Because he knows it teases. (*Ib.*)

It (the Cheshire Cat) vanished quite slowly, beginning with the end of the tail, and ending with the grin, which remained some time after the rest of it had gone. (*Ib.*)

"Then you should say what you mean," the March Hare went on.
    "I do," Alice hastily replied; "at least—at least I mean what I say—that's the same thing, you know." (*Ib.* Chap. 7)

Twinkle, twinkle, little bat!
How I wonder what you're at!
Up above the world you fly,
Like a tea-tray in the sky. (*Ib.*)

Off with her head! (*Ib.* Chap. 8)

Soup of the evening, beautiful Soup! (*Ib.*)

"Begin at the beginning," the King said, gravely, "and go on till you come to the end; then stop." (*Alice in Wonderland*, Chap. 12)

'Twas brillig, and the slithy toves
Did gyre and gimble in the wave;
All mimsy were the borogoves,
And the mome raths outgrabe. (*Through the Looking Glass*, Chap. 1)

Beware the Jabberwock, my son!
The jaws that bite, the claws that catch!
Beware the Jubjub bird, and shun
The frumious Bandersnatch! (*Ib.*)

Now, here, you see, it takes all the running you can do, to stay in the same place. If you want to get somewhere else, you must run at least twice as fast as that! (*Ib.* Chap. 2)

Tweedledum and Tweedledee
Agreed to have a battle;
For Tweedledum said Tweedledee
Had spoiled his nice new rattle. (*Ib.* Chap. 4)

The Walrus and the Carpenter
Were walking close at hand;
They wept like anything to see
Such quantities of sand:
"If this were only cleared away,"
They said, "it would be grand!"

"The time has come," the Walrus said,
"To talk of many things:
Of shoes—and ships—and sealing-wax—
Of cabbages—and kings—
Of why the sea is boiling hot—
And whether pigs have wings." (*Ib.*)

They gave it me . . . for an un-birthday present. (*Ib.* Chap. 6)

In the midst of the word he was trying to say
In the midst of his laughter and glee,
He had softly and suddenly vanished away—
For the Snark was a Boojum, you see. (*Hunting of the Snark*, Fit 8)

RACHEL CARSON 1907–1964

For all at last returns to the sea—the beginning and the end. (*The Sea around Us*)

PHOEBE CARY 1824–1871

And though hard be the task,
"Keep a stiff upper lip." (*Keep a Stiff Upper Lip*)

CATULLUS 87–54? B.C.

There is nothing sillier than a silly laugh. (*Carmina*, No. xxxix. Line 6)

MIGUEL CERVANTES 1547–1616

Wouldn't it be better to stay peacefully at home, and not roam about the world seeking better bread than is made of wheat, never considering that many go for wool and come back shorn? (*Don Quixote*, Pt. I. Chap. 7)

Take care, your worship, those things over there are not giants but windmills. (*Ib.* Pt. I. Chap. 8)

The Knight of the Sad Countenance. (*Ib.* Pt. I. Chap. 19)

One shouldn't talk of halters in the hanged man's house. (*Ib.* Pt. I. Chap. 25)

Hunger is the best sauce in the world. (*Ib.* Pt. II. Chap. 5)

We cannot all be friars, and many are the ways by which God bears his chosen to heaven. (*Ib.* Pt. II. Chap. 8)

Well, now, there's a remedy for everything except death. (*Ib.* Pt. II. Chap. 20)

There are only two families in the world, my old grandmother used to say, the *Haves* and the *Have-nots*. (*Ib.* Pt. II. Chap. 20)

God bless the inventor of sleep, the cloak that covers all men's thoughts, the food that cures all hunger . . . the balancing weight that levels the shepherd with the king and the simple with the wise. (*Don Quixote,* Pt. II. Chap. 68)

NEVILLE CHAMBERLAIN 1869–1940

In war, whichever side may call itself the victor, there are no winners, but all are losers. (Speech at Kettering, July 3, 1938)

I believe it is peace for our time . . . peace with honor. (Wireless speech after Munich Agreement, Oct. 1, 1938)

CHARLES HADDON CHAMBERS
1860–1921

The long arm of coincidence. (*Captain Swift,* Act II)

GEOFFREY CHAUCER 1340?–1400

Whan that Aprille with his shoures sote
The droghte of Marche hath perced to the rote. (*Canterbury Tales,* "Prologue," Line 1)

He was a verray parfit gentil knight. (*Ib.* Line 72)

He was as fresh as is the month of May. (*Ib.* Line 92)

If gold rusts, what shal iren do? (*Ib.* Line 500)

Trouthe is the hyeste thing that man may kepe. ("The Frankeleyns Tale," Line 751)

And therefore, at the kinges court, my brother,
Ech man for him-self, ther is non other. (*Ib.* "The Knightes Tale," Line 323)

The bisy larke, messager of day. (*Ib.* Line 633)

ANTON CHEKHOV 1860–1904

LIUBOV ANDREEVNA: Are you still a student?
TROFIMOV: I expect I shall be a student to the end of my days. (*The Cherry Orchard,* Act I)

Before the cherry orchard was sold everybody was worried and upset, but as soon as it was all settled finally and once for all, everybody calmed down, and felt quite cheerful. (*Ib.* Act IV)

EARL OF CHESTERFIELD 1694–1773

Be wiser than other people if you can, but do not tell them so. (Letter to his son, Nov. 19, 1745)

An injury is much sooner forgotten than an insult. (Letter to his son, Oct. 9, 1746)

Advice is seldom welcome; and those who want it the most always want it the least. (*Ib.* Jan. 29, 1748)

GILBERT KEITH CHESTERTON
1874–1936

For the great Gaels of Ireland
Are the men that God made mad,
For all their wars are merry,
And all their songs are sad. (*Ballad of the White House*, Book ii)

The human race, to which so many of my readers belong. (*The Napoleon of Notting Hill*, Chap. 1)

WINSTON CHURCHILL 1874–

I would say to the House, as I said to those who have joined the Government, "I have nothing to offer but blood, toil, tears and sweat." (Speech in House of Commons, May 13, 1940)

We shall defend our island, whatever the cost may be, we shall fight on the beaches, we shall fight on the landing grounds, we shall fight in the fields and in the streets, we shall fight in the hills; we shall never surrender. (*Ib.* June 4, 1940)

Let us therefore brace ourselves to our duties, and so bear ourselves that, if the British Empire and its Commonwealth last for a thousand years, men will still say: "This was their finest hour." (*Ib.* June 18, 1940)

Never in the field of human conflict was so much owed by so many to so few. (*Ib.* Aug. 20, 1940)

An iron curtain has descended across the Continent. (Address at Westminster College, Fulton, Mo., U.S.A., Mar. 5, 1946)

MARCUS TULLIUS CICERO 106–43 B.C.

Nothing so absurd can be said, that some philosopher has not said it. (*De Divinatione*, Book II. Sect. 58)

The good of the people is the chief law. (*De Legibus*, Book III. Sect. iii. Para. 8)

Summum bonum—The highest good. (*De Officiis*, Book I. Sect. ii. Para. 5)

O tempora, O mores!—What times! What habits! (*In Catilinam*, Oration I. Para. 2)

HENRY CLAY 1777–1852

The gentleman speaks of Virginia being my country. The Union, sir, is my country. (Speech in the Senate, 1848)

I would rather be right than be President! (Speech, 1850)

GROVER CLEVELAND 1837–1908

I believe our Great Maker is preparing the world, in His own good time, to become one nation, speaking one language. (Inaugural Address, 1893)

IRVIN S. COBB 1876–1944

A good storyteller is a person who has a good memory and hopes other people haven't. (*Dictionary of Humorous Quotations*)

Why should a worm turn? It's probably just the same on the other side. (*Ib.*)

JEAN COCTEAU   1891–1963

Tact consists in knowing how far we may go too far. (Quoted in *Treasury of Humorous Quotations*)

SIR EDWARD COKE   1552–1634

How long soever it hath continued, if it be against reason, it is of no force in law. (*Institutes of the Laws of England*, Book I. Chap. 10. Sect. 80)

For a man's house is his castle. (*Ib.* Book III. Sect. 73)

FRANK COLBY   1865–1925

Men will confess to treason, murder, arson, false teeth, or a wig. How many of them will own up to a lack of humor? (*Essays*, Vol. I)

I have found some of the best reasons I ever had for remaining at the bottom simply by looking at the men at the top. (*Ib.* Vol. II)

SAMUEL TAYLOR COLERIDGE
1772–1834

It is an ancient mariner,
And he stoppeth one of three. (*The Ancient Mariner*, Pt. I)

Water, water, everywhere,
Nor any drop to drink. (*Ib.* Pt. II)

He prayeth best, who loveth best
All things both great and small;
For the dear God who loveth us,
He made and loveth all. (*Ib.* Pt. VII)

A sadder and a wiser man,
He rose the morrow morn. (*Ib.*)

In Xanadu did Kubla Khan
A stately pleasure-dome decree;
Where Alph, the sacred river, ran
Through caverns measureless to man
Down to a sunless sea. (*Kubla Khan*)

MORTIMER COLLINS   1827–1876

A man is as old as he's feeling. A woman as old as she looks. (*The Unknown Quantity*)

GEORGE COLMAN, THE YOUNGER
1762–1836

Mum's the word. (*The Battle of Hexham*, Act II. Sc. i)

Not to be sneezed at. (*The Heir-at-Law*, Act II. Sc. i)

His heart runs away with his head. (*Who Wants a Guinea?* Act I. Sc. i)

When taken,
To be well shaken. (*Newcastle Apothecary*)

CHARLES COLTON   1780?–1832

Men will wrangle for religion; write for it; fight for it; anything but—live for it. (*Lacon*, Book I. No. 25)

When you have nothing to say, say nothing. (*Ib.* Book I. No. 183)

WILLIAM CONGREVE   1670–1729

I came upstairs into the world; for I was born in a cellar. (*Love For Love*, Act II. Sc. vii)

O fie miss, you must not kiss and tell. (*Ib.* Act II. Sc. x)

I know that's a secret, for it's whispered everywhere. (*Ib.* Act III. Sc. iii)

He that first cries out stop thief, is often he that has stolen the treasure. (*Ib.* Act III. Sc. xiv)

Music hath charms to soothe a savage breast, To soften rocks, or bend a knotted oak. (*The Mourning Bride*, Act III. Sc. viii)

CALVIN COOLIDGE 1872–1933

He said he was against it. (On being asked what a clergyman had said in a sermon on sin)

One with the law is a majority. (Speech, 1920)

The business of America is business. (Speech, Jan. 17, 1925)

I do not choose to run for president in 1928. (Aug. 2, 1927)

JAMES FENIMORE COOPER 1789–1851

The Last of the Mohicans (Title of novel)

Few men exhibit greater diversity . . . than the native warrior of North America. In war, he is daring, boastful, cunning, ruthless, self-denying, and self-devoted; in peace, just, generous, hospitable, revengeful, superstitious, modest, and commonly chaste. (*The Last of the Mohicans*)

PIERRE CORNEILLE 1606–1684

Do your duty, and leave the rest to the gods. (*Horace, Act II. Sc. viii*)

One often calms one's grief by recounting it. (*Polyeucte, Act I. Sc. iii*)

ÉMILE COUÉ 1857–1926

Every day, in every way, I'm getting better and better. (Formula of his faith-cures)

NORMAN COUSINS 1912–

War is an invention of the human mind. The human mind can invent peace. (*Who Speaks for Man?*)

NOEL COWARD 1899–

Mad dogs and Englishmen go out in the midday sun. (*Words and Music*)

Poor Little Rich Girl (Title of song)

WILLIAM COWPER 1731–1800

But misery still delights to trace
Its semblance in another's case.
(*The Castaway*)

A fool must now and then be right, by chance. (*Conversation, Line 96*)

The man that hails you Tom or Jack,
And proves by thumps upon your back
How he esteems your merit,
Is such a friend, that one had need

Be very much his friend indeed
To pardon or to bear it. (*Friendship*)

Absence from whom we love is worse than
death. (*Hope, Like the Short-lived Ray*)

God moves in a mysterious way,
His wonders to perform;
He plants his footsteps in the sea,
And rides upon the storm.
(*Ohrey Hymns*, 35)

The bud may have a bitter taste,
But sweet will be the flower. (*Ib.*)

Absence of occupation is not rest,
A mind quite vacant is a mind distressed.
(*Retirement, Line* 623)

God made the country, and man made the
town. (*The Task*, Book I. Line 749)

Variety's the very spice of life,
That gives it all its flavour. (*Ib.* Book II.
Line 606)

STEPHEN CRANE   1871–1900

The wayfarer,
Perceiving the pathway to truth,
Was struck with astonishment.
It was thickly grown with weeds,
"Ha," he said,
"I see that no one has passed here
In a long time."
Later he saw that each weed
was a singular knife.
"Well," he mumbled at last,
"Doubtless there are other roads." (*The
Wayfarer*)

MRS. EDMUND CRASTER   ?–1874

The Centipede was happy quite,
Until the Toad in fun
Said, "Pray which leg goes after which?"
And worked her mind to such a pitch,
She lay distracted in the ditch
Considering how to run. (Attr.)

DAVID CROCKETT   1786–1836

Be always sure you're right—then go ahead.
(His motto—then the motto of War of 1812)

OLIVER CROMWELL   1599–1658

A few honest men are better than numbers.
(Letter to Sir W. Spring, Sept., 1643)

WILL CUPPY   1884–1949

The Dodo never had a chance. He seems to
have been invented for the sole purpose of
becoming extinct and that was all he was
good for. (*How to Become Extinct*)

JOHN PHILPOT CURRAN   1750–1817

The condition upon which God hath given
liberty to man is eternal vigilance. (Speech
on the right of election of Lord Mayor of
Dublin, July 10, 1790)

THOMAS AUGUSTINE DALY   1871–

I gotta love for Angela,
   I love Carlotta, too.
I no can marry both o' dem,
   So w'at I gona do? (*Between Two Loves,*
Stanza 1)

Flo was fond of Ebenezer—
   "Eb," for short, she called her beau.
Talk of tides of love, great Caesar!
   You should see them—Eb and Flo. (*The
Tides of Love*)

CHARLES A. DANA 1819–1897

When a dog bites a man that is not news, but when a man bites a dog that is news. ("What Is News?" *New York Sun*, 1882)

DANTE ALIGHIERI 1265–1321

All hope abandon, ye who enter here. (*Divinia Comedia*, "Inferno," Canto iii. Line 9)

There is no greater grief than to recall a time of happiness when in misery. (*Ib.* Canto V. Line 121)

CLARENCE DARROW 1857–1938

To prevent burglary the cause must be removed; it can never be done in any other way. (*The Story of My Life*)

When I was a boy I was told that anybody could become President; I'm beginning to believe it.
(*Dictionary of Humorous Quotations*)

CHARLES DARWIN 1809–1882

I have called this principle, by which each slight variation, if useful, is preserved, by the term of Natural Selection. (*The Origin of Species*, Chap. 3)

We will now discuss in a little more detail the struggle for existence. (*Ib.*)

The expression often used by Mr. Herbert Spencer of the Survival of the Fittest is more accurate, and is sometimes equally convenient. (*Ib.*)

CHARLES DAVENANT 1656–1714

Custom, that unwritten law,
By which the people keep even kings in awe.
(*Circe*, Act II. Sc. iii)

WILLIAM HENRY DAVIES 1870–1940

What is this life if, full of care,
We have no time to stand and stare?
(*Leisure*)

JEFFERSON DAVIS 1808–1889

All we ask is to be let alone. (Inaugural Address as President of the Confederate States of America, 1861. Attr.)

You aggress upon our rights and homes, and under the will of God, we will defend them. (Jan. 10, 1861)

RICHARD HARDING DAVIS 1864–1916

The marines have landed, and the situation is well in hand. (Cablegram from Panama, 1885)

STEPHEN DECATUR 1779–1820

Our country! In her intercourse with foreign nations, may she always be in the right; but our country, right or wrong. (Toast given at Norfolk, Virginia, Apr., 1816)

DANIEL DEFOE 1661?–1731

One day, about noon, going towards my boat, I was exceedingly surprised with the print of a man's naked foot on the shore, which was very plain to be seen in the sand. (*Robinson Crusoe*, Pt. 1)

I takes my man Friday with me. (*Ib.*)

The best of men cannot suspend their fate:
The good die early, and the bad die late.
(*Character of the Late Dr. S. Annesley*)

Wherever God erects a house of prayer,
The Devil always builds a chapel there;
And 'twill be found, upon examination,
The latter has the largest congregation. (*The True-Born Englishman*, Pt. I. Line 1)

WALTER DE LA MARE 1873–1956

Here lies a most beautiful lady,
Light of step and heart was she;
I think she was the most beautiful lady
That ever was in the West Country. (*An Epitaph*)

Do diddle di do,
Poor Jim Jay
Got stuck fast
In Yesterday. (*Jim Jay*)

It's a very odd thing—
As odd as can be—
That whatever Miss T. eats
Turns into Miss T. (*Miss T.*)

ABBÉ JACQUES DELILLE 1738–1813

Fate chooses your relations, you choose your friends. (*Malheur et Pitié*, Canto I)

RENÉ DESCARTES 1596–1650

Traveling is almost like talking with men of other centuries.
(*Le Discours de la Méthode*, I)

I think, therefore I am. (*Ib.* Pt. IV)

GEORGE DEWEY 1835–1917

You may fire when you are ready, Gridley. (To the captain of his flagship, Battle of Manila, May 1, 1898)

CHARLES DICKENS 1812–1870

"There are strings," said Mr. Tappertit, ". . . in the human heart that had better not be vibrated." (*Barnaby Rudge*, Chap. 22)

It's my old girl that advises. She has the head. But I never own to it before her. Discipline must be maintained. (*Bleak House*, Chap. 27)

"Old girl," says Mr. Bagnet, "give him my opinion. You know it." (*Ib.*)

It is a melancholy truth that even great men have their poor relations. (*Ib.* Chap. 28)

"God bless us every one!" said Tiny Tim, the last of all. (*A Christmas Carol*, Chap. 3)

Barkis is willin'.
(*David Copperfield*, Chap. 5)

We are so very 'umble. (*Ib.*)

Uriah, with his long hands slowly twining over one another, made a ghastly writhe from the waist upwards. (*Ib.*)

Papa, potatoes, poultry, prunes and prism, are all very good words for the lips; especially prunes and prism. (*Little Dorrit*, Book II. Chap. 5)

"She's the sort of woman now," said Mould . . . "one would almost feel disposed to bury for nothing: and do it neatly too!" (*Martin Chuzzlewit*, Chap. 25)

He had but one eye and the popular prejudice runs in favor of two. (*Nicholas Nickleby*, Chap. 4)

Known by the *sobriquet* of "The artful Dodger." (*Oliver Twist*, Chap. 8)

"Hard," replied the Dodger. "As nails," added Charley Bates. (*Ib.* Chap. 9)

"It is a far, far better thing that I do, than I have ever done; it is a far, far better rest, that I go to, than I have ever known." (*A Tale of Two Cities*, Book III. Chap. 15)

EMILY DICKINSON 1830–1886

How dreary to be somebody!
How public, like a frog
To tell your name the livelong day
To an admiring bog! (*Life*)

I never saw a moor,
I never saw the sea;
Yet know I how the heather looks,
And what a wave must be. (*Time and Eternity*)

There is no frigate like a book
To take us lands away,
Nor any courses like a page
Of prancing poetry. (*There Is No Frigate Like a Book*)

DIOGENES *fl. c.* 380 B.C.

Stand a little less between me and the sun. ([When asked by Alexander if he lacked anything] Plutarch's *Lives: Alexander*)

BENJAMIN DISRAELI 1804–1881

Is man an ape or an angel? Now I am on the side of the angels. (Speech at Oxford Diocesan Conference, Nov. 25, 1864)

An author who speaks about his own books is almost as bad as a mother who talks about her own children. (Speech at banquet in Glasgow, Nov. 19, 1873)

No Government can be long secure without a formidable Opposition. (*Coningsby*, Book II. Chap. I)

Read no history: nothing but biography, for that is life without theory. (*Contarini Fleming*, Pt. I. Chap. 23)

A *dark* horse, which had never been thought of . . . rushed past the grand stand to sweeping triumph. (*The Young Duke*, Book II. Chap. 5)

JOHN DONNE 1571?–1631

Come live with me, and be my love,
And we will some new pleasures prove
Of golden sands and crystal brooks
With silken lines, and silver hooks.
(*The Bait*)

Death be not proud, though some have
  called thee
Mighty and dreadful, for, thou art not so,
For, those whom thou think'st, thou dost
  overthrow
Die not, poor death. (*Holy Sonnets*, No. X)

Go, and catch a falling star,
Get with child a mandrake root,
Tell me, where all past years are,
Or who cleft the Devil's foot. (Song)

But I do nothing upon myself, and yet I am mine own Executioner. (*Devotions*, No. XII)

No man is an Island, entire of itself; every man is a piece of the Continent, a part of the main. (*Ib.* No. CVII)

Any man's death diminishes me, because I am involved in Mankind; And therefore never send to know for whom the bell tolls; it tolls for thee. (*Ib.*)

STEPHEN A. DOUGLAS 1813–1861

I could travel from Boston to Chicago by the light of my own effigies. (1854)

Support the Constitution and obey the law. (June 3, 1861)

ERNEST DOWSON   1867–1900

I have been faithful to thee, Cynara! in my
    fashion. (*Non Sum Qualis Eram*)

They are not long, the weeping and the
    laughter,
Love and desire and hate:
I think they have no portion in us after
We pass the gate. (*Vitae Summa Brevis*)

SIR ARTHUR CONAN DOYLE   1859–1930

Singularity is almost invariably a clue. The
more featureless and commonplace a crime
is, the more difficult is it to bring it home.
(*The Adventures of Sherlock Holmes*, "The
Boscombe Valley Mystery")

"Excellent!" I cried. "Elementary," said he.
(*The Memoirs of Sherlock Holmes*, "The
Crooked Man")

MICHAEL DRAYTON   1563–1631

Fair stood the wind for France,
When we our sails advance,
Nor now to prove our chance,
Longer will tarry. (*Ballad of Agincourt*)

Upon Saint Crispin's Day
Fought was this noble fray,
Which fame did not delay,
To England to carry.
O when shall English men
With such acts fill a pen,
Or England breed again
Such a King Harry? (*Ib.*)

JOHN DRYDEN   1631–1700

Plots, true or false, are necessary things,
To raise up commonwealths, and ruin kings.
(*Absalom and Achitophel*, Pt. I. Line 83)

Nor is the people's judgment always true;
The most may err as grossly as the few. (*Ib.*
Pt. I. Line 781)

Beware the fury of a patient man. (*Ib.* Pt. I.
Line 1005)

None but the brave deserves the fair. (*Alexander's Feast*, Line 15)

Here lies my wife: here let her lie!
Now she's at rest, and so am I. (Epitaph intended for his wife)

All human things are subject to decay,
And when fate summons, monarchs must
　　obey. (*Mac Flecknoe*, Line 1)

Happy the man, and happy he alone,
He, who can call to-day his own:
He who, secure within, can say,
To-morrow do thy worst, for I have lived
　　today. (*Imitation of Horace*, Book III.
Ode xxix)

Whistling to keep myself from being afraid.
(*Amphitryon*, Act III. Sc. i)

For, Heaven be thanked, we live in such an
　　age,
When no man dies for love, but on the stage.
(*Mithridates*, Epilogue)

ALEXANDRE DUMAS　1803–1870

*Il y a une femme dans toutes les affaires;
aussitôt qu'on me fait un rapport, je dis:
"Cherchez la femme."*—There is a woman
in every case; as soon as they bring me a
report, I say, "Look for the woman." (*Les
Mohicans de Paris*, Act II. Sc. iii)

All for one, one for all. (Motto, *The Three
Musketeers*)

ALEXANDRE DUMAS fils　1824–1895

All generalizations are dangerous, even this
one. (Quoted in *Treasury of Humorous
Quotations*)

FINLEY PETER DUNNE　1867–1936

Th' dead ar-re always pop'lar. I knowed a
society wanst to vote a monyment to a man
an' refuse to help his fam'ly, all in wan night.
(*Mr. Dooley in Peace and War*, "On
Charity")

Life'd not be worth livin' if we didn't keep
our inimies. (*On New Year's Resolutions*)

WILL DURANT　1885–

The finger that turns the dial rules the
air. (*What Is Civilization?*)

The health of nations is more important
than the wealth of nations. (*Ib.*)

MAX EASTMAN　1883–

I don't know why it is we are in such a
hurry to get up when we fall down. You
might think we would lie there and rest
awhile. (*The Enjoyment of Laughter*)

MARY EASTY   d. 1692

I question not but Your Honors do to the utmost of your powers in the discovery and detecting of witchcraft and witches, and would not be guilty of innocent blood for the world. But, by my own innocency, I know you are in the wrong way. (Before her execution in Salem)

THOMAS ALVA EDISON   1847–1931

I am long on ideas, but short on time. I expect to live to be only about a hundred. (Golden Book)

Genius is one per cent inspiration and ninety-nine per cent perspiration. (Newspaper interview)

OLIVER EDWARDS   1711–1791

You are a philosopher, Dr. Johnson. I have tried too in my time to be a philosopher; but I don't know how, cheerfulness was always breaking in. (Quoted in Boswell's Life of Johnson, Apr. 17, 1778)

ALBERT EINSTEIN   1870–1955

Some recent work by E. Fermi and L. Szilard, which has been communicated to me in manuscript, leads me to expect that the element uranium may be turned into a new and important source of energy in the immediate future. (Letter to Pres. Roosevelt, Aug. 2, 1939)

Since I do not foresee that atomic energy is to be a great boon for a long time, I have to say that for the present it is a menace. Perhaps it is well that it should be. It may intimidate the human race into bringing order into its international affairs, which, without the pressure of fear, it would not do. (Atlantic Monthly, Nov., 1945)

Imagination is more important than knowledge. (On Science)

DWIGHT D. EISENHOWER   1890–

People of Western Europe: A landing was made this morning on the coast of France by troops of the Allied Expeditionary Force. . . . I call upon all who love freedom to stand with us now. Together we shall achieve victory. (June 6, 1944, Broadcast)

Whatever America hopes to bring to pass in this world must first come to pass in the heart of America. (Inaugural Address, 1953)

Don't join the book burners. . . . Don't be afraid to go to your library and read every book, as long as any document does not offend our own ideas of decency. That should be the only censorship. (Address at Dartmouth College Commencement, June 14, 1953)

GEORGE ELIOT (MARY ANN EVANS)
1819–1880

He was like a cock who thought the sun had risen to hear him crow.
(Adam Bede, Chap. 33)

We hand folks over to God's mercy, and show none ourselves. (*Adam Bede*, Chap. 42)

Animals are such agreeable friends—they ask no questions, they pass no criticisms. (*Scenes of Clerical Life*, "Mr. Gilfil's Love-Story," Chap. 7)

THOMAS STEARNS ELIOT   1888–

We are the hollow men
We are the stuffed men
Leaning together.
(*The Hollow Men*, Canto I)

This is the way the world ends
Not with a bang but a whimper.
(*Ib.* Canto V)

I grow old . . . I grow old . . .
I shall wear the bottoms of my trousers rolled.
(*Love Song of J. Alfred Prufrock*)

QUEEN ELIZABETH I   1533–1603

I will make you shorter by a head. (Chamberlin, *Sayings of Queen Elizabeth*)

I know I have the body of a weak and feeble woman, but I have the heart and stomach of a king, and of a king of England too. (Speech at Tilbury, on the approach of the Spanish Armada)

RALPH WALDO EMERSON   1803–1882

Here once the embattled farmers stood,
And fired the shot heard round the world.
(*Concord Hymn*)

Some of your hurts you have cured,
And the sharpest you still have survived,
But what torments of grief you endured
From evils which never arrived! (*Quatrains*, "Borrowing" [from the French])

So nigh is grandeur to our dust,
So near is God to man,
When Duty whispers low, *Thou must*,
The youth replies, *I can*. (*Voluntaries*, Canto iii)

The louder he talked of his honor, the faster we counted our spoons. (*Conduct of Life*, "Worship")

Though we travel the world over to find the beautiful, we must carry it with us or we find it not. (*Essays*, "Art")

Nothing great was ever achieved without enthusiasm. (*Ib.* "Circles")

A friend is a person with whom I may be sincere. Before him I may think aloud. (*Ib.* "Friendship")

All mankind loves a lover. (*Ib.* "Love")

Men are conservatives when they are least vigorous, or when they are most luxurious. They are conservatives after dinner. (*Essays, "New England Reformers"*)

Whoso would be a man must be a non-conformist. (*Ib. "Self-Reliance"*)

To be great is to be misunderstood. (*Ib.*)

I like the silent church before the service begins better than any preaching. (*Ib.*)

Hitch your wagon to a star. (*Society and Solitude, "Civilization"*)

If a man write a better book, preach a better sermon, or make a better mousetrap than his neighbor, though he build his house in the woods, the world will make a beaten path to his door. (Lecture, noted down by Mrs. Sarah Yule)

What is a weed? A plant whose virtues have not been discovered. (*Fortune of the Republic, Para. 3*)

DANIEL DECATUR EMMETT   1815–1904

I wish I was in de land ob cotton
Old times dar am not forgotten;
Look away, look away, look away, Dixie
    land! (*Dixie*)

EURIPIDES   480–406 B.C.

Whom God wishes to destroy, he first makes mad. (*Fragments*)

DAVID EVERETT   1770–1813

Large streams from little fountains flow,
Tall oaks from little acorns grow. (*Lines Written for a School Declamation*)

JAMES A. FARLEY   1888–

As Maine goes, so goes Vermont. (Remark in 1936, after election of Franklin D. Roosevelt; Alfred Landon, his opponent, won only the states of Maine and Vermont)

DAVID G. FARRAGUT   1801–1870

Damn the torpedoes! Go ahead! (At the battle of Mobile Bay, Aug. 5, 1864)

GUY FAWKES   1570–1606

Desperate diseases require desperate remedies. ([Gunpowder Plot] *Dic. of Nat. Biog.*)

EMPEROR FERDINAND I   1506–1564

Let justice be done, though the world perish. (Saying)

EUGENE FIELD   1850–1895

Wynken, Blynken and Nod one night
Sailed off in a wooden shoe—
Sailed on a river of crystal light,
Into a sea of dew. (*Wynken, Blynken and Nod*)

Time was when the little toy dog was new
And the soldier was passing fair,
And that was the time when our Little Boy
    Blue
Kissed them and put them there. (*Little Boy Blue*)

Have you ever heard of the Sugar-Plum
    Tree?
'Tis a marvel of great renown!
It blooms on the shore of the Lollipop sea
In the garden of Shut-Eye Town. (*The Sugar-Plum Tree*)

HENRY FIELDING   1707–1754

I am as sober as a judge. (*Don Quixote in England*, Act III. Sc. xiv)

Some folks rail against other folks, because other folks have what some folks would be glad of. (*Ib*. Act IV. Sc. vi)

GUSTAVE FLAUBERT   1821–1880

All one's inventions are true, you can be sure of that. Poetry is as exact a science as geometry. (Letter to Louise Colet, Aug. 14, 1853)

Do not read, as children do, to amuse yourself, or like the ambitious, for the purpose of instruction. No, read in order to live. (Letter to Mlle. de Chantepie, June, 1857)

FERDINAND FOCH   1851–1929

My center is giving way, my right is in retreat; situation excellent. I shall attack. (Message to Joffre, Sept., 1914)

HENRY FORD   1863–1947

History is bunk. (In the witness-box, when suing the *Chicago Tribune*, July, 1919)

I will build a motorcar for the great multitudes. (Launching the Model T Ford in 1909)

THOMAS FORD   1580?–1648

There is a lady sweet and kind,
Was never face so pleased my mind;
I did but see her passing by,
And yet I love her till I die. (*There Is a Lady*)

HOWELL M. FORGY   1908–

Praise the Lord and pass the ammunition.
(Said at Pearl Harbor)

EDWARD MORGAN FORSTER   1879–

Beethoven's Fifth Symphony is the most sublime noise that has ever penetrated into the ear of man. (*Howards End*, Chap. 5)

STEPHEN COLLINS FOSTER   1826–1864

I come down dah wid my hat caved in,
Doodah! doodah!
I go back home wid a pocket full of tin,
Oh, doodah day!
Gwine to run all night!
Gwine to run all day!
I bet my money on the bobtail nag.
Somebody bet on the bay. (*Camptown Races*)

Weep no more, my lady,
Oh! weep no more today!
We will sing one song for the old Kentucky Home,
For the old Kentucky Home far away. (*My Old Kentucky Home*)

O, Susanna! O, don't you cry for me,
I've come from Alabama, wid my banjo on my knee. (*O, Susanna*)

'Way down upon de Swanee Ribber,
Far, far away,
Dere's where my heart is turning ebber:
Dere's where de old folks stay.
All up and down de whole creation
Sadly I roam,
Still longing for de old plantation,
And for de old folks at home. (*Old Folks at Home*)

I'm coming, I'm coming,
For my head is bending low
I hear their gentle voices calling, "Old Black Joe." (*Old Black Joe*)

FELIX FRANKFURTER   1882–

Government is itself an art, one of the subtlest of the arts . . . It is the art of making men live together in peace and with reasonable happiness. (*The Public and Its Government*, Chap. 4)

BENJAMIN FRANKLIN   1706–1790

Remember that time is money. (*Advice to Young Tradesmen*)

Here Skugg lies snug
As a bug in a rug. (Letter to Miss G. Shipley, Sept. 26, 1772)

There never was a good war or a bad peace. (Letter to Quincy, Sept. 11, 1783)

In this world nothing can be said to be certain, except death and taxes. (Letter to Jean-Baptiste Le Roy, Nov. 13, 1789)

A little neglect may breed mischief . . . for want of a nail the shoe was lost; for want of a shoe the horse was lost; and for want of a horse the rider was lost. (*Maxims* . . . prefixed to *Poor Richard's Almanac*)

Some are weather-wise, some are otherwise. (*Poor Richard's Almanac*)

Never leave that till to-morrow which you can do to-day. (*Ib.*)

Yes, we must, indeed, all hang together or, most assuredly, we shall all hang separately. (Remark at signing of Declaration of Independence)

Man is a tool-making animal. (Quoted in Boswell's *Life of Johnson*, Apr. 7, 1778)

. . . This kite is to be raised when a thunder-gust appears to be coming on. . . . As soon as any of the thunder-clouds come over the kite, the pointed wire will draw the electric fire from them, and the kite, with all the twine, will be electrified, and the loose filaments of the string will stand out every way, and be attracted by an approaching finger. (Letter to Peter Collinson, 1752)

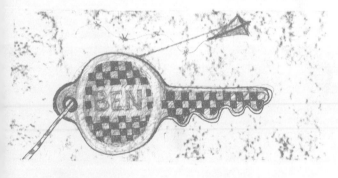

ROBERT FROST   1875–1963

"Home is the place where, when you have to
  go there,
They have to take you in." (*The Death of the Hired Man*)

Some say the world will end in fire,
Some say in ice.
From what I've tasted of desire
I hold with those who favor fire,
But if I had to perish twice,
I think I know enough of hate
To say that for destruction ice
Is also great
And would suffice. (*Fire and Ice*)

My apple trees will never get across
And eat the cones under his pines, I tell him.
He only says, "Good fences make good
  neighbors." (*Mending a Wall*)

I shall be telling this with a sigh
Somewhere ages and ages hence:
Two roads diverged in a wood, and I—
I took the one less travelled by,
And that has made all the difference. (*The Road Not Taken*)

A diplomat is a man who always remembers a woman's birthday but never remembers her age. (Quoted in *Treasury of Humorous Quotations*)

GALILEO GALILEI   1564–1642

Yet it does move. (Attributed saying, after being forced to recant his doctrine that the earth moves around the sun)

HAMLIN GARLAND   1860–1940

To rob me of my memories of the circus would leave me as poor as those to whom life was a drab and hopeless round of toil. It was our brief season of imaginative life. It was an embodiment of all that was skillful and beautiful in manly action. . . . It brought to our ears the latest band pieces and taught us the most popular songs. It furnished us with jokes. It relieved our dullness. It gave us something to talk about.

    Next day as we resumed work in the field the memory of its splendors went with us like a golden cloud. (*A Son of the Middle Border*)

It was worth the while of a boy to live
In the days when the prairie lay wide to the
  herds,
When the sod had a hundred joys to give
And the wind had a thousand words.
  It was well to be led
  Where the wild horses fed
As free as the swarming birds. (*In the Days When the Cattle Ran*)

WILLIAM LLOYD GARRISON
1805–1879

I am in earnest—I will not equivocate—I will not excuse—I will not retreat a single inch—and I will be heard! *(Salutary Address of the Liberator, Jan. 1, 1832)*

I will be as harsh as truth and as uncompromising as justice. *(Liberator, 1831)*

Our country is the world; our countrymen are all mankind. ("Prospectus" of the *Liberator*, Dec. 15, 1837)

JOHN GAY   1685–1732

If with me you'll fondly stray,
Over the hills and far away. *(The Beggar's Opera, Act I. Sc. i)*

In every age and clime we see,
Two of a trade can ne'er agree. *(Fables I. "The Ratcatcher and Cats")*

Those who in quarrels interpose,
Must often wipe a bloody nose. *(Ib. I. "The Mastiffs")*

GEORGE III   1738–1820

I cannot conclude without mentioning how sensibly I feel the dismemberment of America from this empire, and that I should be miserable indeed if I did not feel that no blame on that account can be laid at my door, and did I not also know that knavery seems to be so much the striking feature of its inhabitants that it may not in the end be an evil that they will become aliens to this kingdom. (Letter to Shelburne, Nov. 10, 1782)

HENRY GEORGE   1839–1897

The equal right of all men to the use of the land is as clear as their equal right to breathe the air—it is a right proclaimed by the fact of their existence. *(Progress and Poverty)*

HAROLD N. GILBERT 1896–

Keep 'Em Flying. (Slogan of Air Forces, World War II)

SIR WILLIAM SCHWENCK GILBERT

1836–1911

I'm called Little Buttercup—dear Little
    Buttercup,
Though I could never tell why. (*H.M.S.
Pinafore*, Act I)

And so do his sisters, and his cousins, and
    his aunts! (*Ib.*)

When I was a lad I served a term
As office-boy to an Attorney's firm;
I cleaned the windows and I swept the floor,
And I polished up the handle of the big
    front door,
I polished up that handle so successfullee,
That now I am the Ruler of the Queen's
    Navee! (*Ib.*)

A wandering minstrel I—
A thing of shreds and patches. (*Mikado,*
Act I)

As some day it may happen that a victim
    must be found,
I've got a little list—I've got a little list
Of society offenders who might well be
    underground,
And who never would be missed—who
    never would be missed! (*Ib.*)

Three little maids from school are we,
Pert as a schoolgirl well can be
Filled to the brim with girlish glee! (*Ib.*)

My object all sublime
I shall achieve in time—
To let the punishment fit the crime. (*Ib.
Act II*)

A source of innocent merriment. (*Ib.*)

The flowers that bloom in the spring,
Tra la,
Have nothing to do with the case. (*Ib.*)

On a tree by a river a little tomtit
Sang "Willow, titwillow, titwillow."
(*Mikado*, Act II)

When the foeman bares his steel,
Tarantara, tarantara!
We uncomfortable feel. (*Pirates of Penzance*, Act II)

When constabulary duty's to be done,
The policeman's lot is not a happy one. (*Ib.*)

WILLIAM EWART GLADSTONE

1809–1898

You cannot fight against the future. Time is on our side. (Speech on the Reform Bill, 1866)

All the world over, I will back the masses against the classes. (Speech at Liverpool, June 28, 1886)

HERMANN GOERING 1893–1946

Guns will make us powerful; butter will only make us fat. (Broadcast, 1936)

JOHANN WOLFGANG VON GOETHE
1749–1832

Man errs so long as he strives. (*Faust*, Pt. I, "Prologue in Heaven")

More light! (Reported dying words. Actually he asked for the second shutter of his window to be opened, so that more light could come in)

OLIVER GOLDSMITH 1728–1774

How happy he who crowns in shades like these,
A youth of labour with an age of ease. (*The Deserted Village*, Line 99)

And fools, who came to scoff, remained to pray. (*Ib.* Line 180)

Too fond of the *right* to pursue the expedient. ([Edmund Burke] *Retaliation*, Line 40)

On the stage he was natural, simple, affecting,
'Twas only that, when he was off, he was acting. ([Garrick] *Ib.* Line 101)

You may all go to pot. (*Verses in Reply to an Invitation to Dinner at Dr. Baker's*)

Don't let's make imaginary evils, when you know we have so many real ones to encounter. (*The Good-Natured Man*, Act I.)

As for disappointing them, I should not so much mind; but I can't abide to disappoint myself. (*She Stoops to Conquer*, Act I)

The very pink of perfection. (*Ib.*)

When lovely woman stoops to folly,
And finds too late that men betray,
What charm can soothe her melancholy,
What art can wash her guilt away? (*The Vicar of Wakefield*, Chap. 5)

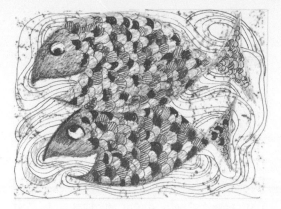

If you were to make little fishes talk, they would talk like whales. ([Said to Johnson] Boswell's *Life of Johnson*, Apr. 27, 1773)

SAMUEL GOLDWYN 1882–

In two words: im-possible. (Quoted in Alva Johnson, *The Great Goldwyn*)

SAMUEL GOMPERS 1850–1924

The trade unions are the legitimate outgrowth of modern societary and industrial conditions. . . . They were born of the necessity of workers to protect and defend themselves from incroachment, injustice and wrong. (Speech, 1898)

RICHARD GRAFTON ?–1572?

Thirty days hath November,
April, June and September,
February hath twenty-eight alone,
And all the rest have thirty-one. (*Abridgement of the Chronicles of England*, Introduction [1570])

KENNETH GRAHAME 1859–1932

Monkeys, who very sensibly refrain from speech, lest they should be set to earn their livings. (*The Golden Age*, "The Magic Ring")

There is nothing—absolutely nothing—half so much worth doing as simply messing about in boats. (*The Wind in the Willows*, Chap. 1)

The clever men at Oxford
Know all that there is to be knowed.
But they none of them know one half as
　much
As intelligent Mr. Toad. (*The Wind in the
Willows*, Chap. 10)

ULYSSES SIMPSON GRANT 1822–1885

I propose to fight it out on this line, if it
takes all summer. (Dispatch to Washington,
May 11, 1864)

No terms except unconditional and immediate surrender can be accepted. (To General
Buckner at Fort Donelson, Feb. 16, 1862)

LORD GRANVILLE 1815–1891

Spheres of action. (Letter, Apr. 29, 1885)

JOHN WOODCOCK GRAVES 1795–1886

D'ye ken John Peel with his coat so gay?
D'ye ken John Peel at the break of the day?
D'ye ken John Peel when he's far far away
With his hounds and his horn in the morn-
　ing? (*John Peel*)

THOMAS GRAY 1716–1771

The curfew tolls the knell of parting day,
The lowing herd winds slowly o'er the lea,
The ploughman homeward plods his weary
　way,
And leaves the world to darkness and to
　me. (*Elegy Written in a Country Churchyard*, Stanza i)

Let not ambition mock their useful toil,
Their homely joys, and destiny obscure;
Nor grandeur hear with a disdainful smile
The short and simple annals of the poor.
(*Elegy Written in a Country Churchyard*,
Stanza viii)

Far from the madding crowd's ignoble strife,
Their sober wishes never learned to stray;
(*Ib.* Stanza xix)

No more; where ignorance is bliss,
'Tis folly to be wise. (*Ode on a Distant
Prospect of Eton College*, Stanza x)

HORACE GREELEY   1811–1872

Go West, young man, and grow up with the country. (*Hints towards Reform*)

The illusion that times that were are better than those that are, has probably pervaded all ages. (*The American Conflict*, Vol. I. Chap. 1)

ÉTIENNE DE GRELLET (STEPHEN GRELLET)   1773–1855

I shall pass through this world but once. If, therefore, there be any kindness I can show, or any good thing I can do, let me do it now; let me not defer it or neglect it, for I shall not pass this way again. (Attr. to Grellet, and to others)

TEXAS GUINAN   1884–1933

Fifty million Frenchmen can't be wrong. (Attr.)

Hello, sucker!
(Said to night club customers)

ARTHUR GUITERMAN   1871–1943

Don't tell your friends about your indigestion:
"How are you!" is a greeting, not a question. (*A Poet's Proverbs*, "Of Tact")

Oh the saddest of sights in a world of sin
Is a little lost pup with his tail tucked in.
(*Little Lost Pup*)

JOHN GUNTHER   1901–

Ours is the only country deliberately founded on a good idea. (*Inside U.S.A.*)

New York City . . . It meets the most severe test that may be applied to definition of a metropolis—it stays up all night. But also it becomes a small town when it rains. (*Inside U.S.A.*, Chap. 33)

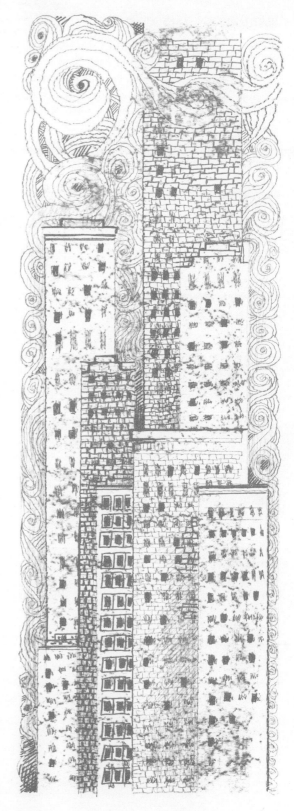

EARL HAIG   1861–1928

Every position must be held to the last man: there must be no retirement. With our backs to the wall, and believing in the justice of our cause, each one of us must fight on to the end. (Order to the British troops, Apr. 12, 1918)

NATHAN HALE   1755–1776

I only regret that I have but one life to lose for my country. (Last words, Sept. 22, 1776)

SARAH HALE   1788–1879

Mary had a little lamb,
Its fleece was white as snow,
And everywhere that Mary went
The lamb was sure to go. (*Mary's Little Lamb*)

CHARLES SPRAGUE HALL   *fl.* 1860

John Brown's body lies a moldering in the
  grave,
His soul is marching on! (*John Brown's Body*)

OWEN HALL (JAMES DAVIS)   1854–1907

Tell me, pretty maiden, are there any more at home like you? (*Florodora*, Act II)

ALEXANDER HAMILTON   1757–1804

Nothing can be more evident than that the thirteen states will be able to support a national government better than one half, or one third, or any number less than the whole. (*For a Strong Central Government*)

To those who, with me, abhorring the practice of dueling, may think that I ought on no account to add to the number of bad examples, I answer, that my *relative* situation, as well in public as private, enforcing all the considerations which men of the world denominate honor, imposed on me (as I thought) a peculiar necessity not to decline the call. (Hamilton's last statement)

JOHN HANCOCK   1737–1793

There, I guess King George will be able to read that. (Placing his signature on the Declaration of Independence, July 4, 1776)

LEARNED HAND   1872–1961

What then is the spirit of liberty? I cannot define it; I can only tell you my own faith. The spirit of liberty is the spirit which is not too sure that it is right. The spirit of liberty is the spirit which seeks to understand the minds of other men and women. The spirit of liberty is the spirit which weighs their interests alongside its own without bias. The spirit of liberty remembers that not even a sparrow falls to earth unheeded. (I Am An American Day Speech, 1944)

ERNST AUGUST, ELECTOR OF HANOVER   1629–1698

The king of France's horses are better housed than I. (On seeing Louis XIV's stables at Versailles)

THOMAS HARDY   1840–1928

We two kept house, the Past and I. (*The Ghost of the Past*)

Well, World, you have kept faith with me,
Kept faith with me;
Upon the whole you have proved to be
Much as you said you were. (*He Never Expected Much*)

Let me enjoy the earth no less
Because the all-enacting Might
That fashioned forth its loveliness
Had other aims than my delight. (*Let Me Enjoy*)

JULIUS and AUGUSTUS HARE
1795–1855 and 1792–1834

Half the failures in life arise from pulling in one's horse as he is leaping. (*Guesses at Truth*)

ROBERT GOODLOE HARPER   1765–1825

Millions for defense but not a cent for tribute. (At dinner in honor of John Marshall, June 18, 1798)

JOEL CHANDLER HARRIS   1848–1908

Hit look lak sparrer-grass, hit feel lak sparrer-grass, hit tas'e lak sparrer-grass, en I bless ef 'taint sparrer-grass. (*Nights with Uncle Remus*, Chap. 27)

A contrapshun what he call a Tar-Baby. (*Uncle Remus*, Chap. 2)

I'm de'f in one year, en I can't hear out'n de udder. (*Ib*. Chap. 19)

NATHANIEL HAWTHORNE   1804–1864

Life is made up of marble and mud. (*The House of the Seven Gables*)

I begin to suspect that a man's bewilderment is the measure of his wisdom. (*Ib.*)

On the breast of her gown, in red cloth, surrounded with an elaborate embroidery and fantastic flourishes of gold-thread, appeared the letter A. (*The Scarlet Letter*, Chap. 2)

The great want which mankind labors under at this present moment is sleep. The world should recline its vast head on the first convenient pillow and take an age-long nap. (*Mosses from an Old Manse*)

IAN HAY (JOHN HAY BEITH)
1876–1952

Funny peculiar, or funny ha-ha? (*The Housemaster*)

WILLIAM HAZLITT   1778–1830

If the world were good for nothing else, it is a fine subject for speculation. (*Characteristics*, No. 302)

His worst is better than any other person's best. ([Scott] *English Literature*, Chap. 14)

I do not think there is anything deserving the name of society to be found out of London. (*On Coffee-House Politicians*)

HEINRICH HEINE   1797–1856

On wings of song. (Title of a song)

FELICIA HEMANS   1793–1835

The boy stood on the burning deck—
Whence all but he had fled. (*Casabianca*)

The stately homes of England,
How beautiful they stand! (*The Homes of England*)

WILLIAM ERNEST HENLEY   1849–1903

Under the bludgeonings of chance
My head is bloody, but unbowed. (*Invictus*)

It matters not how strait the gate,
How charged with punishments the scroll,
I am the master of my fate:
I am the captain of my soul. (*Ib.*)

Night with her train of stars
And her great gift of sleep. (*Margaritae Sororis*)

HENRI IV, OF FRANCE   1553–1610

I want there to be no peasant in my kingdom so poor that he cannot have a chicken in his pot every Sunday. (Attr.)

MATTHEW HENRY   1662–1714

All this and heaven too. (*Life of Philip Henry*)

O. HENRY (W. S. PORTER) 1862–1910

It couldn't have happened anywhere but in little old New York. (*A Little Local Color*)

It was beautiful and simple as all truly great swindles are. (*The Octopus Marooned*)

PATRICK HENRY 1736–1799

Caesar had his Brutus, Charles the First had his Cromwell, and George the Third ("Treason!" cried the Speaker)—may profit by their example. If this be treason, make the most of it. (Speech in the House of Burgesses, Virginia, May 1765)

Is life so dear or peace so sweet as to be purchased at the price of chains and slavery? Forbid it, Almighty God. I know not what course others may take, but as for me, give me liberty or give me death! (Speech in Richmond, Virginia, 1775)

ROBERT HERRICK 1591–1674

You say, to me-wards your affection's strong;
Pray love me little, so you love me long.
(*Hesperides*, "Love Me Little, Love Me Long")

Only to kiss that air,
That lately kissed thee. (*Ib.* "To Electra")

Gather ye rosebuds while ye may,
Old Time is still a-flying. (*Ib.* "To Virgins, to Make Much of Time")

Whenas in silks my Julia goes,
Then, then (methinks) how sweetly flows
That liquefaction of her clothes. (*Ib.* "Upon Julia's Clothes")

JOHN HEYWOOD 1497?–1580?

Let the world slide, let the world go:
A fig for care, and a fig for woe!
If I can't pay, why I can owe,
And death makes equal the high and the
    low. (*Be Merry, Friends*)

All a green willow is my garland. (*The Green Willow*)

THOMAS HEYWOOD 1572?–1641

A Woman Killed with Kindness. (Title of play)

WILLIAM EDWARD HICKSON 1803–1870

'Tis a lesson you should heed,
Try, try again.
If at first you don't succeed,
Try, try again. (*Try and Try Again*)

DR. BREWSTER HIGLEY 19 Cent.

Oh give me a home where the buffalo roam,
Where the deer and the antelope play,
Where seldom is heard a discouraging word
And the skies are not cloudy all day. (*Home on the Range*)

JAMES HILTON 1900–

When the High Lama asked him whether Shangri-la was not unique in his experience, and if the Western world could offer anything in the least like it, he answered with a smile: "Well, yes—to be quite frank, it reminds me very slightly of Oxford." (*Lost Horizon*, Chap. 9)

HIPPOCRATES *c.* 460–357 B.C.

Ars longa, vita brevis. The life so short, the craft so long to learn. (*Aphorisms*, Sect. I. No. i)

Extreme remedies are most appropriate for extreme diseases. (*Ib.* Sect. I. No. vi)

ADOLF HITLER 1889–1945

The great masses of the people . . . will more easily fall victims to a great lie than to a small one. (*Mein Kampf*, Chap. 10)

It (the Sudetenland) is the last territorial claim that I have to make in Europe. (Speech, Sept. 26, 1938)

SAMUEL HOFFENSTEIN 1890–1947

You buy some flowers for your table;
You tend them tenderly as you're able;
You fetch them water from hither and
    thither—
What thanks do you get for it all?
    They wither. (Poems in Praise of Practically Nothing, I)

The apple grows so bright and high,
And ends its days in apple pie. (Songs about Life, XXXIII)

ERNEST THEODOR AMADEUS
HOFFMANN 1776–1822

He's a wicked man that comes after children when they won't go to bed and throws handfuls of sand in their eyes. (The Sandman)

JOHN HAYNES HOLMES 1879–1964

The universe is not hostile, nor yet is it friendly. It is simply indifferent. (Sensible Man's View of Religion)

OLIVER WENDELL HOLMES 1809–1894

I read it in the story-book, that, for to kiss
    his dear,
Leander swam the Hellespont—and I will
    swim this here.
(The Ballad of the Oysterman)

Have you heard of the wonderful one-hoss
    shay,
That was built in such a logical way
It ran a hundred years to a day? (The Deacon's Masterpiece)

For him in vain the envious seasons roll
Who bears eternal summer in his soul. (The Old Player)

Man has his will—but woman has her way. (The Autocrat of the Breakfast Table, Chap. 1)

Build thee more stately mansions, O my
    soul,
As the swift seasons roll! (Ib. Chap. 4, "The Chambered Nautilus")

A moment's insight is sometimes worth a life's experience. (The Professor at the Breakfast Table, Chap. 10)

To be seventy years young is sometimes far more hopeful than to be forty years old. (On the Seventieth Birthday of Julia Ward Howe)

Ay, tear her tattered ensign down!
    Long has it waved on high,
And many an eye has danced to see
    That banner in the sky. (Old Ironsides)

HOMER c. 900 B.C.

Men in their generations are like the leaves of the trees. The wind blows and one year's leaves are scattered on the ground; but the trees burst into bud and put on fresh ones when the spring comes round. (Iliad, Book VI. Line 146)

She (Andromache) was smiling through her tears. (Ib. Book VI. Line 484)

He saw the cities of many peoples and learnt their ways. He suffered many hardships on the high seas in his struggles to preserve his life and bring his comrades home. (Odyssey, Book I. Line 4, transl. E. V. Rieu)

As soon as Dawn with her rose-tinted hands had lit the East. (Ib. Book II. Line 1)

THOMAS HOOD 1799–1845

I remember, I remember,
The house where I was born,
The little window where the sun
Came peeping in at morn. (I Remember)

With fingers weary and worn,
With eyelids heavy and red,
A woman sat in unwomanly rags,
Plying her needle and thread—
Stitch! stitch! stitch!
(*The Song of the Shirt*)

RICHARD HOOKER   1554?–1600

He that goeth about to persuade a multitude
that they are not so well governed as they
ought to be, shall never want attentive and
favourable hearers. (*Ecclesiastical Polity,*
Book I)

ELLEN STURGIS HOOPER   1816–1841

I slept, and dreamed that life was Beauty;
I woke, and found that life was Duty. (*Life
a Duty*)

HERBERT HOOVER   1874–

The American system of rugged individualism. (Campaign speech in New York, Oct.
22, 1928)

Older men declare war. But it is youth that
must fight and die. And it is youth who must
inherit the tribulation, the sorrow, and the
triumphs that are the aftermath of war.
(Speech, Chicago, Ill., June, 1944)

LAURENCE HOPE (ADELA FLORENCE
NICOLSON)   1865–1904

Pale hands I loved beside the Shalimar,
Where are you now? Who lies beneath your
    spell? (*Indian Love Lyrics,* "Pale Hands I
Loved")

HORACE   65–8 B.C.

The wary fox in the fable answered the sick
lion: "Because I am frightened by the footprints. I see them all pointing towards your
den. None of them point away." (*Epistles,*
Book I. Letter No. i)

Anger is a brief madness. (*Ib.* Book I. Letter
No. ii)

Once a word has been allowed to escape, it
cannot be recalled.
(*Ib.* Book I. Letter No. xviii)

When your neighbor's wall is on fire, it
becomes your business. (*Ib.*)

And seek the truth in the groves of Academus. (*Ib.* Book II. Letter No. ii)

*Carpe diem, quam minimum credula pos-
tero.*— Seize today, and put as little trust as
you can in the morrow.
(*Odes,* Book I. No. xi)

Remember, when life's path is steep, to keep
an even mind. (*Ib.* Book II. No. iii)

Dulce et decorum est pro patria mori. It
is a sweet and seemly thing to die for one's
country. (*Ib.* Book III. No. ii. Line 1)

ALFRED EDWARD HOUSMAN
1859–1936

The Grizzly Bear is huge and wild;
He has devoured the infant child.
The infant child is not aware
He has been eaten by the bear.
(*Infant Innocence*)

Clay lies still, but blood's a rover;
Breath's a ware that will not keep.
Up, lad; when the journey's over
There'll be time enough for sleep. (*A Shrop-
shire Lad,* iv, "Reveille")

When I was one-and-twenty
I heard a wise man say,
"Give crowns and pounds and guineas
But not your heart away." (*Ib.* No. xiii)

That is the land of lost content,
I see it shining plain,
The happy highways where I went
And cannot come again.
(A Shropshire Lad, xl)

With rue my heart is laden
For golden friends I had,
For many a rose-lipt maiden
And many a lightfoot lad. (Ib. liv)

JULIA WARD HOWE 1819–1910

Mine eyes have seen the glory of the coming
   of the Lord;
He is trampling out the vintage where the
   grapes of wrath are stored. (Battle-Hymn
of the Republic)

WILLIAM DEAN HOWELLS 1837–1920

Some people can stay longer in an hour than
others can in a week. (Quoted in Treasury
of Humorous Quotations)

ELBERT HUBBARD 1859–1915

This will never be a civilized country until
we expend more money for books than we
do for chewing-gum. (The Philistine)

LANGSTON HUGHES 1902–

Bop comes out of them dark days. That's
why real Bop is mad, wild, frantic, crazy—
and not to be dug unless you've seen dark
days, too. Folks who ain't suffered much
cannot play Bop, neither appreciate it.
(Simple Takes a Wife)

DAVID HUME 1711–1776

Custom, then, is the great guide of human
life. (Inquiry Concerning Human Understanding. Sec. 5. Pt. 1)

Beauty in things exists in the mind which
contemplates them. (Essays, "Of Tragedy")

MARGARET HUNGERFORD 1855?–1897

Beauty is in the eye of the beholder. (Quoted in *Molly Bawn*)

LEIGH HUNT 1784–1859

Abou Ben Adhem (may his tribe increase!) Awoke one night from a deep dream of peace. (*Abou Ben Adhem and the Angel*)

Write me as one that loves his fellowmen. (*Ib.*)

And lo! Ben Adhem's name led all the rest. (*Ib.*)

Jenny kissed me when we met, Jumping from the chair she sat in; Time, you thief, who love to get Sweets into your list, put that in. (*Rondeau*)

ALDOUS HUXLEY 1894–1963

Parodies and caricatures are the most penetrating of criticisms. (*Point Counter Point*, Chap. 28)

HENRIK IBSEN 1828–1906

Home life ceases to be free and beautiful as soon as it is founded on borrowing and debt. (*A Doll's House*, Act I)

One should never put on one's best trousers to go out to battle for freedom and truth. (*An Enemy of the People*, Act IV)

What's a man's first duty? The answer's brief: To be himself. (*Peer Gynt*, Act IV. Sc. i)

WILLIAM RALPH INGE 1860–1954

A man may build himself a throne of bayonets, but he cannot sit on it. (Marchant, *Wit and Wisdom of Dean Inge*)

ROBERT GREEN INGERSOLL 1833–1899

In nature there are neither rewards nor punishments—there are consequences. (*Lectures and Essays, 3rd Series*, "Some Reasons Why")

INSCRIPTIONS

This monument marks the first burying ground in Plymouth of the passengers of the Mayflower. (Inscription on Plymouth Rock Monument)

Proclaim liberty throughout the land unto all the inhabitants thereof. ([Leviticus 25:10] Inscription on the Liberty Bell)

Here Rests in Honored Glory An American Soldier Known But to God (Inscription on the Tomb of the Unknown Soldier)

Washington, the brave, the wise, the good, Supreme in war, in council, and in peace, Valiant without ambition, discreet without fear, Confident without presumption. In disaster, calm; in success, moderate; in all, himself. The hero, the patriot, the Christian. The father of nations, the friend of mankind, Who, when he had won all, renounced all, And sought in the bosom of his family and of nature, retirement, And in the hope of religion, immortality. (Inscription at Mount Vernon)

In this temple as in the hearts of the people for whom he saved the Union the memory of Abraham Lincoln is enshrined forever. (Inscription in Lincoln Memorial, Washington, D.C.)

WASHINGTON IRVING   1783–1859

A sharp tongue is the only edged tool that grows keener with constant use. *(The Sketch Book,* "Rip Van Winkle")

Who ever hears of fat men heading a riot, or herding together in turbulent mobs? . . . . 'tis your lean, hungry men who are continually worrying society, and setting the whole community by the ears. *(Knickerbocker's History of New York,* Book III)

Whenever a man's friends begin to compliment him about looking young, he may be sure that they think he is growing old. *(Bracebridge Hall,* "Bachelors")

ANDREW JACKSON   1767–1845

Our Federal Union! It must and shall be preserved! (Toast at Jefferson birthday banquet, 1830)

ROBERT H. JACKSON   1892–1954

The idea that a State, any more than a corporation, commits crimes is a fiction. Crimes always are committed only by persons. (Opening comments at Nuremberg trial of Nazi war leaders)

THOMAS JONATHAN (STONEWALL) JACKSON   1824–1863

Yell like furies when you charge! (Battle of Bull Run, July, 1861)

JOE JACOBS   1893–

I should of stood in bed. (In 1935, Jacobs left a sickbed to see Detroit and Chicago play in the World Series. He bet on Chicago, but Detroit won. Mr. Jacobs then made the above remark)

JAMES I OF ENGLAND and VI OF SCOTLAND   1566–1625

He was a bold man who first swallowed an oyster. (Quoted in Swift's *Polite Conversation,* Dialogue II)

HENRY JAMES   1843–1916

The only obligation to which in advance we may hold a novel, without incurring the accusation of being arbitrary, is that it be interesting. *(The Art of Fiction)*

WILLIAM JAMES   1842–1910

There is no more miserable human being than one in whom nothing is habitual but indecision. *(Psychology,* Chap. 10)

THOMAS JEFFERSON   1743–1826

When in the Course of human events, it becomes necessary for one people to dissolve the political bands which have connected them with another, and to assume among the powers of the earth, the separate and equal station to which the Laws of Nature and of Nature's God entitle them, a decent respect to the opinions of mankind requires that they should declare the causes which impel them to the separation. *(Declaration of Independence)*

We hold these truths to be self-evident, that all men are created equal, that they are endowed by their Creator with certain un-alienable Rights, that among these are Life, Liberty and the pursuit of Happiness. *(Declaration of Independence)*

Error of opinion may be tolerated where reason is left free to combat it. (First Inaugural Address, Mar. 4, 1801)

Equal and exact justice to all men, of whatever state or persuasion, religious or political; peace, commerce, and honest friendship with all nations—entangling alliances with none. *(Ib.)*

Freedom of religion; freedom of the press; freedom of person under the protection of the habeas corpus; and trial by juries impartially selected,—these principles form the bright constellation which has gone before us, and guided our steps through an age of revolution and reformation. *(Ib.)*

A little rebellion now and then is a good thing. (Letter to James Madison, Jan. 30, 1787)

The tree of liberty must be refreshed from time to time with the blood of patriots and tyrants. It is its natural manure. (Letter to W. S. Smith, Nov. 13, 1787)

PHILANDER JOHNSON   1866–1939

Cheer up, the worst is yet to come. *(Shooting Stars)*

DR. SAMUEL JOHNSON   1709–1784

I put my hat upon my head,
I walked into the Strand,
And there I met another man
Whose hat was in his hand. *(Parodies of the Hermit of Workworth)*

Oats. A grain, which in England is generally given to horses, but in Scotland supports the people. *(Dictionary of the English Language)*

A fly, Sir, may sting a stately horse, and make him wince; but one is but an insect, and the other is a horse still. (Boswell's *Life of Johnson*, Footnote on Warburton, 1754)

You may scold a carpenter who has made you a bad table, though you cannot make a table. It is not your trade to make tables. *(Ib.* June 25, 1763)

A man ought to read just as inclination leads him; for what he reads as a task will do him little good. *(Ib.* July 9, 1763)

If he does really think there is no distinction between virtue and vice, why, Sir, when he leaves our houses let us count our spoons. *(Ib.* July 9, 1763)

Sir, a woman's preaching is like a dog's walking on his hind legs. It is not done well; but you are surprised to find it done at all. *(Ib.* July 31, 1763)

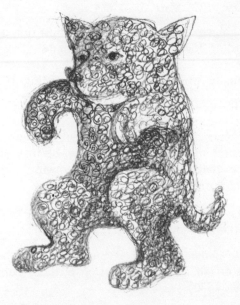

Patriotism is the last refuge of a scoundrel. *(Ib.* Apr. 7, 1775)

I have, all my life long, been lying till noon; yet I tell all young men, and tell them with great sincerity, that nobody who does not rise early will ever do any good. (Boswell, *Tour of the Hebrides*, Sept. 14, 1773)

A cucumber should be well sliced, and dressed with pepper and vinegar, and then thrown out, as good for nothing. (Boswell, *Tour of the Hebrides*, Oct. 5)

AL JOLSON 1886–1950

You ain't heard nothin' yet, folks. (Remark in the first talking film, *The Jazz Singer*, 1927)

JOHN PAUL JONES 1747–1792

I have not yet begun to fight! (Aboard "Bonhomme Richard," Sept. 23, 1779)

BEN JONSON 1573–1637

Apes are apes, though clothed in scarlet. (*The Poetasters*, Act V)

Reader, look
Not on his picture, but his book. (*On the Portrait of Shakespeare*)

Drink to me only with thine eyes,
And I will pledge with mine;
Or leave a kiss but in the cup,
And I'll not look for wine. (*To Celia*)

He was not of an age, but for all time! (*To the Memory of Shakespeare*)

For a good poet's made as well as born. (*Ib.*)

JUVENAL 160–*c.* 130

No one ever reached the depths of wickedness all at once. (*Satires*, No. ii. Line 83)

At Rome, all things can be had at a price. (*Ib.* No. iii. Line 183)

The traveller with empty pockets will sing in the thief's face. (*Ib.* No. x. Line 22)

Two things only the people anxiously desire—bread and circus games. (*Ib.* No. x. Line 80)

Your prayer must be for a sound mind in a sound body. (*Ib.* No. x. Line 356)

IMMANUEL KANT 1724–1804

Two things fill my mind with ever-increasing wonder and awe, the more often and the more intensely the reflection dwells on them: the starry heavens above me and the moral law within me. (*Critique of Pure Reason*, Conclusion)

JOHN KEATS 1795–1821

A thing of beauty is a joy for ever:
Its loveliness increases; it will never
Pass into nothingness. (*Endymion*, Book I. Line 1)

Where's the cheek that doth not fade,
Too much gazed at? (*Fancy*, Line 69)

Heard melodies are sweet, but those unheard
Are sweeter; therefore, ye soft pipes, play on;
Not to the sensual ear, but, more endeared,
Pipe to the spirit ditties of no tone. (*Ode on a Grecian Urn*, Stanza ii)

"Beauty is truth, truth beauty,"—that is all
Ye know on earth, and all ye need to know.
(Ode on a Grecian Urn, Stanza V)

There was a naughty Boy,
And a naughty boy was he,
He ran away to Scotland
The people for to see—
Then he found
That the ground
Was as hard,
That a yard
Was as long,
That a song
Was as merry,
That a cherry
Was as red—
That lead
Was as weighty,
That fourscore
Was as eighty,
That a door
Was as wooden
As in England—
So he stood in his shoes
And he wondered. *(A Song about Myself)*

Bright star, would I were steadfast as thou
art—(Sonnet: *Bright Star*)

To one who has been long in city pent,
'Tis very sweet to look into the fair
And open face of heaven. (Sonnet: *To One
Who Has Been Long in City Pent*)

When I have fears that I may cease to be
Before my pen has gleaned my teeming
   brain. (Sonnet: *When I Have Fears*)

THOMAS A KEMPIS   1380–1471

Sic transit gloria mundi.— Oh, how swiftly
the glory of the world passes away! *(Imitation of Christ*, Chap. I. Pt. vi)

JOHN F. KENNEDY   1917–1963

For those to whom much is given, much is
required. (Speech to Massachusetts State
Legislature, Jan. 9, 1961)

Ask not what your country can do for you;
ask what you can do for your country. (Inaugural Address, Jan. 20, 1961)

But however close we sometimes seem to
that dark and final abyss, let no man of peace
and freedom despair. For he does not stand
alone. If we all can persevere, if we can in
every land and office look beyond our own
shores and ambitions, then surely the age
will dawn in which the strong are just and
the weak secure and the peace preserved.
(Address to the United Nations, Sept. 25,
1961)

FRANCIS SCOTT KEY   1779–1843

'Tis the star-spangled banner, O! long may
   it wave
O'er the land of the free and the home of
   the brave! *(The Star-Spangled Banner)*

OMAR KHAYYÁM   1070–1123
Edward Fitzgerald, Translator   1809–1883

A Book of Verses underneath the Bough,
A Jug of Wine, a Loaf of Bread—and Thou
Beside me singing in the Wilderness—
Oh, Wilderness were Paradise enow.
(The Rubáiyát of Omar Khayyám, Ed. 5.
Stanza 12)

There was the Door to which I found no
  Key;
There was the Veil through which I might
  not see. (*The Rubáiyát of Omar Khayyám*, Ed. 5. Stanza 32)

The Moving Finger writes; and, having writ,
Moves on: nor all your Piety nor Wit
Shall lure it back to cancel half a Line,
Nor all your Tears wash out a Word of it.
(*Ib*. Ed. 5. Stanza 71)

JOYCE KILMER   1888–1918

I think that I shall never see
A poem lovely as a tree. (*Trees*)

Poems are made by fools like me,
But only God can make a tree. (*Ib.*)

CHARLES KINGSLEY   1819–1875

When all the world is young, lad,
And all the trees are green;
And every goose a swan, lad,
And every lass a queen;
Then hey for boot and horse, lad;
And round the world away:
Young blood must have its course, lad,
And every dog his day. (*Songs from the
Water Babies*, "Young and Old")

More ways of killing a cat than choking her
with cream. (*Westward Ho*, Chap. 20)

RUDYARD KIPLING   1865–1936

Oh, East is East, and West is West, and
  never the twain shall meet. (*The Ballad of
East and West*)

And a woman is only a woman, but a good
  cigar is a smoke. (*The Betrothed*)

(Boots—boots—boots—boots—movin' up and
  down again!)
There's no discharge in the war! (*Boots*)

For the female of the species is more deadly
  than the male. (*The Female of the Species*)

You're a better man than I am, Gunga Din!
(*Gunga Din*)

If you can keep your head when all about
  you
Are losing theirs and blaming it on you.
(*If—*)

For the Colonel's Lady an' Judy O'Grady
Are sisters under their skins! (*The Ladies*)

Now this is the Law of the Jungle—as old
  and as true as the sky. (*The Law of the
Jungle*)

On the road to Mandalay,
Where the flyin'-fishes play,
An' the dawn comes up like thunder outer
  China 'crost the Bay! (*Mandalay*)

The tumult and the shouting dies;
The Captains and the Kings depart:
Still stands thine ancient sacrifice,
An humble and a contrite heart.
Lord God of Hosts, be with us yet,
Lest we forget—lest we forget! (Recessional)

Take up the White Man's burden—
And reap his old reward:
The blame of those ye better,
The hate of those ye guard. (The White
Man's Burden)

He travels fastest who travels alone. (The
Winners)

MARQUIS DE LAFAYETTE   1757–1834

The Huron and Iroquois forests are peopled
with my friends; the despots of Europe and
their courts, these to me are the savages.
(Said in 1776)

JEAN DE LA FONTAINE   1621–1695

This fellow did not see further than his own
nose. (Fables, Book III. Fable 5, "The Fox
and the Ram")

Help yourself, and heaven will help you.
(Ib. Book VI. Fable 18, "The Hired Waggoner")

People must help one another; it is nature's
law. (Ib. Book VIII. Fable 17, "The Ass and
the Dog")

FIORELLO H. LA GUARDIA   1882–1947

Some day we will come to realize that the
right to food, shelter, and clothing at reasonable prices is as much an inalienable right as
the right to life, liberty and the pursuit of
happiness. (The Making of an Insurgent)

CHARLES LAMB   1775–1834

Angel-duck, angel-duck, winged and silly,
Pouring a watering-pot over a lily. (Nonsense
Verses)

The human species, according to the best
theory I can form of it, is composed of two
distinct races, the men who borrow and the
men who lend. (Essays of Elia, "The Two
Races of Men")

Your borrowers of books—those mutilators
of collections—spoilers of the symmetry of
shelves, and creators of odd volumes. (Ib.)

Not many sounds in life, and I include all
urban and rural sounds, exceed in interest a
knock at the door. (Ib. "Valentine's Day")

GEORGE MARTIN LANE   1823–1897

The waiter roars it through the hall:
"We don't give bread with one fish-ball!"
(One Fish-Ball)

JAMES LAWRENCE   1781–1813

Don't give up the ship. (As he lay dying
aboard the frigate "The Chesapeake," June
1, 1813)

EMMA LAZARUS   1849–1887

Give me your tired, your poor,
Your huddled masses, yearning to breathe
    free,
The wretched refuse of your teeming shore.
Send these, the homeless, tempest tossed,
    to me;
I lift my lamp beside the golden door.
(Inscription on Statue of Liberty)

STEPHEN LEACOCK   1869–1944

He flung himself from the room, flung himself upon his horse and rode madly off in all
directions. (Nonsense Novels, "Gertrude the
Governess")

EDWARD LEAR   1812–1888

There was an Old Man in a tree,
Who was horribly bored by a bee;
When they said, "Does it buzz?"

He replied, "Yes, it does!
It's a regular brute of a bee!"
(*Book of Nonsense*)

There was an Old Man with a beard,
Who said, "It is just as I feared!—
Two owls and a hen,
Four larks and a wren,
Have all built their nests in my beard!" (*Ib.*)

Far and few, far and few,
Are the lands where the Jumblies live;
Their heads are green, and their hands are
    blue,
And they went to sea in a sieve. (*Nonsense
Songs*, "The Jumblies")

The Owl and the Pussy-Cat went to sea
In a beautiful pea-green boat,
They took some honey, and plenty of money,
Wrapped up in a five-pound note. (*Ib.* "The
Owl and the Pussy-Cat")

HENRY LEE   1756–1818

First in war, first in peace, and first in the
hearts of his countrymen. ([Washington]
Speech in House of Representatives, 1799)

ROBERT EDWARD LEE   1807–1870

The war being at an end, the Southern
states having laid down their arms, and the
questions at issue between them and the
Northern states having been decided, I believe it to be the duty of everyone to unite
in the restoration of the country and the reestablishment of peace and harmony. (1865)

HENRY SAMBROOKE LEIGH   1837–1883

In form and feature, face and limb,
I grew so like my brother
That folks got taking me for him
And each for one another. (*The Twins*)

For one of us was born a twin
And not a soul knew which. (*Ib.*)

DUC DE LÉVIS   1764-1830

Noblesse oblige.—Nobility carries its obligations. (*Maximes et Réflexions*)

SINCLAIR LEWIS   1885–1951

The days of pioneering, of lassies in sunbonnets, and bears killed with axes in piney clearings, are deader now than Camelot; and a rebellious girl is the spirit of that bewildered empire called the American Middlewest. (*Main Street,* Chap. 1)

There is character in spectacles—the pretentious tortoise-shell, the meek pince-nez of the school teacher, the twisted silver-framed glasses of the old villager. Babbitt's spectacles had huge, circular, frameless lenses of the very best glass; the ear-pieces were thin bars of gold. In them he was the modern business man; one who gave orders to clerks and drove a car and played occasional golf and was scholarly in regard to Salesmanship. (*Babbitt,* Chap. 1)

ABRAHAM LINCOLN   1809-1865

The ballot is stronger than the bullet. (Speech, May 19, 1856)

In giving freedom to the slave, we assure freedom to the free,—honorable alike in what we give and what we preserve. (Speech Dec. 1, 1862)

Four score and seven years ago our fathers brought forth on this continent, a new nation, conceived in liberty, and dedicated to the proposition that all men are created equal. (Gettysburg Address, Nov. 19, 1863)

That this nation, under God, shall have a new birth of freedom; and that government of the people, by the people, for the people, shall not perish from the earth. (*Ib.*)

I have not permitted myself, gentlemen, to conclude that I am the best man in the country; but I am reminded in this connection of a story of an old Dutch farmer, who remarked to a companion once that it was not best to swap horses when crossing a stream. (Speech, June 9, 1864)

With malice toward none; with charity for all; with firmness in the right, as God gives us to see the right, let us strive on to finish the work we are in. (Second Inaugural Address, Mar. 4, 1865)

You can fool all the people some of the time, and some of the people all the time, but you cannot fool all of the people all the time. (Attr. words in speech, Sept. 8, 1858)

The Lord prefers common-looking people. That is the reason he makes so many of them. (Attr. by J. Morgan)

I hold that if the Almighty had ever made a set of men that should do all the eating and none of the work, He would have made them with mouths only and no hands. ("Mud-Sill" Theory of Labor)

I believe this government cannot endure permanently half slave and half free. (Speech, Republican State Convention, Springfield, Ill., June 16, 1858)

I would be very happy to oblige you, if my passes were respected. But the fact is, sir, I have, within the last two years, given passes to two hundred and fifty thousand men to go to Richmond, and not one has got there yet. (Answer to man who asked for a safe conduct to Richmond, 1863)

CHARLES A. LINDBERGH 1902–

Sitting in the cockpit, in seconds, minutes long, the conviction surges through me that the wheels *will* leave the ground, that the wings *will* rise above the wires, that it *is* time to start the flight. (*The Spirit of St. Louis*, Pt. II)

The *Spirit of St. Louis* swings around and stops rolling, resting on the solidness of earth, in the center of *Le Bourget*.

I start to taxi back toward the floodlights and hangars—But the entire field ahead is covered with running figures! (*The Spirit of St. Louis*, Pt. II)

VACHEL LINDSAY 1879–1931

It is portentous, and a thing of state
That here at midnight, in our little town
A mourning figure walks, and will not rest,
Near the old courthouse pacing up and
    down.
(*Abraham Lincoln Walks at Midnight*)

He cannot sleep upon his hillside now,
He is among us—as in times before!
And we who toss and lie awake for long,
Breathe deep, and start, to see him pass the
    door. (*Ib.*)

It breaks his heart that kings must murder
    still,
That all his hours of travail here for me
Seem yet in vain. And who will bring white
    peace
That he may sleep upon his hill again. (*Ib.*)

The flower-fed buffaloes of the spring
In the days of long ago,
Ranged where the locomotives sing
And the prairie flowers lie low. (*The Flower-Fed Buffaloes*)

But the flower-fed buffaloes of the spring
Left us long ago.
They gore no more, they bellow no more,
They trundle around the hills no more:
With the Pawnees lying low. (*Ib.*)

Then I saw the Congo, creeping through the
    black,
Cutting through the jungle with a golden
    track. (*The Congo*, Pt. 1)

Mumbo-Jumbo is dead in the jungle. (*Ib.*
Pt. 3)

ROBERT LLOYD 1733–1764

Slow and steady wins the race. (*The Hare and the Tortoise*)

JOHN LOCKE 1632–1704

New opinions are always suspected, and usually opposed, without any other reason but because they are not already common. (*Essay on the Human Understanding*, Dedication)

~~~~~~~~~~

HENRY WADSWORTH LONGFELLOW
1807–1882

I shot an arrow into the air,
It fell to earth, I know not where. (*The Arrow and the Song*)

Thou, too, sail on, O Ship of State!
Sail on, O Union, strong and great!
Humanity with all its fears,
With all the hopes of future years,
Is hanging breathless on thy fate! (*The Building of the Ship*)

Between the dark and the daylight,
When the night is beginning to lower,
Comes a pause in the day's occupations,
That is known as the Children's Hour. (*The Children's Hour*)

Archly the maiden smiled, with eyes over-
running with laughter,
Said, in a tremulous voice, "Why don't you
speak for yourself, John?" (*The Courtship of Miles Standish*)

The cares that infest the day
Shall fold their tents, like the Arabs,
And as silently steal away. (*The Day Is Done*)

This is the forest primeval. (*Evangeline*, "Prelude")

The shades of night were falling fast,
As through an Alpine village passed
A youth, who bore, 'mid snow and ice,
A banner with the strange device,
Excelsior! (*Excelsior*)

A boy's will is the wind's will,
And the thoughts of youth are long, long
thoughts. (*My Lost Youth*)

Tell me not in mournful numbers,
Life is but an empty dream!
For the soul is dead that slumbers,
And things are not what they seem.

Life is real! Life is earnest!
And the grave is not its goal.
Dust thou art, to dust returnest,
Was not spoken of the soul. (*A Psalm of Life*)

Lives of great men all remind us
We can make our lives sublime,
And, departing, leave behind us
Footprints on the sands of time. (*Ib.*)

By the shores of Gitchee Gumee,
By the shining Big-Sea-Water,
Stood the wigwam of Nokomis,
Daughter of the Moon, Nokomis. (*The Song of Hiawatha*, Canto iii)

From the waterfall he named her,
Minnehaha, Laughing Water. (*Ib.* Canto iv)

Ships that pass in the night, and speak each
other in passing; (*Tales of a Wayside Inn*, "The Theologian's Tale")

Listen, my children, and you shall hear
Of the midnight ride of Paul Revere. (*Ib.* "Paul Revere's Ride")

There was a little girl
Who had a little curl
Right in the middle of her forehead;
And when she was good
She was very, very good,
But when she was bad she was horrid. (*There Was a Little Girl*)

Under the spreading chestnut tree
The village smithy stands;
The smith, a mighty man is he,
With large and sinewy hands;
And the muscles of his brawny arms
Are strong as iron bands. (*The Village Blacksmith*)

Looks the whole world in the face,
For he owes not any man. (*Ib.*)

LOUIS XIV 1638–1715

L'État c'est moi.— I am the state. (Attr. to speech, Apr. 13, 1655)

RICHARD LOVELACE 1618–1658

Stone walls do not a prison make
Nor iron bars a cage;
Minds innocent and quiet take
That for an hermitage. (*To Althea from Prison*)

AMY LOWELL 1874–1925

Sea Shell, Sea Shell,
Sing me a song, O please!
A song of ships, and sailormen,
And parrots, and tropical trees. (*Sea Shell*)

JAMES RUSSELL LOWELL 1819–1891

Dear common flower, that grow'st beside
  the way
Fringing the dusty road with harmless gold.
(*To the Dandelion*)

And what is so rare as a day in June?
Then, if ever, come perfect days. (Prelude, *The Vision of Sir Launfal*, Pt. I. Stanza 5)

There is no good in arguing with the inevitable. The only argument available with an east wind is to put on your overcoat. (*Democracy and Addresses*, "Democracy")

ST. IGNATIUS LOYOLA 1491–1556

To give and not to count the cost;
To fight and not to heed the wounds;
To toil and not to seek for rest;
To labor and not ask for any reward
Save that of knowing that we do Thy will.
(*Prayer for Generosity*)

LUCRETIUS 99–55 B.C.

What is food to one man is bitter poison to others. (*On the Nature of Things*, Book IV. Line 637)

HENRY FRANCIS LYTE 1793–1847

Abide with me! Fast falls the eventide;
The darkness deepens; Lord, with me abide!
When other helpers fail, and comforts flee,
Help of the helpless, O abide with me!
(*Hymn*)

EDWARD BULWER-LYTTON 1809–1873

Beneath the rule of men entirely great,
The pen is mightier than the sword. (*Richelieu*, Act II. Sc. ii)

DOUGLAS MacARTHUR 1880–1964

In war there is no substitute for victory. (Address before Joint Meeting of Congress, Apr. 19, 1951)

I shall return. (Upon leaving the Philippines, Mar. 11, 1942)

THOMAS MACAULAY 1800–1859

The gallery in which the reporters sit has become a fourth estate of the realm. (*Historical Essays*, "Hallam's Constitutional History")

Perhaps no person can be a poet, or can even enjoy poetry, without a certain unsoundness of mind.
(*Literary Essays*, "Milton")

ANTHONY CLEMENT McAULIFFE   1898–

Nuts! (Reply to German request to surrender, Bastogne, Belgium, Dec. 22, 1944)

GEORGE McCLELLAN   1826–1885

All quiet along the Potomac. (Attr., in the American Civil War)

JOHN McCRAE   1872–1918

In Flanders fields the poppies blow
Between the crosses, row on row. (*In Flanders Fields*)

FIONA MACLEOD (WILLIAM SHARP)
1856–1905

My heart is a lonely hunter that hunts on a
   lonely hill. (*The Lonely Hunter*, Stanza vi)

SIR THOMAS MALORY   ?–1471

And much more am I sorrier for my good knights' loss than for the loss of my fair queen; for queens I might have enough, but such a fellowship of good knights shall never be together in no company. (*Morte d'Arthur*, Book XX. Chap. 9)

THOMAS ROBERT MALTHUS   1766–1834

The perpetual struggle for room and food. (*On Population*, Chap. 3)

W. R. MANDALE   19 Cent.

Up and down the City Road,
In and out the Eagle,
That's the way the money goes—
Pop goes the weasel? (*Pop Goes the Weasel*)

HORACE MANN   1796–1859

Be ashamed to die until you have won some victory for humanity. (Commencement Address, Antioch College, 1859)

WILLIAM MARCY   1786–1857

They see nothing wrong in the rule that to the victors belong the spoils of the enemy. (Speech in U.S. Senate, Jan., 1832)

QUEEN MARIE-ANTOINETTE   1755–1793

Let them eat cake. (Attr. [on being told that the people could not afford bread])

EDWIN MARKHAM   1852–1940

He drew a circle that shut me out—
Heretic, rebel, a thing to flout.
But Love and I had the wit to win:
We drew a circle that took him in!
(*Outwitted*)

Bowed by the weight of centuries he leans
Upon his hoe and gazes on the ground,
The emptiness of ages in his face,
And on his back the burden of the world.
(*The Man with the Hoe*)

CHRISTOPHER MARLOWE   1564–1593

Was this the face that launched a thousand
   ships,
And burnt the topless towers of Ilium?
Sweet Helen, make me immortal with a
   kiss! (*The Tragical History of Doctor Faustus*, Lines 1328–1331)

Accursed be he that first invented war. (*Ib.*)

Who ever loved, that loved not at first sight? (*Hero and Leander*, Line 176)

Come live with me and be my love,
And we will all the pleasures prove
That hills and valleys, dales and fields,
Woods, or steepy mountain yields. (*The Passionate Shepherd to His Love*)

DON MARQUIS 1878–1937

now and then
there is a person born
who is so unlucky
that he runs into accidents
which started out to happen
to somebody else *(archy's life of mehitabel.)*

toujours gai, archy, toujours gai *(Ib.)*

i have noted that when chickens quit quarrelling
over their food they often find that there is
 enough
for all of them i wonder if it might not be
 the same
way with the human race *(Ib.)*

there is always
a comforting thought
in time of trouble when
it is not our trouble. *(archy does his part.)*

GEORGE C. MARSHALL 1880–1959

If man does find the solution for world peace
it will be the most revolutionary reversal of
his record we have ever known. (Report of
Chief of Staff, 1945)

THOMAS RILEY MARSHALL 1854–1925

What this country needs is a good five-cent
cigar. (Said to John Crockett)

KARL MARX 1818–1883

The workers have nothing to lose but their
chains. They have a world to gain. Workers
of the world, unite.
(The Communist Manifesto)

From each according to his abilities, to
each according to his needs.
(Critique of the Gotha Program)

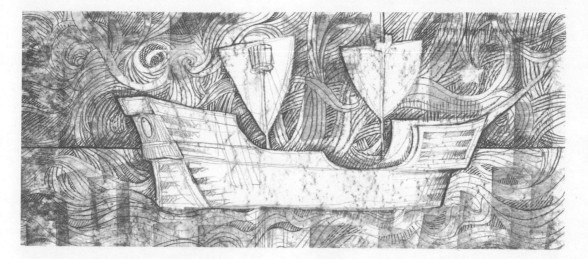

CAPTAIN FREDERICK MARRYAT
  1792–1848

It's just six of one and half-a-dozen of the
other. *(The Pirate,* Chap. 4)

Every man paddle his own canoe. *(Settlers
in Canada,* Chap. 8)

JOHN MASEFIELD 1878–

One road leads to London,
One road runs to Wales,
My road leads me seawards
To the white dipping sails. *(Roadways)*

I must down to the seas again, to the lonely
 sea and the sky,
And all I ask is a tall ship and a star to steer
 her by. *(Sea Fever)*

DAVID FRANCIS MASON 1914–

Sighted sub. Sank same. (Report to base of naval pilot, March, 1942)

EDGAR LEE MASTERS 1869–1949

I am Anne Rutledge who sleeps beneath
  these weeds,
Beloved in life of Abraham Lincoln,
Wedded to him, not through union,
But through separation. (*Anne Rutledge*)

WILLIAM SOMERSET MAUGHAM 1874–

A woman will always sacrifice herself if you give her the opportunity. It is her favourite form of self-indulgence.
(*The Circle*, Act III)

People ask you for criticism, but they only want praise.
(*Of Human Bondage*, Chap. 50)

I would sooner read a time-table or a catalogue than nothing at all. . . . They are much more entertaining than half the novels that are written. (*The Summing Up*, Chap. 25)

Sentimentality is only sentiment that rubs you up the wrong way. (*A Winter's Notebook*, 1941)

WILLIAM H. ("BILL") MAULDIN 1921–

Look at an infantryman's eyes and you can tell how much war he has seen. (*Up Front*)

HUGHES MEARNS 1875–

As I was going up the stair
I met a man who wasn't there.
He wasn't there again today.
I wish, I wish he'd go away. (*The Psychoed*)

HERMAN MELVILLE 1819–1891

Call me Ishmael. Some years ago—never mind how long precisely—having little or no money in my purse, and nothing particular to interest me on shore, I thought I would sail about a little and see the watery part of the world. (*Moby Dick*)

A whale ship was my Yale College and my Harvard. (*Ib.*)

To produce a mighty book, you must choose a mighty theme. No great and enduring volume can ever be written on the flea, though many there be that have tried it. (*Ib.*)

OWEN MEREDITH (EARL OF LYTTON)   1831–1891

Genius does what it must, and Talent does what it can. (*Last Words of a Sensitive Second-Rate Poet*)

JOHN STUART MILL   1806–1873

The worth of a State, in the long run, is the worth of the individuals composing it. (*On Liberty*, Chap. 5)

EDNA ST. VINCENT MILLAY   1892–1950

My candle burns at both ends;
It will not last the night;
But, ah, my foes, and oh, my friends—
It gives a lovely light. (*Figs from Thistles*, "First Fig")

And if I loved you Wednesday,
Well what is that to you?
I do not love you Thursday—
So much is true. (*Thursday*)

I like Americans.
You may say what you will, they are the nicest people in the world.
They sleep with their windows open.
Their bathtubs are never dry.
(*I Like Americans*)

O world, I cannot hold thee close enough!
Thy winds, thy wide gray skies!
Thy mists that roll and rise! (*God's World*)

ARTHUR MILLER   1915–

LINDA: I don't say he's a great man. Willy Loman never made a lot of money. His name was never in the paper. He's not the finest character that ever lived. But he's a human being, and a terrible thing is happening to him. So attention must be paid. He's not to be allowed to fall into his grave like an old dog. Attention, attention must be finally paid to such a person. (*Death of a Salesman*, Act I)

JOAQUIN MILLER   1841–1913

"Brave Adm'r'l, speak; what shall I say?"
"Why, say, 'Sail on! sail on! and on!' "
(*Columbus*)

WILLIAM MILLER   1810–1872

Wee Willie Winkie runs through the town,
Upstairs and downstairs in his nicht-gown.
(*Willie Winkie*)

A. A. MILNE   1882–1956

James James
Morrison Morrison
Weatherby George Dupree
Took great
Care of his Mother
Though he was only three. (*When We Were Very Young*, "Disobedience")

Hush! Hush! Whisper who dares!
Christopher Robin is saying his prayers.
(*Ib.* "Vespers")

And nobody knows
(Tiddely pom),
How cold my toes
(Tiddely pom),
How cold my toes
(Tiddely pom),
Are growing.
(*House at Pooh Corner*, Chap. 1)

Tiggers don't like honey. (*Ib.* Chap. 2)

JOHN MILTON 1608–1674

Hence loathed Melancholy,
Of Cerberus and blackest Midnight born.
(*L'Allegro*, Line 1)

Haste thee, nymph, and bring with thee
Jest and youthful jollity,
Quips and cranks, and wanton wiles,
Nods, and becks, and wreathed smiles. (*Ib.*
Line 25)

Yet shall I temper so
Justice with mercy. (*Paradise Lost*, Book X.
Line 77)

Eyeless in Gaza at the mill with slaves. (*Samson Agonistes*, Line 41)

How soon hath Time, the subtle thief of
youth,
Stoln on his wing my three and twentieth
year! (Sonnet: *On Being Arrived at the
Age of Twenty-three*)

When I consider how my light is spent
Ere half my days in this dark world and
wide,
And that one talent which is death to hide,
Lodged with me useless. (Sonnet: *On His
Blindness*)

Doth God exact day-labour, light denied,
I fondly ask; but patience, to prevent
That murmur, soon replies, God doth not
need
Either man's work or his own gifts; who best
Bear his mild yoke, they serve him best; his
state
Is kingly; thousands at his bidding speed,
And post o'er land and ocean without rest,
They also serve who only stand and wait.
(Sonnet: *On His Blindness*)

Fame is the spur that the clear spirit doth
raise
(The last infirmity of noble mind)
To scorn delights, and live laborious days.
(*Lycidas*, Line 70)

MOHAMMED 570–632

He deserves paradise who makes his companions laugh. (*The Koran*)

Riches are not from an abundance of worldly goods, but from a contented mind. (*Sunnah: Sayings of Muhammad*)

EMILIO MOLA ?–1936

The fifth column. (Radio speech during Spanish Civil War)

J. B. POQUELIN, called MOLIÈRE
1622–1673

M. JOURDAIN: Gracious me! I've been talking prose for the last forty years and have never known it. (*Le Bourgeois Gentilhomme*, Act II. Sc. iv)

I live on good soup, not on fine words. (*Les Femmes Savantes*, Act II. Sc. vii)

I assure you that a learned fool is more foolish than an ignorant fool. (*Ib.* Act IV. Sc. iii)

One should examine oneself for a very long time before thinking of condemning others. (*Le Misanthrope*, Act III. Sc. iv)

JAMES MONROE 1758–1831

The American continents . . . are henceforth not to be considered as subjects for future colonization by any European powers. . . .

We owe it, therefore, to candor, and to the amicable relations existing between the United States and those powers to declare that we should consider any attempt on their part to extend their system to any portion of this hemisphere as dangerous to our peace and safety. With the existing colonies or dependencies of any European power we have not interfered and shall not interfere. But with the governments who have declared their independence and maintained it, and whose independence we have, on great consideration and on just principles, acknowledged, we could not view any interposition for the purpose of oppressing them, or controlling in any other manner their destiny, by any European power, in any other light than as the manifestation of an unfriendly disposition toward the United States. (From message to Congress, Dec. 2, 1823)

MICHEL DE MONTAIGNE 1533–1592

Unless a man feels he has a good enough memory, he should never venture to lie. (*Essays*, Book I. Chap. ix)

The value of life lies, not in the length of the days, but in the use we make of them; a man may live long, yet live very little. Satisfaction in life depends not on the number of your years, but on your will. (*Ib*. Book I. Chap. xx)

The greatest thing in the world is to know how to be self-sufficient.
(*Ib*. Book I. Chap. xxxix)

When I play with my cat, who knows whether she is not amusing herself with me more than I with her.
(*Ib*. Book II. Chap. xii)

Poverty of goods is easily cured; poverty of soul, impossible. (*Ib*. Book III. Chap. x)

CHARLES, BARON DE MONTESQUIEU
1689–1755

An empire founded by war has to maintain itself by war. (*Considérations sur les Causes de la Grandeur des Romains et de Leur Décadence*, Chap. 8)

CLEMENT MOORE 1779–1863

'Twas the night before Christmas, when all through the house
Not a creature was stirring, not even a mouse;
The stockings were hung by the chimney with care,
In hopes that St. Nicholas soon would be there. (*A Visit from St. Nicholas*)

EDWARD MOORE   1712–1757

This is adding insult to injuries. (*The Foundling*, Act V. Sc. ii)

THOMAS MOORE   1779–1852

Believe me, if all those endearing young
  charms,
Which I gaze on so fondly to-day. (*Irish Melodies*, "Believe Me, If All Those Endearing Young Charms")

The harp that once through Tara's halls
The soul of music shed,
Now hangs as mute as Tara's walls
As if that soul were fled. (*Ib.* "The Harp That Once through Tara's Halls")

No, there's nothing half so sweet in life
As love's young dream. (*Ib.* "Love's Young Dream")

The Minstrel Boy to the war is gone,
In the ranks of death you'll find him;
His father's sword he has girded on,
And his wild harp slung behind him. (*Ib.* "The Minstrel Boy")

'Tis the last rose of summer
Left blooming alone;
All her lovely companions
Are faded and gone. (*Ib.* " 'Tis the Last Rose of Summer")

SIR THOMAS MORE   1478–1535

I pray you, Master Lieutenant, see me safe up, and for my coming down let me shift for myself. ([On mounting the scaffold] Roper, *Life of Sir Thomas More*)

THOMAS MORELL   1703–1784

See, the conquering hero comes!
Sound the trumpets, beat the drums!
(*Joshua*, Pt. 3)

GEORGE POPE MORRIS   1802–1864

Woodman, spare that tree!
Touch not a single bough!
In youth it sheltered me,
And I'll protect it now. (*Woodman, Spare That Tree*)

NAPOLEON BONAPARTE   1769–1821

Soldiers, consider that from the summit of these pyramids, forty centuries look down upon you. (Speech before the Battle of the Pyramids, 1798)

The bullet that is to kill me has not yet been molded. (Said in 1814, when the Spanish king asked whether he had ever been hit by a cannon-ball)

An army marches on its stomach. (Attr.)

OGDEN NASH 1902–

Ask Daddy, He Won't Know. (Title of poem)

The song of canaries
Never varies,
And when they're molting
They're pretty revolting. (*The Canary*)

To be an Englishman is to belong to the most exclusive club there is. (*England Expects*)

Children aren't happy with nothing to ignore,
And that's what parents were created for. (*The Parent*)

A bit of talcum
Is always walcum. (*Reflection on Babies*)

I think that I shall never see
A billboard lovely as a tree.
Perhaps unless the billboards fall,
I'll never see a tree at all. (*Song of the Open Road*)

HORATIO, VISCOUNT NELSON
  1758–1805

It is warm work; and this day may be the last to any of us at a moment. But mark you! I would not be elsewhere for thousands. ([Battle of Copenhagen] Southey's *Life of Nelson*, Chap. 7)

England expects every man will do his duty. ([Battle of Trafalgar] *Ib*. Chap. 9)

EMPEROR NERO 37–68

What an artist dies in me! (Dying words)

ALLAN NEVINS   1890–

The former allies had blundered in the past by offering Germany too little, and offering even that too late, until finally Nazi Germany had become a menace to all mankind. (*Current History*, May, 1935)

CARDINAL NEWMAN   1801–1890

It is almost a definition of a gentleman to say that he is one who never inflicts pain. (*The Idea of a University*, "Knowledge and Religious Duty")

Lead, Kindly Light, amid the encircling
   gloom,
Lead Thou me on!
The night is dark, and I am far from home—
Lead Thou me on! (Hymn)

FRIEDRICH NIETZSCHE   1844–1900

I teach you the superman. Man is something that is to be surpassed. (*Thus Spake Zarathustra*, Prologue, Chap. 3)

FLORENCE NIGHTINGALE   1820–1910

Too kind—too kind. (When handed the insignia of the Order of Merit on her deathbed)

CHESTER WILLIAM NIMITZ   1885–

A ship is always referred to as "she" because it costs so much to keep one in powder and paint. (Talk before the Society of Sponsors of the Navy, Feb., 1940)

CHRISTOPHER NORTH (JOHN WILSON)   1785–1854

His Majesty's dominions, on which the sun never sets. (*Noctes Ambrosianae*, Sect. 20)

Laws were made to be broken. (*Ib.* Sect. 24)

ALFRED NOYES   1880–1958

Go down to Kew in lilac-time, in lilac-time, in lilac-time. (*The Barrel Organ*)

ADOLPH OCHS   1858–1935

All the news that's fit to print. (Motto of the *New York Times*)

PATRICK O'KEEFE   1872–1934

Say it with flowers. (Slogan for Society of American Florists)

EUGENE O'NEILL   1888–1954

For de little stealin' dey gits you in jail soon or late. For de big stealin' dey makes you emperor and puts you in de Hall o' Fame when you croaks. (*The Emperor Jones*)

The child was diseased at birth, stricken with a hereditary ill that only the most vital men are able to shake off. I mean poverty—that most deadly and prevalent of all diseases. (*Ib.*)

BARONESS ORCZY   1865–1947

We seek him here, we seek him there,
Those Frenchies seek him everywhere.
Is he in heaven?— Is he in hell?
That demmed, elusive Pimpernel? (*The Scarlet Pimpernel*, Chap. 12)

GEORGE ORWELL   1903–1950

All animals are equal, but some animals are more equal than others. (*Animal Farm*, Chap. 10)

Big Brother is watching you. (*1984*, Pt. I. Chap. 1)

JAMES OTIS   1725–1783

Taxation without representation is tyranny. (Watchword of the American Revolution Attr.)

ROBERT OWEN 1771–1858

All the world is queer save thee and me, and even thou art a little queer. (When ending his partnership with William Allen)

LEROY "SATCHEL" PAIGE 1900?–

Don't look back. Something might be gaining on you. ("How To Keep Young," *Colliers*, June 13, 1953)

ALBERT BIGELOW PAINE 1861–1937

The Great White Way (Title of novel)

THOMAS PAINE 1737–1809

These are the times that try men's souls. ("The American Crisis," *Pennsylvania Journal*, 1776)

The summer soldier and the sunshine patriot will, in this crisis, shrink from the service of their country. (*Ib.* 1785)

Government, even in its best state, is but a necessary evil; in its worst state, an intolerable one. (*Common Sense*, Chap. 1)

My country is the world, and my religion is to do good. (*The Rights of Man*, Pt. ii. Chap. 5)

DOROTHY PARKER 1893–

Men seldom make passes
At girls who wear glasses. (*News Item*)

Guns aren't lawful;
Nooses give;
Gas smells awful;
You might as well live. (*Résumé*)

Excuse my dust. (Her own epitaph)

She ran the whole gamut of her emotions from A to B. (Quoted in *Treasury of Humorous Quotations*)

JOHN PARKER 1729–1775

Stand your ground. Don't fire unless fired upon, but if they mean to have a war let it begin here. (To his Minute Men, on Lexington Green, Apr. 19, 1775)

ROSS PARKER 1914–
  and HUGHIE CHARLES 1907–

There'll always be an England
While there's a country lane,
Wherever there's a cottage small
Beside a field of grain. (*There'll Always Be an England*)

ANDREW PATERSON 1864–1941

Once a jolly swagman camped by a billy-bong,
Under the shade of a kulibar tree,
And he sang as he sat and waited for his billy-boil,
"You'll come a-waltzing, Matilda, with me."
(*Waltzing Matilda*)

JOHN HOWARD PAYNE 1792–1852

'Mid pleasures and palaces though we may roam,
Be it ever so humble, there's no place like home. (*Clari, the Maid of Milan*, "Home, Sweet Home")

ROBERT EDWIN PEARY 1856–1920

The Eskimo had his own explanation. Said he: "The devil is asleep or having trouble with his wife, or we should never have come back so easily." *(The North Pole)*

WILLIAM PENN 1644–1718

Men are more careful of the breed of their horses and dogs than of their children. *(Reflexions and Maxims, "Right Marriage," No. 85)*

SAMUEL PEPYS 1633–1703

And so to bed. *(Diary, Apr. 20, 1660 etc.)*

Strange to say what delight we married people have to see these poor fools decoyed into our condition. *(Ib. Dec. 25, 1665)*

And so I betake myself to that course, which is almost as much as to see myself go into my grave; for which, and all the discomforts that will accompany my being blind, the good God prepare me. *(Ib. final entry)*

OLIVER HAZARD PERRY 1785–1819

We have met the enemy and they are ours—two ships, two brigs, one schooner and one sloop. (Battle of Lake Erie, Sept. 10, 1813)

WILLIAM LYON PHELPS 1865–1943

The only war I ever approved of was the Trojan war; it was fought over a woman and the men knew what they were fighting for. (Sermon, Riverside Church, New York City, June 25, 1933)

WENDELL PHILLIPS 1811–1884

We live under a government of men and morning newspapers. (Speech, Jan. 28, 1852)

One, on God's side is a majority. (Speech at Brooklyn, Nov. 1, 1859)

Every man meets his Waterloo at last. *(Ib.)*

The rock underlies all America; it only crops out here. (Speech, Plymouth, Dec. 21, 1855)

EDEN PHILLPOTTS 1862–

His father's sister had bats in the belfry and was put away. *(Peacock House, "My First Murder")*

PLATO c. 428–347 B.C.

Necessity, who is the mother of invention.
(*The Republic*, Book II. Chap. XI. 369)

Astronomy compels the soul to look upwards
and leads us from this world to another. (*Ib.*
Book VII. Chap. X. 529)

The people have always some champion
whom they set over them and nurse into
greatness. . . . This and no other is the root
from which a tyrant springs; when he first
appears he is a protector. (*The Republic*,
Book VIII. Chap. XVI. 565)

PLAUTUS 254–184 B.C.

He whom the gods favor dies young. (*Bacchides*, Act IV. Line 816)

EDGAR ALLAN POE 1809–1849

It was many and many a year ago,
In a kingdom by the sea,
That a maiden there lived whom you may
    know
By the name of Annabel Lee. (*Annabel Lee*)

I was a child and she was a child,
In this kingdom by the sea;
But we loved with a love that was more than
    love—
I and my Annabel Lee. (*Ib.*)

Once upon a midnight dreary, while I
    pondered, weak and weary,
Over many a quaint and curious volume of
    forgotten lore,
While I nodded, nearly napping, suddenly
    there came a tapping,
As of someone gently rapping. (*The Raven*,
Stanza i)

Take thy beak from out my heart, and take
    thy form from off my door!
Quoth the Raven, "Nevermore."
(*Ib.* Stanza xvii)

Helen, thy beauty is to me
Like those Nicean barks of yore. (*To Helen*)

Thy Naiad airs have brought me home
To the glory that was Greece,
And the grandeur that was Rome. (*Ib.*)

MME. DE POMPADOUR 1721–1764

Après nous le déluge.— After us the deluge.
(After Battle of Rossbach, 1757)

ALEXANDER POPE 1688–1744

I mount! I fly!
O grave! where is thy victory?
O death! where is thy sting? (*The Dying Christian to His Soul*)

Pride, the never failing vice of fools. (*An Essay on Criticism*, Line 204)

A little learning is a dang'rous thing;
Drink deep, or taste not the Pierian spring:
There shallow draughts intoxicate the brain,
And drinking largely sobers us again. (*Ib.* Line 215)

To err is human, to forgive, divine. (*Ib.* Line 525)

For fools rush in where angels fear to tread. (*Ib.* Line 625)

Hope springs eternal in the human breast;
Man never is, but always to be blessed. (*An Essay on Man*, Epistle I. Line 95)

Know then thyself, presume not God to scan;
The proper study of mankind is man. (*Ib.* Epistle II. Line 1)

Happy the man whose wish and care
A few paternal acres bound,
Content to breathe his native air,
In his own ground. (*Ode on Solitude*)

I never knew any man in my life who could not bear another's misfortunes perfectly like a Christian. (*Thoughts on Various Subjects*)

ADELAIDE PROCTER 1825–1864

Seated one day at the organ,
I was weary and ill at ease,
And my fingers wandered idly
Over the noisy keys. (*A Lost Chord*)

PROTAGORAS c. 485–415 B.C.

Man is the measure of all things. (Quoted by Plato in *Theaetetus*, 160D)

ISRAEL PUTNAM 1715–1790

Men, you are all marksmen—don't one of you fire until you see the whites of their eyes. (Battle of Bunker Hill, June 17, 1775. Also attr. to W. Prescott)

ERNIE PYLE 1900–1945

If you go long enough without a bath even the fleas will let you alone. (*Here Is Your War*)

I'm a rabid one-man movement bent on tracking down and stamping out everybody in the world who doesn't fully appreciate the common front-line soldier. (*Brave Men*)

QUINTUS ENNIUS 239–169 B.C.

No sooner said than done—so acts your man of worth.
(*Annals*, Book 9, Quoted by Priscianus)

FRANÇOIS RABELAIS c. 1492–1553

Appetite comes with eating. (*Gargantua*, Chap. 5)

Better to write of laughter than of tears, Because to laugh is proper to a man. (*Ib.* "To the Readers")

I owe much; I have nothing; the rest I leave to the poor. (His will)

Ring down the curtain, the farce is over. (Attr. last words)

SIR WALTER RALEIGH c. 1552–1618

So the heart be right, it is no matter which way the head lieth. (When laying his head on the block)

JAMES RYDER RANDALL 1839–1908

Avenge the patriotic gore
That flecked the streets of Baltimore,
And be the battle-queen of yore,
  Maryland! My Maryland! (*My Maryland*, written when Union troops attacked Baltimore, Apr. 26, 1861)

JOHN RAY 1627–1705?

When the cat's away the mice will play. (*English Proverbs*)

Never too old to learn. (*Ib.*)

THOMAS B. REED 1839–1902

The terrible, rumble, grumble and roar
Telling the battle was on once more—
And Sheridan twenty miles away! (*Sheridan's Ride*)

ERICH MARIA REMARQUE 1898–

All Quiet on the Western Front. (Title of novel)

GRANTLAND RICE 1880–1954

For when the One Great Scorer comes
To write against your name,
He marks—not what you won or lost—
But how you played the game. (*Alumnus Football*)

JAMES WHITCOMB RILEY 1852–1916

An' the gobble-uns 'll git you
Ef you don't watch out! (*Little Orphant Annie*)

Oh! the old swimmin'-hole! where the crick
    so still and deep
Looked like a baby-river that was laying half
    asleep. (The Old Swimmin'-hole)

ROBERT L. RIPLEY 1893–1949

Believe it or not. (Title of newspaper feature)

EDWIN ARLINGTON ROBINSON

1869–1935

Miniver Cheevy, child of scorn,
Grew lean while he assailed the seasons;
He wept that he was ever born,
    And he had reasons. (Miniver Cheevy)

I would have rid the earth of him
    Once, in my pride.
I never knew the worth of him
    Until he died. (An Old Story)

JACKIE ROBINSON 1919–

At the beginning of the World Series of
1947, I experienced a completely new emotion, when the National Anthem was played.
This time, I thought, it is being played for
me, as much as for anyone else. This is
organized major league baseball, and I am
standing here with all the others; and everything that takes place includes me. (This I
Believe)

DUC DE LA ROCHEFOUCAULD

1613–1680

We have all enough strength to bear other
people's troubles. (Les Maximes, Maxim 19)

We need greater virtues to bear good fortune
than bad. (Ib. Maxim 25)

One gives nothing so freely as advice. (Ib.
Maxim 110)

One's over-great haste to repay an obligation
is a kind of ingratitude. (Ib. Maxim 226)

We seldom attribute common sense except
to those who agree with us. (Les Maximes,
Maxim 347)

SAMUEL ROGERS 1763–1855

Oh! she was good as she was fair.
None—none on earth above her!
As pure in thought as angels are,
To know her was to love her. (Jacqueline,
Stanza I)

WILLIAM PENN ADAIR ("WILL")

ROGERS 1879–1935

All Wrigley had was an idea. He was the first
man to discover that American jaws must
wag. So why not give them something to wag
against? (The Illiterate Digest)

Everything is funny as long as it is happening to somebody else. (Ib.)

Everybody is ignorant, only on different
subjects. (Ib.)

All I know is what I see in the papers.

I never met a man I didn't like. (Address,
Boston, June, 1930)

I always like to hear a man talk about himself because then I never hear anything but
good.

ELEANOR ROOSEVELT 1884–1962

Up to a certain point it is good for us to
know that there are people in the world who
will give us love and unquestioned loyalty to
the limit of their ability. I doubt, however, if
it is good for us to feel assured of this without the accompanying obligation of having
to justify this devotion by our behavior.
(This Is My Story)

And the important thing was that you never let down doing the best that you were able to do—it might be poor because you might not have very much within you to give, or to help people with, or to live your life with. But as long as you did the very best that you were able to do, then that was what you were put here to do and that was what you were accomplishing by being here.
(This I Believe)

FRANKLIN DELANO ROOSEVELT

1882–1945

The forgotten man at the bottom of the economic pyramid. (Broadcast speech, Apr. 7, 1932)

I pledge you—I pledge myself—to a new deal for the American people. (Speech at Convention, Chicago, July 2, 1932)

Let me assert my firm belief that the only thing we have to fear is fear itself. (First Inaugural Address, Mar. 4, 1933)

In the field of world policy I would dedicate this nation to the policy of the good neighbor. *(Ib.)*

This generation of Americans has a rendezvous with destiny.
(Address, June 27, 1936)

I see one-third of a nation ill-housed, ill-clad, ill-nourished. (Second Inaugural Address, Jan. 20, 1937)

We must be the great arsenal of democracy. (Fireside Chat, Dec. 29, 1940)

A world founded upon four essential freedoms. The first is freedom of speech and expression—everywhere in the world. The second is freedom of every person to worship God in his own way—everywhere in the world. The third is freedom from want . . . everywhere in the world. The fourth is freedom from fear . . . anywhere in the world. (Speech, Jan. 6, 1941)

Yesterday, December 7, 1941—a date that will live in infamy—the United States of America was suddenly and deliberately attacked by naval and air forces of the Empire of Japan. (Address, Dec. 8, 1941)

We have learned that we cannot live alone, in peace; that our own well-being is dependent on the well-being of other nations, far away. . . . We have learned to be citizens of the world, members of the human community.
(Fourth Inaugural Address, Jan. 20, 1945)

THEODORE ROOSEVELT   1858–1919

The lunatic fringe in all reform movements.
(*Autobiography*, Chap. 7)

Speak softly and carry a big stick; you will go far. (Speech at Minnesota, Sept. 2, 1901)

No man is justified in doing evil on the ground of expediency.
(*The Strenuous Life*, "Latitude and Longitude among Reformers")

The most successful politician is he who says what everybody is thinking most often and in the loudest voice. (Quoted in *Treasury of Humorous Quotations*)

CHRISTINA ROSSETTI   1830–1894

My heart is like a singing bird
Whose nest is in a watered shoot;
My heart is like an apple-tree
Whose boughs are bent with thickset fruit;
My heart is like a rainbow shell
That paddles in a halcyon sea;
My heart is gladder than all these
Because my love is come to me.
(*A Birthday*)

Better by far you should forget and smile
Than that you should remember and be sad. (*Remember*)

Who has seen the wind?
Neither you nor I:
But when the trees bow down their heads
The wind is passing by. (*Sing-Song*)

When I am dead, my dearest,
Sing no sad songs for me; (Song: *When I Am Dead, My Dearest*)

The city mouse eats bread and cheese;—
The garden mouse eats what he can;
We will not grudge him seeds and stocks,
Poor little timid furry man. (*The City Mouse*)

DANTE GABRIEL ROSSETTI   1828–1882

The blessed damozel leaned out
From the gold bar of heaven;
Her eyes were deeper than the depth
Of waters stilled at even;
She had three lilies in her hand,
And the stars in her hair were seven. (*The Blessed Damozel*, Stanza i)

GIOACCHINO ROSSINI   1792–1868

Give me a laundry-list and I'll set it to music. (Quoted in *Treasury of Humorous Quotations*)

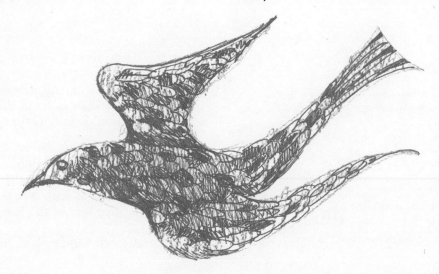

JOSEPH ROUGET DE LISLE 1760–1836

Allons, enfants de la patrie,
Le jour de gloire est arrivé.
Come, children of our native land,
The day of glory has arrived.
(*La Marseillaise*)

JEAN-JACQUES ROUSSEAU 1712–1778

Man was born free, and everywhere he is in chains. (*The Social Contract*, Chap. I)

JOHN RUSKIN 1819–1900

Remember that the most beautiful things in the world are the most useless; peacocks and lilies for instance. (*The Stones of Venice*, I. Chap. 2. §17)

The purest and most thoughtful minds are those which love colour the most. (*Ib.* I. Chap. 5. §30)

Fine art is that in which the hand, the head, and the heart of man go together. (*The Two Paths*, Lecture 2)

BERTRAND RUSSELL 1872–

Mathematics possesses not only truth, but supreme beauty—a beauty cold and austere, like that of sculpture. (*Mysticism and Logic*, "The Study of Mathematics")

The secret of happiness is this: let your interests be as wide as possible, and let your reactions to the things and persons that interest you be as far as possible friendly rather than hostile. (*The Conquest of Happiness*)

SAKI (H. H. MUNRO) 1870–1916

In baiting a mouse-trap with cheese, always leave room for the mouse. (*The Infernal Parliament*)

I might have been a gold-fish in a glass bowl for all the privacy I got. (*The Innocence of Reginald*)

CARL SANDBURG 1878–

The fog comes
on little cat feet. (*Fog*)

Pile the bodies high at Austerlitz and Waterloo,
Shovel them under and let me work—
I am the grass; I cover all. (*Grass*)

The people will live on.
The learning and blundering people will live on.
They will be tricked and sold and again sold
And go back to the nourishing earth for rootholds. (*The People, Yes*)

In the darkness with a great bundle of grief the people march.
In the night, and overhead a shovel of stars for keeps, the people march: "Where to? what next?" (*Ib.*)

When Abraham Lincoln was shovelled into the tombs, he forgot the copperheads and the assassin. . . . in the dust, in the cool tombs. (*Cool Tombs*)

O prairie mother, I am one of your boys.
I have loved the prairie as a man with a heart shot full of pain over love. (*Prairie*)

The sea folds away from you like a mystery. You can look and look at it and mystery never leaves it. (*Remembrance Rock*)

GEORGE SANTAYANA   1863–1952

There is no cure for birth and death save to enjoy the interval. (*Soliloquies in England*, "War Shrines")

It is a great advantage for a system of philosophy to be substantially true.
(*The Unknowable*)

JOHN SINGER SARGENT   1856–1925

Every time I paint a portrait I lose a friend. (Quoted in *Treasury of Humorous Quotations*)

WILLIAM SAROYAN   1908–

In the time of your life—live! (*The Time of Your Life*)

FRIEDRICH VON SCHILLER   1759–1805

There are three lessons I would write,
   Three words as with a burning pen,
In tracings of eternal light,
   Upon the hearts of men. (*Hope, Faith, and Love*, Stanza 1)

Against stupidity the gods themselves struggle in vain. (*The Maid of Orleans*, Act III. Sc. 6)

ARTHUR SCHOPENHAUER   1788–1860

To be alone is the fate of all great minds— a fate deplored at times, but still always chosen as the less grievous of two evils. (*Essays*, "Our Relation to Ourselves," Sect. 24)

The most general survey shows us that the two foes of human happiness are pain and boredom. (*Ib.* "Personality, or What a Man Is")

Hatred comes from the heart; contempt from the head; and neither feeling is quite within our control. (*Studies in Pessimism. Psychological Observations*)

Every man takes the limits of his own field of vision for the limits of the world. (*Ib.*)

CARL SCHURZ   1829–1906

Our country right or wrong. When right, to be kept right; when wrong, to be put right! (Speech, United States Senate, 1872)

SIR WALTER SCOTT   1771–1832

Hail to the chief who in triumph advances!
(*The Lady of the Lake*, Canto II. Stanza xix)

Breathes there the man, with soul so dead,
Who never to himself hath said,
This is my own, my native land! (*The Lay of the Last Minstrel*, Canto VI. Stanza i)

O, young Lochinvar is come out of the west,
Through all the wide Border his steed was the best. (*Marmion*, Canto V. Stanza xii)

And dar'st thou then
To beard the lion in his den,
The Douglas in his hall? (*Ib.* Canto VI. Stanza xiv)

O, what a tangled web we weave,
When first we practice to deceive! (*Ib.* Canto VI. Stanza xvii)

My heart's in the Highlands, my heart is not here,
My heart's in the Highlands a-chasing the deer. (*Waverly*, Chap. 28)

ALAN SEEGER   1888–1916

I have a rendezvous with Death
At some disputed barricade. (*I Have a Rendezvous with Death*)

JOHN SELDEN 1584–1654

Old friends are best. King James used to call for his old shoes; they were easiest for his feet. (*Table Talk*, "Friends")

Ignorance of the law excuses no man; not that all men know the law, but because 'tis an excuse every man will plead, and no man can tell how to refute him. (*Ib.* "Law")

Preachers say, Do as I say, not as I do. (*Ib.* "Preaching")

ROBERT W. SERVICE 1874–1958

This is the Law of the Yukon, that only the
    Strong shall thrive;
That surely the Weak shall perish, and only
    the Fit survive. (*The Law of the Yukon*)

Back of the bar, in a solo game, sat Danger-
    ous Dan McGrew,
And watching his luck was his light o' love,
    the lady that's known as Lou. (*The Shoot-
ing of Dan McGrew*)

WILLIAM SHAKESPEARE 1564–1616

References are to the Oxford single-volume edition, ed. W. J. Craig.

All's Well That Ends Well

My friends were poor but honest. (Act I. Sc. iii. Line 203)

Antony and Cleopatra

My salad days,
When I was green in judgement. (Act I. Sc. v. Line 73)

The barge she sat in, like a burnished throne,
Burned on the water; the poop was beaten
    gold,
Purple the sails, and so perfumed, that
The winds were lovesick with them, the oars
    were silver
Which to the tune of flutes kept stroke,
    and made
The water which they beat to follow faster,

As amorous of their strokes. For her own
  person,
It beggared all description. (Act II. Sc. ii.
Line 199)

Age cannot wither her, nor custom stale
Her infinite variety; other women cloy
The appetites they feed, but she makes
  hungry
Where most she satisfies. (Act II. Sc. ii.
Line 243)

As You Like It

Sweet are the uses of adversity,
Which, like the toad, ugly and venomous,
Wears yet a precious jewel in his head;
And this our life, exempt from public haunt,
Finds tongues in trees, books in the running
  brooks,
Sermons in stones, and good in everything.
(Act II. Sc. i. Line 12)

And thereby hangs a tale. (Act II. Sc. vii.
Line 26)

All the world's a stage,
And all the men and women merely players:
They have their exits and their entrances;
And one man in his time plays many parts,
His acts being seven ages. (Act II. Sc. vii.
Line 139)

Blow, blow, thou winter wind,
Thou art not so unkind
As man's ingratitude.
(Act II. Sc. vii. Line 174)

Cymbeline

Hark! hark! the lark at heaven's gate sings.
(Act II. Sc. iii. Line 22)

Hamlet

A little more than kin, and less than kind.
(Act I. Sc. ii. Line 65)

O! that this too too solid flesh would melt.
(Act I. Sc. ii. Line 129)

Neither a borrower nor a lender be;
For loan oft loses both itself and friend,
And borrowing dulls the edge of husbandry.
This above all: to thine own self be true,
And it must follow, as the night the day,
Thou canst not then be false to any man.
(Act I. Sc. iii. Line 75)

But to my mind,—though I am native here,
And to the manner born,—it is a custom
More honoured in the breach than the
observance. (Act I. Sc. iv. Line 14)

Something is rotten in the state of Denmark.
(Act I. Sc. iv. Line 90)

Leave her to heaven,
And to those thorns that in her bosom lodge,
To prick and sting her.
(Act I. Sc. v. Line 86)

There are more things in heaven and earth,
Horatio,
Than are dreamt of in your philosophy.
(Act I. Sc. ii. Line 166)

Brevity is the soul of wit. (Act II. Sc. ii.
Line 90)

Though this be madness, yet there is method
in't. (Act II. Sc. ii. Line 259)

There is nothing either good or bad, but
thinking makes it so.
(Act II. Sc. ii. Line 259)

O! what a rogue and peasant slave am I.
(Act II. Sc. ii. Line 593)

The play's the thing
Wherein I'll catch the conscience of the
king. (Act II. Sc. ii. Line 641)

To be or not to be: that is the question:
Whether 'tis nobler in the mind to suffer
The slings and arrows of outrageous fortune,
Or to take arms against a sea of troubles,

And by opposing end them? To die: to sleep;
No more; and by a sleep to say we end
The heart-ache and the thousand natural
shocks
That flesh is heir to, 'tis a consummation
Devoutly to be wished. To die, to sleep;
To sleep: perchance to dream: ay, there's
the rub. (Act III. Sc. i. Line 56)

The lady doth protest too much, methinks.
(Act III. Sc. ii. Line 242)

There's rosemary, that's for remembrance.
(Act IV. Sc. v. Line 174)

Alas! Poor Yorick, I knew him, Horatio.
(Act V. Sc. i. Line 201)

Sweets to the sweet: farewell! (Act V. Sc. i.
Line 265)

Let Hercules himself do what he may,
The cat will mew and dog will have his day.
(Act V. Sc. i. Line 313)

The rest is silence. (Act V. Sc. ii. Line 372)

Now cracks a noble heart. Good-night, sweet
  prince,
And flights of angels sing thee to thy rest!
(Act V. Sc. ii. Line 373)

Henry IV, Pt. 1

The better part of valour is descretion. (Act
V. Sc. iv. Line 120)

Henry IV, Pt. 2

He hath eaten me out of house and home.
(Act II. Sc. i. Line 82)

Uneasy lies the head that wears a crown.
(Act III. Sc. i. Line 31)

Henry V

We few, we happy few, we band of brothers;
For he today that sheds his blood with me
Shall be my brother.
(Act IV. Sc. iii. Line 60)

Julius Caesar

Beware the ides of March. (Act I. Sc. ii.
Line 18)

Men at some time are masters of their fates;
The fault, dear Brutus, is not in our stars,
But in ourselves, that we are underlings.
(Act I. Sc. ii. Line 134)

Yond Cassius has a lean and hungry look;
He thinks too much: such men are dangerous. (Act I. Sc. ii. Line 191)

For my own part, it was Greek to me. (Act
I. Sc. ii. Line 288)

When beggars die, there are no comets seen;
The heavens themselves blaze forth the
  death of princes. (Act II. Sc. ii. Line 30)

Cowards die many times before their deaths;
The valiant never taste of death but once.
(Act II. Sc. ii. Line 32)

Et tu, Brute! (Act III. Sc. i. Line 77)

Cry "Havoc!" and let slip the dogs of war.
(Act III. Sc. i. Line 273)

Friends, Romans, countrymen, lend me
    your ears;
I come to bury Caesar, not to praise him.
The evil that men do lives after them,
The good is oft interred with their bones.
(Act III. Sc. ii. Line 79)

This was the most unkindest cut of all. (Act
III. Sc. ii. Line 188)

When love begins to sicken and decay,
It useth an enforced ceremony!
There are no tricks in plain and simple faith.
(Act IV. Sc. ii. Line 20)

You yourself
Are much condemned to have an itching
    palm. (Act IV. Sc. iii. Line 9)

There is a tide in the affairs of men,
Which, taken at the flood, leads on to
    fortune;
Omitted, all the voyage of their life
Is bound in shallows and in miseries. (Act
IV. Sc. iii. Line 217)

This was the noblest Roman of them all.
All the conspirators save only he
Did that they did in envy of great Caesar.
(Act V. Sc. v. Line 68)

King John

Bell, book and candle shall not drive me
    back
When gold and silver becks me to come on.
(Act III. Sc. iii. Line 12)

To gild refined gold, to paint the lily. (Act
IV. Sc. ii. Line 11)

I beg cold comfort. (Act V. Sc. vii. Line 42)

King Lear

How sharper than a serpent's tooth it is
To have a thankless child! (Act I. Sc. iv.
Line 312)

I am a man
More sinned against than sinning. (Act III.
Sc. ii. Line 59)

The prince of darkness is a gentleman. (Act
III. Sc. iv. Line 148)

Her voice was ever soft,
Gentle and low, an excellent thing in
    woman. (Act V. Sc. iii. Line 274)

Macbeth

Methought I heard a voice cry, "Sleep no
    more!
Macbeth does murder sleep," the innocent
    sleep,
Sleep that knits up the ravelled sleave of
    care, (Act II. Sc. ii. Line 36)

Double, double, toil and trouble;
Fire burn and cauldron bubble. (Act IV.
Sc. i. Line 10)

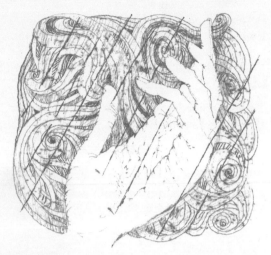

Out, damned spot! out, I say! One; two: why then, 'tis time to do't. Hell is murky! Fie, my lord, fie! a soldier, and afeared? (Act V. Sc. i. Line 38)

To-morrow, and to-morrow, and to-morrow,
Creeps in this petty pace from day to day,
To the last syllable of recorded time;
And all our yesterdays have lighted fools
The way to dusty death. Out, out, brief
    candle!
Life's but a walking shadow, a poor player
That struts and frets his hour upon the stage,
And then is heard no more: it is a tale
Told by an idiot, full of sound and fury,
Signifying nothing. (Act V. Sc. v. Line 17)

I bear a charmed life.
(Act V. Sc. vii. Line 41)

Lay on, Macduff;
And damned be him that first cries, "Hold,
    enough!" (Act V. Sc. vii. Line 62)

Measure for Measure

What's mine is yours, and what is yours is
    mine. (Act V. Sc. i. Line 539)

The Merchant of Venice

It is a wise father that knows his own child.
(Act II. Sc. ii. Line 83)

But love is blind, and lovers cannot see
The pretty follies that themselves commit.
(Act II. Sc. vi. Line 36)

If you prick us, do we not bleed? if you tickle us, do we not laugh? if you poison us, do we not die? and if you wrong us, shall we not revenge? (Act III. Sc. i. Line 69)

The quality of mercy is not strained,
It droppeth as the gentle rain from heaven
Upon the place beneath: it is twice blessed;
It blesseth him that gives and him that
    takes. (Act IV. Sc. i. Line 184)

How far that little candle throws his beams!
So shines a good deed in a naughty world.
(Act V. Sc. i. Line 90)

The Merry Wives of Windsor

Why then the world's mine oyster,
Which I with sword will open. (Act II. Sc.
ii. Line 2)

A Midsummer Night's Dream

For aught that ever I could read,
Could ever hear by tale or history,
The course of true love never did run
    smooth. (Act I. Sc. i. Line 123)

Lord, what fools these mortals be! (Act III.
Sc. ii. Line 115)

Much Ado About Nothing

Speak low, if you speak love. (Act II. Sc. i.
Line 104)

Othello

But I will wear my heart upon my sleeve
For daws to peck at. (Act I. Sc. i. Line 64)

Put money in thy purse. (Act I. Sc. iii.
Line 345)

Good name in man and woman, dear my
    lord,
Is the immediate jewel of their souls;
Who steals my purse, steals trash; 'tis some-
    thing, nothing;
'Twas mine, 'tis his and has been slave to
    thousands;
But he that filches from me my good name
Robs me of that which not enriches him,
And makes me poor indeed. (Act III. Sc. iii.
Line 153)

O! beware, my lord, of jealousy;
It is the green-eyed monster which doth mock
The meat it feeds on.
(Act III. Sc. iii. Line 165)

'Tis neither here nor there. (Act IV. Sc. iii. Line 59)

When you shall these unlucky deeds relate,
Speak of me as I am; nothing extenuate,
Nor set down aught in malice: then must you speak
Of one that loved not wisely but too well.
(Act V. Sc. ii. Line 337)

Richard II

This happy breed of men, this little world,
This precious stone set in the silver sea,
Which serves it in the office of a wall,
Or as a moat defensive to a house,
Against the envy of less happier lands.
This blessed plot, this earth, this realm, this England. (Act II. Sc. i. Line 40)

For God's sake, let us sit upon the ground
And tell sad stories of the death of kings.
(Act III. Sc. ii. Line 155)

Richard III

Now is the winter of our discontent
Made glorious summer by this sun of York.
(Act I. Sc. i. Line 1)

A horse! a horse! my kingdom for a horse!
(Act V. Sc. iv. Line 7)

Romeo and Juliet

A pair of star-crossed lovers. (Prologue, Line 6)

My only love sprung from my only hate!
(Act I. Sc. v. Line 142)

He jests at scars, that never felt a wound.
But, soft! what light through yonder window breaks?
It is the east, and Juliet is the sun. (Act II. Sc. ii. Line 1)

See! how she leans her cheek upon her hand:
O! that I were a glove upon that hand,

That I might touch that cheek. (Act II. Sc. ii. Line 23)

O Romeo, Romeo! wherefore art thou Romeo? (Act II. Sc. ii. Line 33)

What's in a name? that which we call a rose
By any other name would smell as sweet.
(Act II. Sc. ii. Line 43)

O! swear not by the moon, the inconstant moon,
That monthly changes in her circled orb,
Lest that thy love prove likewise variable.
(Act II. Sc. ii. Line 109)

Good-night, good-night! parting is such sweet sorrow
That I shall say good-night till it be morrow.
(Act II. Sc. ii. Line 184)

A plague o' both your houses!
They have made worms' meat of me. (Act III. Sc. i. Line 112)

The Taming of the Shrew

Kiss me, Kate. (Act II. Sc. i. Line 318)

This is the way to kill a wife with kindness.
(Act IV. Sc. i. Line 211)

The Tempest

Full fathom five thy father lies;
Of his bones are coral made:
Those are pearls that were his eyes:
Nothing of him that doth fade,
But doth suffer a sea-change
Into something rich and strange. (Act I.
Sc. ii. Line 394)

Misery acquaints a man with strange bedfellows. (Act II. Sc. ii. Line 42)

How beauteous mankind is! O brave new
world,
That has such people in't. (Act V. Sc. i.
Line 183)

Timon of Athens

We have seen better days. (Act IV. Sc. ii.
Line 27)

Twelfth Night

If music be the food of love, play on;
Give me excess of it, that, surfeiting,
The appetite may sicken, and so die. (Act I.
Sc. i. Line 1)

Be not afraid of greatness: some men are
born great, some achieve greatness, and some
have greatness thrust upon them. (Act II.
Sc. v. Line 158)

The Two Gentlemen of Verona

Who is Silvia? What is she,
That all our swains commend her? (Act
IV. Sc. ii. Line 40)

The Winter's Tale

Daffodils,
That come before the swallow dares, and
take
The winds of March with beauty; violets
dim,
But sweeter than the lids of Juno's eyes
Or Cytherea's breath. (Act IV. Sc. iii.
Line 116)

Poems

Shall I compare thee to a summer's day?
Thou art more lovely and more temperate.
(Sonnets, 18)

When to the sessions of sweet silent thought
I summon up remembrance of things past.
(*Ib.* 30)

Farewell! thou art too dear for my possessing,
And like enough thou know'st thy estimate.
(*Ib.* 87)

Let me not to the marriage of true minds
Admit impediments. Love is not love
Which alters when it alteration finds.
(*Ib.* 116)

GEORGE BERNARD SHAW 1856–1950

We have no more right to consume happiness without producing it than to consume wealth without producing it. (*Candida*, Act I)

The worst sin towards our fellow creatures is not to hate them, but to be indifferent to them; that's the essence of inhumanity. (*The Devil's Disciple*, Act II)

He knows nothing; and he thinks he knows everything. That points clearly to a political career. (*Major Barbara*, Act III)

The true artist will let his wife starve, his children go barefoot, his mother drudge for his living at seventy, sooner than work at anything but his art. (*Man and Superman*, Act I)

It is a woman's business to get married as soon as possible, and a man's to keep unmarried as long as he can. (*Ib*. Act II)

He who can, does. He who cannot, teaches. (*Ib. Maxims for Revolutionists*)

The reasonable man adapts himself to the world; the unreasonable one persists in trying to adapt the world to himself. Therefore all progress depends on the unreasonable man. (*Ib.*)

HENRY WHEELER SHAW (JOSH BILLINGS) 1818–1885

Thrice is he armed that hath his quarrel just,
But four times he who gets his blow in fust.
(*Josh Billings, His Sayings*)

PERCY BYSSHE SHELLEY 1792–1822

I weep for Adonais—he is dead!
O, weep for Adonais! though our tears
Thaw not the frost that binds so dear a head!
(*Adonais*, Stanza 1)

I arise from dreams of thee
In the first sweet sleep of night.
When the winds are breathing low,
And the stars are shining bright. (*The Indian Serenade*)

My name is Ozymandias, king of kings:
Look on my works, ye mighty, and despair!
(*Ozymandias*)

Music, when soft voices die,
Vibrates in the memory—
Odours, when sweet violets sicken,
Live within the sense they quicken.

Rose-leaves, when the rose is dead,
Are heaped for the beloved's bed;
And so thy thoughts, when thou art gone,
Love itself shall slumber on. (*To—, Music, When Soft Voices Die*)

Hail to thee, blithe spirit!
Bird thou never wert,
That from heaven, or near it,
Pourest thy full heart
In profuse strains of unpremeditated art.
(*To a Skylark*, Stanza 1)

PHILIP H. SHERIDAN 1831–1888

The only good Indian is a dead Indian. (Attr. at Fort Cobb, 1869)

The crow that flies over the Valley of Virginia must henceforth carry his rations with him. (After scorching Virginia's earth, 1865)

RICHARD BRINSLEY SHERIDAN 1751–1816

All that can be said is, that two people happened to hit on the same thought—and Shakespeare made use of it first, that's all. (*The Critic*, Act III. Sc. i)

My valour is certainly going!—it is sneaking off!—I feel it oozing out as it were at the palms of my hands!
(*The Rivals*, Act V. Sc. iii)

SIDNEY SHERMAN 1805–1873

Remember the Alamo! (Battle cry of Sam Houston's troops, San Jacinto, April 21, 1836)

WILLIAM TECUMSEH SHERMAN 1820–1891

I am tired and sick of war. Its glory is all moonshine. . . . War is hell. (Attr. words in Address at Michigan Military Academy, June 19, 1879)

Hold the fort! I am coming. (Message to General John M. Corse, Oct. 5, 1864)

MARTHA ("MOTHER") SHIPTON 1488–1561

Carriages without horses shall go,
And accidents fill the world with woe. (*Prophecy*)

Around the world thoughts shall fly
In the twinkling of an eye. (*Ib.*)

Under water men shall walk,
Shall ride, shall sleep, and talk;
In the air men shall be seen
In white, in black, and in green. (*Ib.*)

SIR PHILIP SIDNEY 1554–1586

My true love hath my heart and I have his,
By just exchange one for another given. (*Arcadia*, Book 3)

EDITH SITWELL 1887–

Jane, Jane,
Tall as a crane,
The morning light creaks down again. (*Aubade*)

The King of China's daughter,
She never would love me
Though I hung my cap and bells upon
Her nutmeg tree. (*The King of China's Daughter*)

SAMUEL SMILES 1812–1904

A place for everything, and everything in its place. (*Thrift*, Chap. 5)

LOGAN PEARSALL SMITH 1865–1946

There are two things to aim at in life: first, to get what you want; and, after that, to enjoy it. Only the wisest of mankind achieve the second. (*All Trivia*, "Afterthoughts." Sect. I)

There are few sorrows, however poignant, in which a good income is of no avail. (*Ib.*)

SAMUEL F. SMITH 1808–1895

My country 'tis of thee,
Sweet land of liberty,
Of thee I sing. (*America*)

SOCRATES 469–399 B.C.

Nothing can harm a good man, either in life or after death. (Plato, *Apology*)

I am a citizen, not of Athens or Greece, but of the world. (Plutarch's *Morals*, Vol. III. "Of Banishment")

Crito, we ought to offer a cock to Asclepius. See to it, and don't forget. (Last words. Plato, *Phaedo*)

SOPHOCLES 495–406 B.C.

Wonders are many, and none is more wonderful than man. (*Antigone*)

To err
From the right path is common to mankind. (*Ib.*)

A woman should be seen, not heard. (*Ajax*)

To him who is in fear everything rustles. (*Acrisius*, Fragment 58)

JOHN BABSONE LANE SOULE 1815–1891

Go west, young man. (Article in the *Terre Haute Express*, 1851)

ROBERT SOUTHEY 1774–1843

How then was the Devil dressed?
O, he was in his Sunday best;
His coat was red, and his breeches were blue,
And there was a hole where his tail came
    through. (*The Devil's Walk*, written in collaboration with Coleridge)

You are old, Father William, the young man
    cried,
And pleasures with youth pass away,
And yet you lament not the days that are
    gone,
Now tell me the reason, I pray. (*The Old Man's Comforts*)

HERBERT SPENCER 1820–1903

Progress, therefore, is not an accident, but a necessity. . . . It is a part of nature. (*Social Statics*, Pt. I. Chap. 2)

No one can be perfectly free till all are free; no one can be perfectly moral till all are moral; no one can be perfectly happy till all are happy. (*Ib.* Pt. IV. Chap. 30)

EDMUND SPENSER 1552?–1599

Sleep after toil, port after stormy seas,
Ease after war, death after life, does greatly
   please. (*The Faerie Queene*, Book I.
Canto ix. Stanza 40)

And all for love, and nothing for reward. (*Ib.*
Book II. Canto viii. Stanza 2)

BENEDICT SPINOZA 1632–1677

Nature abhors a vacuum. (*Ethics*, Pt. I.
Prop. 15, note)

Man is a social animal. (*Ib*. Pt. IV. Prop. 35,
note)

We feel and know that we are eternal. (*Ib.*
Pt. V. Prop. 23, note)

MME. DE STAËL 1766–1817

To understand all is to forgive all. (Common misquotation of *Corinne*, Book XVIII.
Chap. 5)

JOSEPH STALIN 1879–1953

In case of a forced retreat of Red Army
units, all rolling stock must be evacuated; to
the enemy must not be left a single engine, a
single railway car, not a single pound of
grain or a gallon of fuel. Collective farmers
must drive off their cattle and turn over
their grain to the safekeeping of State authorities for transportation to the rear. All
valuable property including non-ferrous
metals, grain and fuel which cannot be withdrawn must without fail be destroyed.

In areas occupied by the enemy, guerilla
units, mounted and foot, must be formed,
diversionist groups must be organized to
combat enemy troops, to foment guerilla
warfare everywhere, to blow up bridges,
roads, damage telephone and telegraph
lines, and to set fire to forest, stores and
transports. (Declaration of War, July 3,
1941. Russia was invaded by Germany June
22, 1941)

HENRY MORTON STANLEY 1841–1904

Dr. Livingstone, I presume. (*How I Found
Livingstone*, Chap. 11)

CHARLES E. STANTON 1859–1933

Lafayette, we are here. (Address delivered at
grave of Lafayette, July 4, 1917)

EDWIN McMASTERS STANTON
1814–1869

Now he belongs to the ages. (Said after
Abraham Lincoln's death, Apr. 15, 1865)

JOHN STARK 1728–1822

My men, yonder are the Hessians. They were
bought for seven pounds and ten pence a
man. Are you worth more? Prove it. Tonight, the American flag floats from yonder
hill or Molly Stark sleeps a widow! (Aug.
16, 1777, before the Battle of Bennington)

SIR RICHARD STEELE 1672–1729

There are so few who can grow old with a
good grace. (*The Spectator*, No. 263)

Reading is to the mind what exercise is to
the body. (*The Tatler*, No. 147)

GERTRUDE STEIN   1874–1946

Rose is a rose is a rose is a rose. (*Sacred Emily*)

Pigeons on the grass alas. (*Four Saints in Three Acts*, Act III. Sc. ii)

In the United States there is more space where nobody is than where anybody is. That is what makes America what it is. (*The Geographical History of America*)

HENRI BEYLE called STENDHAL
1783–1842

Almost all our misfortunes in life come from the wrong notions we have about the things that happen to us. To know men thoroughly, to judge events sanely is, therefore, a great step towards happiness.
(*Journal*, Dec. 10, 1801)

JAMES STEPHENS   1882–1950

I heard a bird at dawn
Singing sweetly on a tree,
That the dew was on the lawn,
And the wind was on the lea;
But I didn't listen to him,
For he didn't sing to me. (*The Rivals*)

LAURENCE STERNE   1713–1768

I am positive I have a soul; nor can all the books with which materialists have pestered the world ever convince me of the contrary. (A *Sentimental Journey*, "Maria Moulines")

A man should know something of his own country, too, before he goes abroad. (*Tristram Shandy*, Book VI. Chap. 2)

THADDEUS STEVENS   1792–1868

I Repose in This Quiet and Secluded Spot
Not from Any Natural Preference for Solitude,
But Finding Other Cemeteries Limited as to Race,
By Charter Rules,
I Have Chosen This That I Might Illustrate In My Death
The Principles Which I Advocated
Through a Long Life:
Equality of Man Before His Creator
(Epitaph on his grave at Schreiners Cemetery, Lancaster, Penn.)

ADLAI STEVENSON   1900–

I sometimes marvel at the extraordinary docility with which Americans submit to speeches. (Chicago, 1950)

My definition of a free society is a society where it is safe to be unpopular. (Detroit, Oct., 1952)

The problem of cat versus bird is old as time. If we attempt to resolve it by legislation, who knows but what we may be called upon to take sides as well in the age-old problem of dog versus cat, bird versus bird, or even bird versus worm. (Veto of "Cat Bill," Apr. 23, 1949)

ROBERT LOUIS STEVENSON   1850–1894

Every one lives by selling something. (*Across the Plains*, "Beggars," Sect. III)

To be what we are, and to become what we are capable of becoming, is the only end of life. (*Familiar Studies of Men and Books*)

Politics is perhaps the only profession for which no preparation is thought necessary. (*Ib.* "Yoshida-Torajiro")

For my part, I travel not to go anywhere, but to go. I travel for travel's sake. The great affair is to move. (*Travels with a Donkey*, "Cheylard and Luc")

Fifteen men on the Dead Man's Chest—
Yo-ho-ho, and a bottle of rum!
(*Treasure Island*, Chap. 1)

There is no duty we so much underrate as the duty of being happy. (*Virginibus Puerisque*, "An Apology for Idlers")

In winter I get up at night
And dress by yellow candle-light.
In summer quite the other way,
I have to go to bed by day. (*A Child's Garden of Verses*, Stanza i, "Bed in Summer")

A child should always say what's true
And speak when he is spoken to,
And behave mannerly at table:
At least as far as he is able. (*Ib.* "Whole Duty of Children")

I have a little shadow that goes in and out with me,
And what can be the use of him is more than I can see. (*Ib.* "My Shadow")

The world is so full of a number of things,
I'm sure we should all be as happy as kings.
(*Ib.* "Happy Thought")

Under the wide and starry sky,
Dig the grave and let me lie.
Glad did I live and gladly die,
And I laid me down with a will.
This be the verse you grave for me:
"*Here he lies where he longed to be;*
Home is the sailor, home from sea,
And the hunter home from the hill."
(*Underwoods*, "Requiem")

You cannot run away from a weakness; you must some time fight it out or perish; and if that be so, why not now, and where you stand? (*The Amateur Emigrant*, Chap. 4)

Let any man speak long enough, he will get believers.
(*The Master of Ballantrae*, Chap. 1)

HARRIET BEECHER STOWE 1811–1896

"Who was your mother?" "Never had none," said the child, with another grin. "Never had any mother? What do you mean? Where were you born?" "Never was born," persisted Topsy; "never had no father, nor mother, nor nothin'. I was raised by a speculator." (*Uncle Tom's Cabin*, Chap. 20)

"Do you know who made you?" "Nobody as I knows on," said the child, with a short laugh. . . . "I 'spect I growed." (*Ib.*)

I's wicked—I is. I's mighty wicked, anyhow. I can't help it. (*Ib.*)

SIR JOHN SUCKLING   1609–1642

Why so pale and wan, fond lover?
Prithee, why so pale?
Will, when looking well can't move her,
Looking ill prevail?
Prithee, why so pale? (*Aglaura*, Act IV. Sc. i)

SUETONIUS   *c.* 70–*c.* 140

Hail, Emperor, those about to die salute you. (*Lives of the Twelve Caesars*, "Claudius." Para. 21)

JONATHAN SWIFT   1667–1745

'Tis an old maxim in the schools,
That flattery's the food of fools;
Yet now and then your men of wit
Will condescend to take a bit. (*Cadenus and Vanessa*, Line 758)

Hail fellow, well met,
All dirty and wet:
Find out, if you can,
Who's master, who's man. (*My Lady's Lamentation*, Line 165)

Satire is a sort of glass, wherein beholders do generally discover everybody's face but their own. (*The Battle of the Books*, Preface)

He gave it for his opinion, that whoever could make two ears of corn or two blades of grass to grow upon a spot of ground where only one grew before, would deserve better of mankind, and do more essential service to his country than the whole race of politicians put together. (*Gulliver's Travels*, "Voyage to Brobdingnag," Part II. Chap.7)

We are so fond of one another, because our ailments are the same. (*Journal to Stella*, Feb. 1, 1711)

Promises and pie-crust are made to be broken. (*Polite Conversation*, Dialogue 1)

Why every one as they like; as the good woman said when she kissed her cow. (*Ib.*)

ALGERNON CHARLES SWINBURNE
1837–1909

Maiden, and mistress of the months and stars
Now folded in the flowerless fields of heaven. (*Atalanta in Calydon*, opening)

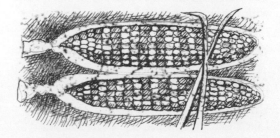

When the hounds of spring are on winter's
    traces,
The mother of months in meadow or plain
Fills the shadows and windy places
With lisp of leaves and ripple of rain. (*Ib.*
Chorus)

And the best and the worst of this is
That neither is most to blame,
If you have forgotten my kisses
And I have forgotten your name.
(*An Interlude*)

JOHN MILLINGTON SYNGE   1871–1909

They're cheering a young lad, the champion
playboy of the Western World. (*The Playboy
of the Western World*, Act III)

TACITUS   *c.* 55–*c.* 117

It is a characteristic of the human mind to
hate the man one has injured. (*Agricola*,
Pt. 45)

Arbiter of taste. ([Of Petronius] *Annals*,
Book xvi. Para. 18)

THE TALMUD

A child tells in the street what its father and
mother say at home.

Respect for God demands that the face, the
hands and the feet be washed once a day.

The wise man indulges himself not in gossip
with women, not even his own wife.

JANE TAYLOR   1783–1827

Twinkle, twinkle, little star,
How I wonder what you are!
Up above the world so high,
Like a diamond in the sky! (*The Star*)

TECUMSEH (CHIEF OF THE
SHAWNEES)   1768–1813

These lands are ours. No one has a right to
remove us, because we were the first owners.
The Great Spirit above has appointed this
place for us, on which to light our fires, and
here we will remain. (To the messenger
from the President, 1810)

ALFRED, LORD TENNYSON   1809–1892

I come from haunts of coot and hern,
I make a sudden sally,
And sparkle out among the fern,
To bicker down a valley. (*The Brook*, song)

For men may come and men may go,
But I go on for ever. (*Ib.*)

Half a league, half a league,
Half a league onward.
All in the valley of Death
Rode the six hundred. (*The Charge of the
Light Brigade*)

Someone had blundered:
Theirs not to make reply,
Theirs not to reason why,
Theirs but to do and die. (*Ib.*)

May there be no moaning of the bar,
When I put out to sea. (*Crossing the Bar*)

I hold it true, whate'er befall;
I feel it when I sorrow most;
'Tis better to have loved and lost
Than never to have loved at all. (In Memoriam, Pt. xxvii)

He seems so near and yet so far.
(Ib. Pt. xcvii)

Ring out, wild bells, to the wild sky.
(Ib. Pt. cvi)

Ring out the old, ring in the new,
Ring, happy bells, across the snow:
The year is going, let him go;
Ring out the false, ring in the true. (Ib.)

'Tis only noble to be good.
Kind hearts are more than coronets,
And simple faith than Norman blood. (Lady Clara Vere de Vere)

He said, "She has a lovely face;
God in his mercy lend her grace,
The Lady of Shalott." (The Lady of Shalott, Canto iv)

In the spring a young man's fancy lightly
    turns to thoughts of love. (Locksley Hall, Line 20)

For I'm to be Queen o' the May, mother,
    I'm to be
Queen o' the May. (The May Queen)

Sweet and low, sweet and low,
Wind of the western sea. (The Princess, Pt. III, song)

Sleep, my little one, sleep, my pretty one,
    sleep. (Ib.)

My strength is as the strength of ten,
Because my heart is pure. (Sir Galahad, Stanza i)

And after many a summer dies the swan.
(Tithonus, Stanza 1)

Elaine, the lily maid
Of Astolat. (Idylls of the King, Lancelot and Elaine. Line 2)

TERENCE   c. 195–159 B.C.

Fortune favors the brave.
(Phormio, Line 203)

As many opinions as there are men; each a law to himself. (Ib. Line 454)

WILLIAM MAKEPEACE THACKERAY
1811–1863

'Tis strange what a man may do, and a woman yet think him an angel. (Henry Esmond, Book I. Chap. 7)

Remember, it is as easy to marry a rich woman as a poor woman.
(Pendennis, Chap. 28)

Them's my sentiments.
(Vanity Fair, Chap. 21)

ERNEST LAWRENCE THAYER 1863–1940

Oh, somewhere in this favored land the sun
 is shining bright;
The band is playing somewhere, and some-
 where hearts are light,
And somewhere men are laughing, and
 somewhere children shout;
But there is no joy in Mudville—mighty
 Casey has struck out. (*Casey at the Bat*)

BRANDON THOMAS   1857–1914

I am Charley's aunt from Brazil, where the
nuts come from. (*Charley's Aunt*, Act I)

JAMES THOMSON   1700–1748

"Rule, Britannia, rule the waves;
Britons never will be slaves." (*Alfred: a
Masque*, Act II. Sc. v)

HENRY DAVID THOREAU   1817–1862

The mass of men lead lives of quiet desperation. (*Walden*, "Economy")

Beware of all enterprises that require new
clothes. (*Ib.*)

Our life is frittered away by detail. . . .
Simplify, Simplify. (*Ib.* "Where I Lived, and
What I Lived For")

Time is but the stream I go a-fishing in. (*Ib.*)

I never found the companion that was so
companionable as solitude. (*Ib.* "Solitude")

I had three chairs in my house; one for
solitude, two for friendship, three for society.
(*Ib.* "Visitors")

I frequently tramped eight or ten miles
through the deepest snow to keep an appointment with a beech-tree, or a yellow
birch, or an old acquaintance among the
pines. (*Ib.* "Winter Visitors")

It takes two to speak the truth,—one to
speak, and another to hear. (*A Week on the*

Concord and Merrimack Rivers, "Wednesday")

Some circumstantial evidence is very strong, as when you find a trout in the milk. (*Miscellanies*)

Thank God, men cannot as yet fly, and lay waste the sky as well as the earth! We are safe on that side for the present. (*Journal*, Jan. 3, 1861)

ROSE H. THORPE   1850–1939

As she climbed the dusty ladder on which
  fell no ray of light,—
Up and up, her white lips saying, "Curfew
  shall not ring tonight." (*Curfew Must Not Ring Tonight*)

JAMES THURBER   1894–1962

Well, if I called the wrong number, why did you answer the phone? (*Men, Women and Dogs*, cartoon caption)

Her own mother lived the latter years of her life in the horrible suspicion that electricity was dripping invisibly all over the house. (*My Life and Hard Times*, Chap. 2)

Then, with that faint fleeting smile playing about his lips, he faced the firing squad; erect and motionless, proud and disdainful, Walter Mitty, the undefeated, inscrutable to the last. (*My World and Welcome to It*, "The Secret Life of Walter Mitty")

LEO TOLSTOY   1828–1910

All happy families resemble one another, each unhappy family is unhappy in its own way. (*Anna Karenina*, Pt. I. Chap. 1)

All, everything that I understand, I understand only because I love. (*War and Peace*, Book VII)

Love is God, and to die means that I, a particle of love, shall return to the general and eternal source. (*Ib.*)

Pure and complete sorrow is as impossible as pure and complete joy. (*War and Peace*, Book XV. Chap. 1)

HARRY S. TRUMAN   1884–

Sixteen hours ago an American airplane dropped one bomb on Hiroshima. . . . It is a harnessing of the basic power of the universe. The force from which the sun draws its powers has been loosed against those who brought war to the Far East.
(Aug. 6, 1945)

When Kansas and Colorado have a quarrel over the water in the Arkansas River they don't call out the National Guard in each State and go to war over it. They bring a suit in the Supreme Court of the United States and abide by the decision. There isn't a reason in the world why we cannot do that internationally. (Speech, Kansas City, Apr., 1945)

MARK TWAIN (SAMUEL LANGHORNE
CLEMENS)   1835–1910

If there was two birds sitting on a fence, he would bet you which one would fly first. (*The Celebrated Jumping Frog of Calaveras County*)

I'll resk forty dollars that he can outjump any frog in Calaveras county. (*Ib.*)

Cauliflower is nothing but cabbage with a college education. (*Pudd'nhead Wilson's Calendar*)

It is difference of opinion that makes horse races. (*Ib.*)

There was things which he stretched, but mainly he told the truth. (*The Adventures of Huckleberry Finn*, Chap. 1)

All kings is mostly rapscallions.
(*Ib.* Chap. 23)

This poor little one-horse town. (*The Undertaker's Chat*)

A classic is something that everybody wants to have read and nobody wants to read. (Speech, *The Disappearance of Literature*)

The report of my death was an exaggeration. (Cable from Europe to the Associated Press)

If there is one thing in the world that will make a man peculiarly and insufferably self-conceited, it is to have his stomach behave itself, the first day at sea, when nearly all his comrades are sick. (*The Innocents Abroad*, Chap. 3)

My books are water: those of the great geniuses are wine. Everybody drinks water. (*Notebook*, 1935)

Among the three or four million cradles now rocking in the land are some which this nation would preserve for ages as sacred things, if we could know which ones they are. (Banquet in honor of General U. S. Grant, Chicago, Nov. 14, 1879)

RALPH R. UPTON   Late 19 Cent.

Stop; look; listen. (Notice devised in 1912 for American railway crossings)

LOUIS UNTERMEYER   1885–

And though these shattering walls are thin,
May they be strong enough to keep hate out
And hold love in. (*Prayer for a New House*, Stanza 4)

From compromise and things half-done,
Keep me, with stern and stubborn pride.
And when, at last, the fight is won,
God, keep me still unsatisfied. (*Prayer*, Stanza 5)

WILLIAM H. VANDERBILT 1821–1885

The public be damned! ([Reply to a question whether the public should be consulted about luxury trains] A. W. Cole's letter, *New York Times*, Aug. 25, 1918)

BARTOLOMEO VANZETTI 1888–1927

I might have lived out my life, talking on street corners to scorning men. I might have died unmarked, unknown, a failure. Now we are not a failure. . . . Our words—our lives—our pains—nothing! The taking of our lives—lives of a good shoemaker and a poor fish-peddler—all! The last moment belongs to us—that agony is our triumph. (Letter to his son, Apr., 1927)

QUEEN VICTORIA 1819–1901

I will be good.([Resolution on ascending the throne] Martin, *The Prince Consort*)

We are not interested in the possibilities of defeat. (To A. J. Balfour, Dec., 1899)

We are not amused. (*Notebooks of a Spinster Lady*, Jan. 2, 1900)

FRANCOIS VILLON 1431–1465

Where are the snows of yesteryear? (*Ballad of Old-Time Ladies*)

VIRGIL 70–19 B.C.

I sing of arms and of the hero who first came from the shores of Troy, exiled by Fate, to Italy and its Lavinian shore. (*Aeneid*, Book I. Line 1)

I fear the Greeks, even though they offer gifts. (*Ib.* Book II. Line 49)

Fear lent wings to his feet. (*Ib.* Book VIII. Line 224)

FRANÇOIS MARIE A. VOLTAIRE
1694–1778

If God did not exist, it would be necessary to invent Him. (*A l'Auteur du Livre des Trois Imposteurs*)

In this best of all possible worlds. (*Candide*, Chap. 1 etc.)

Work banishes those three great evils, boredom, vice, and poverty. (*Candide*, Chap. 30)

I disapprove of what you say, but I will defend to the death your right to say it. (Attr. to Voltaire in S. G. Tallentyre, *The Friends of Voltaire*, 1907)

HENRY WALLACE 1888–

The century on which we are entering can and must be the century of the common man. (Address, May 8, 1942)

WILLIAM ROSS WALLACE ?–1881

The hand that rocks the cradle
Is the hand that rules the world. (*John o' London's Treasure Trove*)

HORACE WALPOLE 1717–1797

The world is a comedy to those that think, a tragedy to those that feel. (Letter to the Countess of Upper Ossory, Aug. 16, 1776)

IZAAK WALTON 1593–1683

As no man is born an artist, so no man is born an angler. (*Compleat Angler*, "Epistle to the Reader")

No man can lose what he never had. (*Ib.* Pt. I. Chap. 5)

I love any discourse of rivers, and fish and fishing. (*Ib.* Pt. I. Chap. 18)

ARTEMUS WARD (CHARLES FARRAR BROWN) 1834–1867

I girded up my Lions & fled the Seen. (*Artemus Ward His Book*, "A Visit to Brigham Young")

Did you ever hav the measels, and if so how many? (*Ib.* "The Census")

I'm not a politician and my other habits are good. (*Ib.* "Fourth of July Oration")

He (Brigham Young) is dreadfully married. He's the most married man I ever saw in my life. (*Artemus Ward's Lecture*)

Why is this thus? What is the reason of this thusness? (*Ib.*)

Let us be happy and live within our means, even if we have to borrer the money to do it with. (*Science and Natural History*)

EUGENE FITCH WARE 1841–1911

O Dewey was the morning
Upon the first of May,
And Dewey was the Admiral
Down in Manila Bay;
And Dewey were the Regent's eyes,
Them orbs of royal blue!
And Dewey feel discouraged?
I Dew not think we Dew. (*Manila*)

CHARLES DUDLEY WARNER 1829–1900

Politics makes strange bedfellows. (*My Summer in a Garden*, Chap. 14)

BOOKER T. WASHINGTON 1732–1799

We are crawling up, working up, yea, bursting up . . . there is no power on earth that can permanently stay our progress. (*The American Standard*)

GEORGE WASHINGTON 1732–1799

Father, I cannot tell a lie. I did it with my little hatchet. (Attr.)

It is our true policy to steer clear of permanent alliance with any portion of the foreign world.
(Farewell Address, Sept. 17, 1796)

The time is now near at hand which must probably determine whether Americans are to be freemen or slaves. (Address to American troops before the Battle of Long Island, July, 1776)

The fate of unborn millions will now depend, under God, on the courage and conduct of this army. (*Ib.*)

Liberty, when it begins to take root, is a plant of rapid growth. (Letter to James Madison, Mar. 2, 1788)

ISAAC WATTS 1674–1748

Let dogs delight to bark and bite,
For God has made them so,
Let bears and lions growl and fight,
For 'tis their nature to.

But, children, you should never let
Such angry passions rise;
Your little hands were never made
To tear each other's eyes.
(*Divine Songs for Children*, xvi. "Against Quarreling and Fighting!")

How doth the little busy bee
Improve each shining hour,
And gather honey all the day
From every opening flower! (*Ib.* xx, "Against Idleness and Mischief")

Our God, our help in ages past,
Our hope for years to come,
Our shelter from the stormy blast,
And our eternal home. (*Psalms*, xc)

A thousand ages in Thy sight
Are like an evening gone;
Short as the watch that ends the night
Before the rising sun. (*Ib.*)

DANIEL WEBSTER   1782–1852

There is always room at the top. (When advised not to become a lawyer, since the profession was overcrowded)

The past, at least, is secure. (Second speech on Foot's Resolution, Jan. 26, 1830)

Liberty and Union, now and forever, one and inseparable! (Reply to Hayne, 1830)

CHARLES E. WELLER   1840–1925

Now is the time for all good men to come to the aid of the party. (Sentence used to test first typewriter, built by Christopher Sholes, 1867)

ARTHUR WELLESLEY, DUKE OF WELLINGTON   1769–1852

A battle of giants. (Referring in conversation with Samuel Rogers to the battle of Waterloo)

The battle of Waterloo was won on the playing fields of Eton. (Attr.)

HERBERT GEORGE WELLS   1866–1946

Human history becomes more and more a race between education and catastrophe. (*The Outline of History*, Chap. 15)

JOHN WESLEY   1703–1791

I look upon all the world as my parish. (*Journal*, June 11, 1739)

MAE WEST   1893–

Come up and see me some time. (*Diamond Lil* [film, 1932])

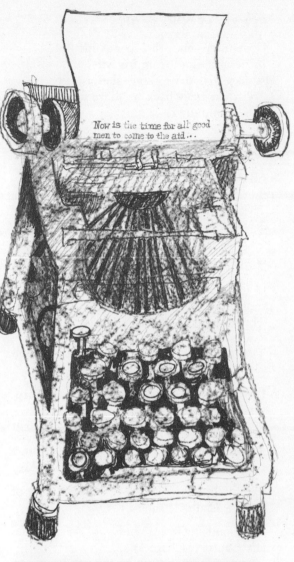

JAMES ABBOTT McNEILL WHISTLER   1834–1903

I am not arguing with you—I am telling you. (*The Gentle Art of Making Enemies*)

I'm lonesome. They are all dying. I have hardly a warm personal enemy left. (D. C. Seitz, *Whistler Stories*)

ELWYN BROOKS WHITE 1899–

Commuter—one who spends his life
In riding to and from his wife;
A man who shaves and takes a train,
And then rides back to shave again.
(*The Commuter*)

WILLIAM ALLEN WHITE 1868–1944

All dressed up, with nowhere to go.
(On the Progressive Party in 1916, after
Theodore Roosevelt retired from the Presi-
dential campaign)

WALT WHITMAN 1819–1892

O Captain! my Captain! our fearful trip is
    done,
The ship has weathered every rack, the prize
    we sought is won,
The port is near, the bells I hear, the people
    all exulting. (*O Captain! My Captain!*)

Have you your pistols? have you your sharp-
    edged axes?
Pioneers! O pioneers! (*Pioneers! O Pioneers!*)

A great city is that which has the greatest
    men and women. (*Song of the Broad-Axe*)

I celebrate myself, and sing myself. (*Song of
Myself*, Canto 1, Line 1)

I loaf and invite my soul.
(*Ib.* Canto 1. Chap. 4)

When lilacs last in the dooryard bloomed,
And the great star early dropped in the
    western sky in the night,
I mourned, and yet shall mourn with ever-
    returning spring. (*When Lilacs Last in
the Dooryard Bloomed*, Canto 1. Line 1)

I hear America singing, the varied carols I
    hear. (*I Hear America Singing*)

To have great poets there must be great
audiences, too. (*Notes Left Over*, "Ventures,
on an Old Theme")

Out of the cradle endlessly rocking,
Out of the mocking-bird's throat, the musical
    shuttle. (*Out of the Cradle Endlessly
Rocking*)

JOHN GREENLEAF WHITTIER
    1807–1892

"Shoot, if you must, this old gray head,
But spare your country's flag," she said.
(*Barbara Frietchie*, Line 35)

For all sad words of tongue or pen,
The saddest are these: "It might have been!"
(*Maud Muller*, Line 105)

The Indian Summer of the heart. (*Memories*,
Stanza ix)

Blessings on thee, little man,
Barefoot boy, with cheek of tan! (*The Barefoot Boy*, Stanza 1)

ELLA WHEELER WILCOX 1855–1919

Laugh and the world laughs with you;
Weep, and you weep alone;
For the sad old earth must borrow its mirth,
But has trouble enough of its own. (*Solitude*)

OSCAR WILDE 1856–1900

I never saw a man who looked
With such a wistful eye
Upon that little tent of blue
Which prisoners call the sky. *(The Ballad of Reading Gaol,* Pt. I. Stanza iii)

Yet each man kills the thing he loves,
By each let this be heard,
Some do it with a bitter look,
Some with a flattering word.
The coward does it with a kiss,
The brave man with a sword!
(Ib. I. Stanza vii)

Other people are quite dreadful. The only possible society is oneself. *(An Ideal Husband,* Act III)

Truth is never pure, and rarely simple. *(The Importance of Being Earnest,* Act I)

I can resist everything except temptation. *(Lady Windermere's Fan,* Act I)

A man cannot be too careful in the choice of his enemies. *(The Portrait of Dorian Gray,* Chap. I)

Ah! don't say you agree with me. When people agree with me I always feel that I must be wrong. *(The Critic as Artist,* Pt. ii)

I have nothing to declare except my genius. ([At the New York Customs House] F. Harris, *Oscar Wilde)*

THORNTON WILDER 1897–

EMILY: I can't. I can't go on. Oh! Oh. It goes so fast. We don't have time to look at one another. I didn't realize. So all that was going on and we never noticed. Take me back —up the hill—to my grave. But first: Wait! One more look. Good-by, Good-by, world. Good-by, Grover's Corners . . . Mama and Papa. Good-by to clocks ticking . . . and Mama's sunflowers. And food and coffee. And new-ironed dresses and hot baths . . . and sleeping and waking up. Oh, earth, you're too wonderful for anybody to realize you. Do any human beings ever realize life while they live it?—every, every minute? *(Our Town,* Act III)

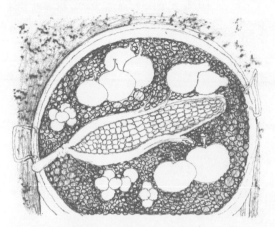

SARA PAYSON WILLIS (FANNY FERN) 1811–1872

The way to a man's heart is through his stomach. *(Willis Parton)*

WENDELL WILLKIE 1892–1944

There exists in the world today a gigantic reservoir of good will toward us, the American people. *(One World,* Chap. 10)

The Constitution does not provide for first and second class citizens. *(An American Program,* Chap. 2)

CHARLES E. WILSON 1890–

What is good for the country is good for General Motors, and what's good for General Motors is good for the country. (To a Congressional Committee, 1952)

WOODROW WILSON 1856–1924

Business underlies everything in our national life, including our spiritual life. Witness the fact that in the Lord's Prayer, the first petition is for daily bread. No one can worship God or love his neighbor on an empty stomach. (Speech, New York, 1912)

We shall not, I believe, be obliged to alter our policy of watchful waiting. (Message to Congress, Dec. 2, 1913)

There is such a thing as a man being too proud to fight. (Address at Philadelphia, May 10, 1915)

Armed neutrality. (Message to Congress, Feb. 26, 1917)

The world must be made safe for democracy. (Address to Congress, Apr. 2, 1917)

OWEN WISTER   1860–1938

When you call me that, smile! (*The Virginian*, Chap. II)

PELHAM GRENVILLE WODEHOUSE 1881–

He spoke with a certain what-is-it in his voice, and I could see that, if not actually disgruntled, he was far from being gruntled. (*The Code of the Woosters*)

WILLIAM WORDSWORTH   1770–1850

Who is the happy warrior? Who is he
That every man in arms should wish to be?
(*Character of the Happy Warrior*)

I travelled among unknown men,
In lands beyond the sea;
Nor, England! did I know till then
What love I bore to thee. (*I Travelled among Unknown Men*)

I wandered lonely as a cloud
That floats on high o'er vales and hills,
When all at once I saw a crowd,
A host, of golden daffodils. (*I Wandered Lonely as a Cloud*)

The world is too much with us; late and
    soon,
Getting and spending, we lay waste our
    powers. (*Miscellaneous Sonnets*)

My heart leaps up when I behold
A rainbow in the sky. (*My Heart Leaps Up*)

The child is father of the man;
And I could wish my days to be
Bound each to each by natural piety. (*Ib.*)

Milton! thou shouldst be living at this hour:
England hath need of thee: she is a fen
Of stagnant waters. (*Poems Dedicated to National Independence and Liberty*, Pt. I. No. 14. "London, 1802")

Though nothing can bring back the hour
Of splendour in the grass, of glory in the
    flower. (*Ode, Intimations of Immortality*, Stanza x)

She dwelt among the untrodden ways
Beside the springs of Dove,
A maid whom there were none to praise
And very few to love:
A violet by a mossy stone
Half hidden from the eye!
—Fair as a star, when only one
Is shining in the sky. (*She Dwelt among the Untrodden Ways*)

She was a phantom of delight
When first she gleamed upon my sight;
A lovely apparition, sent
To be a moment's ornament. (*She Was a Phantom of Delight!*)

Behold her, single in the field,
Yon solitary Highland lass!
(The Solitary Reaper)

HERMAN WOUK   1915–

I kid you not. *(The Caine Mutiny)*

FRANK LLOYD WRIGHT   1869–1959

The physician can bury his mistakes, but the architect can only advise his client to plant vines. *(New York Times,* "Magazine," Oct. 4, 1953)

ORVILLE WRIGHT   1871–1948
WILBUR WRIGHT   1867–1912

Success four flights Thursday morning all against twenty-one mile wind started from level with engine power alone average speed through air thirty-one miles longest 59 seconds inform press home Christmas (Telegram to their father, Kitty Hawk, North Carolina, Dec. 17, 1903)

I do not believe (the airplane) will surplant surface transportation. I believe it will always be limited to special purposes. It will be a factor in war. It may have a future as a carrier of mail. (Interview, March, 1906, Wilbur Wright)

JOHN WYCLIFFE   ?–1471

I believe that in the end the truth will conquer. (To the Duke of Lancaster, 1381, quoted in J. R. Green's *Short History of the English People)*

WILLIAM BUTLER YEATS   1865–1939

Down by the salley gardens my love and I
   did meet;
She passed the salley gardens with little
   snow-white feet.
She bid me take love easy, as the leaves grow
   on the tree;
But I, being young and foolish, with her
   would not agree. *(Down by the Salley Gardens)*

EDWARD YOUNG   1683–1765

Be wise with speed;
A fool at forty is a fool indeed. *(Love of Fame,* Satire II. Line 281)

ÉMILE ZOLA   1840–1902

Truth is on the march; nothing can stop it now. (Article on the Dreyfus case)

J'accuse.—I accuse. (Title of an open letter to the French President concerning the Dreyfus case)

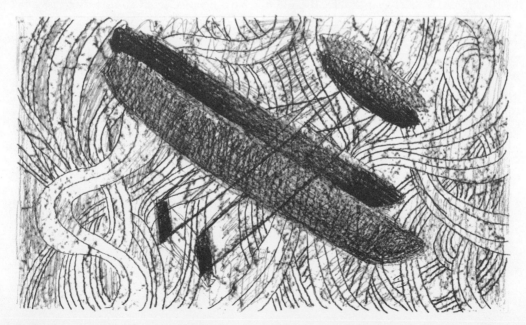

INDEX

THE INDEX is made up of key words and phrases from every quotation in this book. If you are trying to find a specific quotation you remember only partially, look up any of the important words that you recall. The phrases that follow each word guide you to the page and column where the quotation may be found. *The letter* a *refers to the first column on any page; the letter* b, *to the second column.*

You can also use the index to find interesting or useful quotations about a great many different subjects. Under key words such as *America, death, God, life, man,* and *war,* there are phrases from quotations reflecting many diverse opinions. Wherever possible, the phrases have been selected so as to suggest the point of view of each quotation.

Key words that have only an *s* added for the plural or third person singular are indexed together under the singular or first person singular form: *heart* and *hearts* are indexed under *heart; time* and *times* under *time; love* and *loves* under *love.* But pairs such as *hurry* and *hurries* and *march* and *marches,* in which the change involves more than just the addition of an *s,* are indexed separately.

Words that may be spelled more than one way, including ancient, dialect, and comic spellings, are indexed as if they were spelled in the ordinary way. The identifying phrase, however, shows the actual spelling in the quotation. Thus, *sumer is icumen in* appears under *summer.* An exception is made only when the unusual spelling is likely to be better known. The same quotation also appears under *icumen.*

A: appeared the letter A 59a
    gamut of her emotions from A to B 85a
Abandon: all hope abandon 41a
Abideth: and now abideth 25b
Abilities: from each according to his abilities
    77b
Abou: Abou Ben Adhem 64a
Abroad: know something of his own country
    . . . abroad 107b
Absalom: O Absalom, my son 22b
Absence: absence from whom we love 40a
    absence of occupation 40a
Abhor: nature abhors a vacuum 106a
Abide: abide with me 75b
Absurd: nothing so absurd 37b
Abundance: not from an abundance of worldly
    goods 80b
Abyss: that dark and final abyss 68b
Academus: seek the truth in the groves of Acade-
    mus 62b
Acceptable: acceptable in thy sight 23a
Accident: accidents fill the world with woe 104b
    progress . . . is not an accident 105b
    so unlucky that he runs into accidents 77a
Accursed: accursed be he that first invented war
    76b
Accuse: I accuse 121b
Acid: she drank prussic acid 18a
Acorn: tall oaks from little acorns 49b
Acquaintance: auld acquaintance be forgot 29a
Act: doest every act of thy life 16a
Acting: when he was off, he was acting 55a
Action: beautiful in manly action 52b
    spheres of action 56a
Adams: every Adams 11a
Adapt: reasonable man adapts himself 103a
Admiral: Dewey was the Admiral 116a
Adonais: weep for Adonais—he is dead 103a
Adversity: hundred that will stand adversity 32b
    sweet are the uses of adversity 96a
Advice: advice is seldom welcome 37a
    woman seldom asks advice 12a

Advise: my old girl that advises 43a
Affair: tide in the affairs of men 99a
Affecting: on the stage he was . . . affecting 55a
Affection: to me-wards your affection's strong
    60a
A-flying: Time is still a-flying 60a
Afraid: nor be afraid 28a
    whistling to keep . . . from being afraid 46a
After: after us the deluge 87b
Again: try, try again 60b
Against: not with me is against me 25a
    said he was against it 39a
Age: acts being seven ages 96b
    age cannot wither her 96a
    ages and ages hence 52b
    he was not of an age 67a
    in every age and clime we see 53b
    mighty ages of eternity 32b
    never remembers her age 52b
    now he belong to the ages 106b
    think, at your age, it is right 34a
    thousand ages in Thy sight 116b
    we live in such an age 46a
    with an age of ease 55a
Aggress: aggress upon our rights and homes 41b
Agony: agony is our triumph 115a
Agree: except to those who agree with us 90b
    two of a trade can ne'er agree 53b
    when people agree with me 119a
Agreeable: just as agreeable as optimism 21a
Ahead: go ahead 49b
Ailment: our ailments are the same 109b
Aim: other aims than my delight 58b
Ain't: ain't heard nothin' yet 67a
Air: in the air men shall be seen 104b
Airplane: not believe (the airplane) will surplant
    121a
Airy: up the airy mountain 12b
Alabama: I've come from Alabama 51a
Alamo: remember the Alamo! 104a
Alas: alas! Poor Yorick 97b
Alice: "I do," Alice hastily replied 34a

Alien: aliens to this kingdom 53b
All: all at last returns to the sea 35b
  all for love 106a
  all for one 46b
  all generalizations are dangerous 46b
  all the news . . . fit to print 84b
  all the world as my parish 117a
  all this and heaven too 59b
  all we ask 41b
  all's right with the world 28a
  liberty . . . is all in all 31b
  some of the people all the time 73a
  this above all 97a
Alley: she lives in our alley 32a
Alliance: entangling alliances with none 66a
  steer clear of permanent alliance 116b
Allied: Allied Expeditionary Force 47b
Allies: former allies had blundered 84a
Allons: allons, enfants de la patrie 93a
Alone: to be alone is the fate 94a
  to be let alone 41b
Aloud: before him I may think aloud 48b
Alph: Alph, the sacred river, ran 38a
Alpha: Alpha and Omega 25b
Alter: alters when it alteration finds 102b
Am: I think, therefore I am 43a
Ambition: let not ambition mock their useful
    toil 56b
  valiant without ambition 64b
Ambitious: like the ambitious 50a
America: America! America! 18b
  America hopes to bring to pass 47b
  and all lost, wild America 21a
  business of America 39a
  dismemberment of America from this empire
    53b
  epoch in the history of America 11a
  I hear America singing 118a
  makes America what it is 107a
  rock underlies all America 86b
American: American continents . . . not . . . sub-
    jects for future colonization 81a
  American Soldier Known But to God 64b
  American system of rugged individualism 62a
  bewildered empire called the American Mid-
    dlewest 72a
  good will toward us, the American people 119b
  I like Americans 79a
  whether Americans are to be freemen or slaves
    116b
Ammunition: pass the ammunition 51a
Amused: we are not amused 115a
Amusing: amusing herself with me more than I
    with her 81a
Ancient: it is an ancient mariner 38a
Anderson: John Anderson my jo 29b

Angel: angels sing thee to thy rest 98a
  golden hours on angel wings 29b
  on the side of the angels 44a
  tongues of men and of angels 25b
  where angels fear to tread 88a
  woman yet think him an angel 111b
Angela: gotta love for Angela 40b
Anger: anger is a brief madness 62b
Angler: no man is born an angler 115b
Angry: angry with my friend 26a
  such angry passions rise 116b
Animal: all animals are equal 84b
  animals are such agreeable friends 48a
  man is a tool-making animal 52a
Annabel: I and my Annabel Lee 87a
Annal: short and simple annals of the poor 56b
Anniversary: great anniversary festival 11a
Annoy: only does it to annoy 34a
Another: bear another's misfortunes perfectly
    88a
Answer: why did you answer the phone? 113a
Antagonist: antagonist is our helper 29a
Anybody: anybody can win 11b
Anywhere: anywhere but in little old New York
    60a
Ape: apes are apes 67a
Apparition: lovely, apparition, sent 120b
Appetite: appetite comes with eating 88b
  appetite may sicken, and so die 102a
  cloy the appetites they feed 96a
Apple: apple grows so bright and high 61a
  apple of his eye 22b
  my apple trees will never get across 52a
Apple-tree: heart is like an apple-tree 92a
Appointment: appointment with a beech-tree
    112a
April: now that April's there 28a
  whan that Aprille 36b
Arab: fold their tents, like the Arabs 74a
Arbiter: arbiter of taste 110a
Arbitrary: incurring the accusation of being arbi-
    trary 65b
Architect: architect can only advise 121a
  architect of his own fate 15a
Archy: toujours gai, archy 77a
Arduous: however arduous the task 27a
Arguing: no good in arguing with the inevitable
    75a
  not arguing with you 117b
Arm: I sing of arms 115a
Armageddon: place called . . . Armageddon 25b
Armed: armed neutrality 120a
Armies: ignorant armies clash by night 15b
Army: army marches on its stomach 82b
  courage and conduct of this army 116b
Arrayed: arrayed like one of these 24b

Arrow: shot an arrow into the air 74a
Ars: ars longa 60b
Arsenal: arsenal of democracy 91b
Arson: confess to . . . arson 38a
Art: fine art is that in which 93a
   one of the subtlest of the arts 51b
   profuse strains of unpremeditated art 103b
   what art can wash her guilt away 55a
Artful: artful Dodger 43b
Artist: no man is born an artist 115b
   true artist will let his wife starve 103a
   what an artist dies 83a
Asclepius: offer a cock to Asclepius 105a
Ashamed: ashamed to die 76a
Ask: ask Daddy 83a
   ask not what your country 68b
Asleep: soon will be asleep 18a
Astolat: Elaine, the lily maid of Astolat 111b
Astronomy: astronomy compels the soul 87a
Asunder: let not man put asunder 24b
Atmosphere: cold, thin atmosphere 28b
Atomic: not foresee that atomic energy is . . .
   great boon 47a
Attack: I shall attack 50a
Attention: attention must be paid 79a
Audience: must be great audiences, too 118a
Auld: auld lang syne 29b
Aunt: and so do his sisters, and his cousins, and
   his aunts 54a
   I am Charley's aunt 112a
Austerlitz: at Austerlitz and Waterloo 93b
Author: author who speaks about his own books
   44a
Autumn: something in the Autumn 32b
Avenge: avenge the patriotic gore 89a
Avenged: South is avenged 26b
Awake: toss and lie awake for long 73b
A-waltzing: come a-waltzing, Matilda 85b
Awe: fill my mind with . . . wonder and awe 67b
Axe: have you your sharp-edged axes? 118a
   Lizzie Borden took an axe 14a

B

Babbitt: Babbitt's spectacles had huge 72a
Babe: mouths of babes and sucklings 25a
   out of the mouth of babes 22b
Baby: first baby laughed 18a
Back: backs to the wall 58a

thumps upon your back 39b
Bad: altogether irreclaimably bad 32b
   bad die late 42b
   great men are always bad men 11a
   nothing either good or bad 97a
   when bad men combine 29a
   when she was bad she was horrid 74b
Badness: badness of her badness 18a
Bagnet: "Old girl," says Mr. Bagnet 43a
Baiting: in baiting a mouse-trap 93b
Ballot: ballot is stronger than the bullet 72a
Baltimore: flecked the streets of Baltimore 89a
Band: band is playing somewhere 112a
   latest band pieces 52b
Bandersnatch: shun the frumious Bandersnatch
   34b
Bang: not with a bang but a whimper 48a
Banjo: wid my banjo on my knee 51a
Banner: banner in the sky 61b
   banner with the strange device 74a
   star-spangled banner 68b
Bar: back of the bar, in a solo game 95b
   no moaning of the bar 110b
   nor iron bars a cage 75a
Barefoot: barefoot boy, with cheek of tan 118b
Barge: barge she sat in 95b
Barkis: Barkis is willin' 43a
Barometer: barometer, n. 26a
Baseball: this is . . . major league baseball 90a
Bat: bats in the belfry 86b
   twinkle, twinkle, little bat 34a
Bath: long enough without a bath 88b
Bathtub: bathtubs are never dry 79a
Battle: agreed to have a battle 34b
   battle and the breeze 32a
   battle for freedom and truth 64a
   battle of giants 117b
   battle of Waterloo was won 117a
   midst of the battle 22b
   nor the battle to the strong 23b
   telling the battle was on 89a
Bay: somebody bet on the bay 51a
Bayonet: throne of bayonets 64b
Be: fears that I may cease to be 68a
   to be or not to be 97a
   to be what we are 108a
Beaches: shall fight on the beaches 37a
Bean: bean and the cod 26b
Bear: bears and lions growl and fight 116b
   Grizzly Bear is huge and wild 62b
   to pardon or to bear it 40a
Beard: beard the lion in his den 94b
   was an Old Man with a beard 71b
Beast: birds and beasts and flowers 18a
Beastie: cow-rin', tim'rous beastie 30a
Beat: beat him when he sneezes 34a

Beau: she called her beau 40b
Beauteous: how beauteous mankind is 102a
Beautiful: here lies a most beautiful lady 42b
   how beautiful they stand 59b
   most beautiful things in the world 93a
   travel . . . to find the beautiful 48b
Beauty: beauty cold and austere 93a
   beauty in distress 29a
   beauty in things exists in the mind 63b
   beauty is in the eye of the beholder 64a
   beauty is truth, truth beauty 68a
   dreamed that life was beauty 14a
   England, home and beauty 15b
   Helen, thy beauty is to me 87a
   she walks in beauty 31b
   simple beauty and nought else 28a
   slept, and dreamed that life was Beauty 62a
   thing of beauty is a joy for ever 67b
Become: become what we are capable of 108a
Bed: and so to bed 86a
   have to go to bed by day 108b
   should of stood in bed 65b
   when they won't go to bed 61a
Bedfellow: politics makes strange bedfellows 116a
   strange bedfellows 102a
Bee: bringest home the bee 31b
   how doth the little busy bee 116b
   regular brute of a bee 71b
Beethoven: Beethoven's Fifth Symphony 51a
Beggar: when beggars die 98b
Beggared: beggared all description 96a
Begin: begin at the beginning 34b
Beginning: beginning and the end 25b
   in the beginning 22a
   sea—the beginning and the end 35b
Behave: behave mannerly at table 108b
Behavior: justify this devotion by our behavior 90b
Behind: get thee behind me, Satan 24b
Beholder: in the eye of the beholder 64a
Belfry: bats in the belfry 86b
Believe: believe it or not 90a
   believe me, if all 82a
Believed: I have ever believed 27b
Believers: he will get believers 108b
Bell: bell, book and candle 99b
   for whom the bell tolls 44b
   port is near, the bells I hear 118a
   ring out, wild bells 111a
Bellow: bellow no more 73b
Beloved: beloved in life of Abraham Lincoln 78a
   never be beloved by men 26a
Best: best and the worst of this is 110a
   best is yet to be 28a
   best man in the country 72a
   best of all possible worlds 115b

better than any other person's best 59b
   doing the best that you were able 91a
Bet: bet you which one would fly first 113b
Betray: finds too late that men betray 55a
Better: better bread than is made of wheat 35b
   better man than I am, Gunga Din 69b
   far, far better thing that I do 43b
   getting better and better 39b
   man write a better book 49a
   no better than you should be 18b
   seen better days 102a
   worst is better 59b
Beware: beware . . . enterprises . . . require new clothes 112a
   beware, my lord, of jealousy 101a
   beware of false prophets 24b
   beware the fury 45a
   beware the ides of March 98b
   beware the Jabberwock 34b
Bewilderment: man's bewilderment 59a
Bias: their interests alongside its own without bias 58b
Bicker: bicker down a valley 110b
Billboard: billboard lovely as a tree 83a
Biographies: essence of innumerable biographies 32a
Biography: biography is about chaps 21b
   read . . . nothing but biography 44a
Bird: birds and beasts and flowers 18a
   bird thou never wert 103b
   free as the swarming birds 52b
   heard a bird at dawn 107a
   heart is like a singing bird 92a
   if there was two birds sitting 113b
   problem of cat versus bird 107b
   time of the singing of birds 23b
Birth: no cure for birth and death 94a
Birthday: always remembers a woman's birthday 52b
   for an un-birthday present 34b
Birthright: Esau selleth his birthright 22a
Bite: man bites a dog that is news 41a
Black: creeping through the black 73b
   Old Black Joe 51b
Blame: blame of those ye better 70a
   neither is most to blame 110a
Bleed: prick us, do we not bleed? 100b
Bless: God bless us every one 43a
Blessed: always to be blessed 88a
   blessed are the poor 24a
   blessed are the pure in heart 24a
   blessed damozel leaned out 92b
   it is twice blessed 100b
   more blessed to give 25b
Blessing: blessings on thee, little man 118b
   blessings on this House 11a

Blind: discomforts . . . accompany my being blind 86a
  love is blind 100a
Bliss: where ignorance is bliss 56b
Blithe: hail to thee, blithe spirit 103b
Blood: blood of patriots and tyrants 66a
  blood, toil, tears and sweat 37a
  blood's a rover 62b
  native to my blood 32b
  simple faith than Norman blood 111a
  that shed his blood with me 98a
  white in the blood of the Lamb 25b
  young blood must have its course 69b
Bloody: must often wipe a bloody nose 53b
  my head is bloody, but unbowed 59b
Blow: blow, blow, thou winter wind 96b
  blow up bridges 106a
  gets his blow in fust 103a
Bludgeoning: bludgeonings of chance 59b
Blue: our Little Boy Blue 50a
Blundered: former allies had blundered 84a
  someone had blundered 110b
Blynken: Wynken, Blynken and Nod 50a
Boat: messing about in boats 55b
Bobtail: bet my money on the bobtail nag 51a
Bodies: pile the bodies high 93b
Body: sound mind in a sound body 67b
Bog: to an admiring bog 43b
Bold: bold man who first swallowed an oyster 65b
Bomb: one bomb on Hiroshima 113b
Bone: of his bones are coral made 102a
Bonum: summum bonum 37b
Boojum: Snark was a Boojum 34b
Book: author who speaks about his own books 44a
  bell, book and candle 99b
  Book of Verses underneath the Bough 68b
  books in the running brooks 96a
  demand for books 19a
  don't join the book burners 47b
  expend more money for books than . . . for chewing-gum 63b
  his books were read 19b
  man write a better book 49a
  my books are water 114a
  no frigate like a book 43b
  reader look . . . on his book 67a
  some books are to be tasted 16b
  to produce a mighty book 78b
  your borrowers of books 70b
Boone: when Daniel Boone goes by at night 21a
Boot: boots—boots—boots 69b
Bop: real Bop is . . . crazy 63b
Bore: Bores and Bored 31a
Bored: Bores and Bored 31a
Boredom: boredom, vice and poverty 115b

Born: born in a cellar 38b
  good poet's made as well as born 67a
  house where I was born 61b
  man is born unto trouble 22b
  "Never was born," persisted Topsy 108b
  time to be born 23b
  to the manner born 97a
Borogoves: all mimsy were the borogoves 34b
Borrow: even if we have to borrer the money 116a
  men who borrow and the men who lend 70b
Borrower: neither a borrower nor a lender 97a
  your borrowers of books 70b
Borrowing: founded on borrowing and debt 64a
Boston: good old Boston 26b
  travel from Boston to Chicago 44b
Bottom: remaining at the bottom 38a
Bowed: bowed by the weight of centuries 76b
Boy: boy stood on the burning deck 59b
  boy's will is the wind's will 74a
  dog teaches a boy 19b
  our Little Boy Blue 50a
  speak roughly to your little boy 34a
  there was a naughty Boy 68a
  worth the while of a boy 52b
Brain: before my pen has gleaned my teeming brain 68a
  feared it might injure the brain 34a
Brass: become as sounding brass 25b
Brave: brave man with a sword 119a
  brave new world 102a
  fortune favors the brave 111b
  home of the brave 68b
  none but the brave 46a
  too late tomorrow to be brave 15b
Brazil: Brazil, where the nuts come from 112a
Breach: custom more honoured in the breach 97a
Bread: all the trees were bread and cheese 13b
  bread and circus games 67b
  cast thy bread 23b
  don't give bread with one fish-ball 70b
  first petition is for daily bread 119a
  Jug of Wine, a Loaf of Bread 68b
  man doth not live by bread only 22b
  our daily bread 24b
Breakfast: hope is a good breakfast 16b
Breath: breath's a ware 62b
  hot and cold with the same breath 12a
Breathe: breathes there the man 94b
  content to breathe his native air 88a
Breeches: and his breeches were blue 105b
Breed: more careful of the breed of their horses 86a
  this happy breed of men 101a
Brevity: brevity is the soul of wit 97a
Bright: young lady named Bright 28b

C

killed the cats 28a
more ways of killing a cat 69b
play with my cat 81a
problem of cat versus bird 107b
when the cat's away 89a
Catalogue: sooner read a time-table or a catalogue 78a
Catastrophe: race between education and catastrophe 117a
Cauliflower: cauliflower is nothing but 113b
Cause: cause must be removed 41a
Cavern: caverns measureless to man 38a
Celebrate: I celebrate myself 118a
Cemeteries: Other Cemeteries Limited as to Race 107b
Censorship: should be the only censorship 47b
Cent: not a cent for tribute 59a
Center: my center is giving way 50a
Centipede: centipede was happy quite 40a
Centuries: bowed by the weight of centuries 76b
forty centuries look down upon you 82b
men of other centuries 43a
Century: century of the common man 115b
Cerberus: of Cerberus and blackest Midnight 80a
Ceremony: useth an enforced ceremony 99a
Certain: certain we can carry nothing out 25b
nothing can be said to be certain 51b
Chain: at the price of chains and slavery 60a
everywhere he is in chains 93a
nothing to lose but their chains 77b
Chair: three chairs in my house 112a
Champion: people have always some champion 87a
Chance: bludgeonings of chance 59b
right, by chance 39b
Change: remember that to change your mind 16a
think you that I would change 11a
Chap: biography is about chaps 21b
Character: very great, very important character 21b
Charge: yell like furies when you charge 65b
Charity: charity begins at home 27b
charity for all 73a
faith, hope, charity 25b
have not charity 25b
in charity . . . no excess 16b
Charles: Charles the First had his Cromwell 60a
Charley: I am Charley's aunt 112a
Charm: music hath charms 38b
those endearing young charms 82a
what charm can soothe her melancholy 55a
Charmed: bear a charmed life 100a
Cheek: barefoot boy, with cheek of tan 118b
cheek that doth not fade 67b
might touch that cheek 101b
on thy right cheek 24b

Cheer: cheer up 66b
Cheerful: maketh a cheerful countenance 23b
Cheerfulness: cheerfulness was always breaking in 47a
Cheering: they're cheering a young lad 110a
Cheevy: Miniver Cheevy, child of scorn 90a
Cherchez: cherchez la femme 46a
Cherry: before the cherry orchard was sold 36b
Chestnut: under the spreading chestnut tree 75a
Chewing: chewing little bits of string 19b
Chewing-gum: expend more money for books than . . . for chewing-gum 63b
Chicago: travel from Boston to Chicago 44b
Chicken: chicken in his pot every Sunday 59b
don't count your chickens 12a
when chickens quit quarrelling 77a
Chief: hail to the chief 94b
Child: child is father of the man 120b
child is known by his doings 23b
child should always say what's true 108b
child tells in the street 110a
child was diseased at birth 84b
every time a child says 18a
I was a child 87a
infant child is not aware 62b
little child shall lead them 24a
to have a thankless child 99b
train up a child 23b
wise father that knows his own child 100a
Children: breed . . . of their children 86a
children aren't happy 83a
children, you should never let 116b
children of God 24a
do not read, as children do 50a
known as the Children's Hour 74a
mother who talks about her own children 44a
somewhere children shout 112a
suffer the little children 25a
wicked man that comes after children 61a
China: outer China crost the Bay 69b
Choose: do not choose to run 39a
Chopin: gap between Dorothy and Chopin 11b
Christian: onward, Christian soldiers 18a
Christmas: inform press home Christmas 121a
night before Christmas 81b
Christopher: Christopher Robin is saying his prayers 79b
Church: I will build my church 24b
silent church before the service 49a
Cigar: country needs is a good five-cent cigar 77b
good cigar is a smoke 69b
smokes a fifty-cent cigar 11a
Circle: drew a circle that took him in 76b
Circumstantial: some circumstantial evidence 113a
Circus: bread and circus games 67b

memories of the circus 52b
Cities: saw the cities of many peoples 61b
Citizen: citizen of the world 16b
  citizens of the world 91b
  I am a citizen . . . of the world 105a
  not provide for first and second class citizens 119b
City: great city is that which 118a
  long in city pent 68a
Civil: dire effects from civil discord 11b
Civilized: never be a civilized country 63b
Claim: last territorial claim . . . in Europe 61a
Clash: ignorant armies clash by night 15b
Class: not provide for first and second class citizens 119b
Classes: back the masses against the classes 54b
Classic: classic is something that everybody 114a
Clay: Clay lies still 62b
Clever: clever men at Oxford 56a
Clime: in every age and clime we see 53b
Clothed: though clothed in scarlet 67a
Clothes: beware . . . enterprises . . . require new clothes 112a
  that liquefaction of her clothes 60a
Clothing: right to food, shelter, and clothing 70a
Cloud: wandered lonely as a cloud 120a
Cloudy: skies are not cloudy all day 60b
Club: most exclusive club there is 83a
Clue: singularity . . . invariably a clue 45a
Coat: coat was red, and his breeches were blue 105b
Cock: cock who thought the sun had risen 47b
  offer a cock to Asclepius 105a
Cockpit: sitting in the cockpit 73a
Cod: bean and the cod 26b
Coincidence: long arm of coincidence 36b
Cold: hot and cold with the same breath 12a
  how cold my toes 79b
  I beg cold comfort 99b
  midst of a cold war 18a
  we called a cold a cold 21a
Colonization: American continents . . . not . . . subjects for future colonization 81a
Color: those which love colour the most 93a
Colt: twirled an old Colt forty-five 21a
Column: fifth column 80b
Come: come live with me 44a, 76b
  come up and see me 117a
Comedy: world is a comedy 115b
Comet: there are no comets seen 98b
Comfort: I beg cold comfort 99b
  rod and thy staff they comfort me 23a
Comforting: comforting thought in time of trouble 77a
Coming: coming of the Lord 63a
  I'm coming, I'm coming 51b

Commander: task of a commander 27a
Common: century of the common man 115b
  dear common flower 75a
  happiness of the common man 21b
  Lord prefers common-looking people 73a
  seldom attribute common 90a
  suspected . . . because they are not already common 74a
Commonwealth: British Empire and its Commonwealth 37a
  raise up commonwealths 45a
Community: administer . . . for the good of the community 32b
Commuter: commuter—one who 118a
Companionable: so companionable as solitude 112a
Compare: compare thee to a summer's day 102b
Complainers: loudest complainers for the public 29a
Compliment: friends . . . compliment him about looking young 65a
Compromise: from compromise and things 114a
Conceited: insufferably self-conceited 114a
Condemning: before thinking of condemning others 80b
Confess: men will confess 38a
Conflict: never in the field of human conflict 37a
Congo: then I saw the Congo 73b
Congregation: latter has the largest congregation 42b
Conquer: truth will conquer 121b
Conquered: I came, I saw, I conquered 31b
  perpetually to be conquered 29a
Conquering: conquering hero comes 82a
Conscience: catch the conscience of the king 97a
Consequence: in nature . . . there are consequences 64b
Conservative: conservatives after dinner 49a
Consider: consider the lilies 24b
Conspirator: all the conspirators save only he 99a
Constitution: Constitution does not provide 119b
  support the Constitution 44b
Consume: consume wealth without producing it 103a
Consumed: bush was not consumed 22a
Consummation: consummation devoutly to be wished 97b
Contempt: contempt from the head 94b
Content: land of lost content 63a
Contented: riches are . . . from a contented mind 80b
Continent: man is a piece of the Continent 44b
Control: control stops with the shore 31a
Coonskin: whose wit was a coonskin sack 21a

Coral: of his bones are coral made 102a
Corner: some corner of a foreign field 27a
Coronet: kind hearts are more than coronets 111a
Corrupt: power tends to corrupt 11a
Cost: give and not to count the cost 75b
Cotton: in de land ob cotton 49a
Count: don't count your chickens 12a
   let me count the ways 27b
Countenance: expression of countenance 18b
   Knight of the Sad Countenance 35b
   maketh a cheerful countenance 23b
Country: ask not what your country 68b
   country needs is a good five-cent cigar 77b
   God made the country 40a
   know something of his own country 107b
   more essential service to his country 109a
   my country is the world 85a
   my country 'tis of thee 105a
   never be a civilized country 63b
   one life to lose for my country 58a
   only country deliberately founded on a good idea 57a
   our country is the world 53b
   our country, right or wrong 42b, 94b
   save in his own country 24b
   seemly thing to die for one's country 62b
   spare your country's flag 118b
   Union, sir, is my country 37b
   what is good for the country 119b
Countrymen: first in the hearts of his countrymen 71b
   our countrymen are all mankind 53b
Courage: courage and conduct of this army 116b
Course: course of true love 100b
   courses like a page 43b
Courteous: courteous to strangers 16b
Cousin: and so do his sisters, and his cousins, and his aunts 54a
Cow: never saw a Purple Cow 28b
   said when she kissed her cow 109b
Coward: coward does it with a kiss 119a
   coward, n. 26a
   cowards die many times 98b
   only cowards insult 12b
Cradle: hand that rocks the cradle 115b
   million cradles now rocking 114a
   out of the cradle endlessly rocking 118a
Craft: craft so long to learn 60b
Crane: tall as a crane 104b
Crawling: we are crawling up 116a
Crazy: real Bop is . . . crazy 63b
Created: God created the heaven and the earth 22a
   male and female created he them 22a
   thou hast created us 15b

Creator: endowed by their Creator 66a
Cried: cried unto thee, O Lord 23a
Crime: crimes . . . are committed only by persons 65a
   featureless and commonplace a crime 45a
   let the punishment fit the crime 54a
Crisis: in this crisis, shrink 85a
Crispin: upon Saint Crispin's Day 45a
Criticism: pass no criticisms 48a
   people ask you for criticism 78a
Crocodile: how doth the little crocodile 34a
Cross: upon a cross of gold 28a
   with the Cross of Jesus 18a
Crosses: between the crosses, row on row 76a
Crow: crow that flies over the Valley of Virginia 104a
   risen to hear him crow 47b
Crowd: crowd, a host, of golden daffodils 120a
   madding crowd's ignoble strife 56b
Crown: head that wears a crown 98a
   crown of thorns 28a
Crucify: shall not crucify mankind 28a
Cry: don't you cry for me 51a
Crystal: river of crystal light 50a
Cucumber: cucumber . . . good for nothing 67a
Cup: leave a kiss but in the cup 67a
   this cup pass from me 25a
Cur: ears of the old cur 30b
Cure: no cure for birth and death 94a
Cured: hurts you have cured 48b
Curfew: curfew shall not ring tonight 113a
   curfew tolls the knell of parting day 56a
Curiouser: curiouser and curiouser 34a
Curl: who had a little curl 74b
Curtain: iron curtain 37a
Custom: custom . . . great guide of human life 63b
   custom more honoured in the breach 97a
   custom, that unwritten law 41a
Cut: most unkindest cut 99a
Cymbal: tinkling cymbal 25b
Cynara: faithful to thee, Cynara 45a

D

Daddy: ask Daddy 83a
Daffodil: crowd, a host, of golden daffodils 120a
   daffodils that come before 102b
Daily: our daily bread 24b

Damn: damn the torpedoes 49b
Damned: and damned be him 100a
　　public be damned 115a
Damozel: blessed damozel leaned out 92b
Dandy: Yankee Doodle dandy 17a
Dangerous: little learning is a dang'rous thing 88a
　　such men are dangerous 98b
Dark: between the dark and the daylight 74a
　　dark horse 44a
　　in this dark world and wide 80a
　　night is dark 84a
Darkling: as on a darkling plain 15b
Darkness: darkness was upon the face of the
　　　　deep 22a
　　leaves the world to darkness and to me 56a
　　prince of darkness is a gentleman 99b
Date: date that will live in infamy 91b
Daughter: King of China's daughter 104b
David: David his ten thousands 22b
Dawn: dawn comes up like thunder 69b
　　Dawn with her rose-tinted hands 61b
Day: and the day but one 26b
　　as thy days 22b
　　cares that infest the day 74a
　　curfew tolls the knell of parting day 56a
　　day's at the morn 28a
　　dearly love but one day 32a
　　messager of day 36b
　　must follow, as does the night the day 97a
　　now the day is over 18a
　　seen better days 102a
　　sufficient unto the day 24b
　　this day may be the last 83a
　　twenty-four hour day 19a
Daylight: between the dark and the daylight 74a
Dead: dead ar-re always pop'lar 46b
　　fifteen men on the Dead Man's Chest 108a
　　Mumbo-Jumbo is dead in the jungle 73b
　　soul is dead that slumbers 74b
　　weep for Adonais—he is dead 103a
　　when I am dead 19b
　　when I am dead, my dearest 92b
Deadly: more deadly than the male 69b
Deaf: I'm de'f in one year 59a
Deal: new deal for the American people 91a
Dear: too dear for my possessing 102b
Death: all in the valley of Death 110b
　　any man's death diminishes 44b
　　blaze forth the death of princes 98b
　　death after life 106a
　　death and taxes 51b
　　death be not proud 44a
　　death makes equal the high and the low 60a
　　death, where is thy sting 25b, 88a
　　give me liberty or give me death 60a
　　hard at death's door 23a

I have a rendezvous with Death 94b
love thee better after death 27b
no cure for birth and death 94a
ranks of death you'll find him 82a
remedy for everything except death 35b
report of my death . . . exaggeration 114a
sad stories of the death of kings 101a
valley of the shadow of death 23a
wages of sin is death 25b
worse than death 40a
Debt: founded on borrowing and debt 64a
Decay: human things are subject to decay 46a
Deceive: first we practice to deceive 94b
Decency: not offend . . . ideas of decency 47b
Decision: valley of decision 24a
Deck: boy stood on the burning deck 59b
Declare: nothing to declare except my genius
　　119a
Decoyed: poor fools decoyed 86a
Deed: so shines a good deed in a naughty world
　　100b
Deep: darkness was upon the face of the deep
　　22a
　　wonders in the deep 23a
Deer: a-chasing the deer 30a, 94b
　　and the deer and the antelope play 60b
　　phantom deer arise 21a
Defeat: not interested in the possibilities of de-
　　feat 115a
Defect: chief defect of Henry King 19b
Defend: defend to the death your right 115b
　　necessity of workers to protect and defend
　　themselves 55b
　　shall defend our island 37a
　　we will defend them 41b
Defense: millions for defense 59a
Defer: let me not defer it or neglect it 57a
Deferred: hope deferred 23b
Delight: other aims than my delight 58b
　　phantom of delight 120b
　　scorn delights, and live laborious days 80b
　　what delight we married people have 86a
Déluge: après nous le déluge 87b
Democracy: arsenal of democracy 91b
　　made safe for democracy 120a
Denmark: rotten in the state of Denmark 97a
Depth: depths of wickedness 67b
　　out of the depths 23a
Designing: designing St. Paul's 21b
Description: beggared all description 96a
Desire: from what I've tasted of desire 52a
　　love and desire and hate 45a
Despair: let no man of peace and freedom de-
　　spair 68b
　　ye mighty, and despair 103b
Desperate: desperate diseases 49b

Desperation: men lead lives of quiet desperation 112a

Despot: despots of Europe . . . are the savages 70a

Destiny: homely joys, and destiny obscure 56b
  rendezvous with destiny 91a

Destroy: whom God wishes to destroy 49b

Destroyed: must without fail be destroyed 106a

Destruction: for destruction ice is also great 52a
  pride goeth before destruction 23b

Detail: life is frittered away by detail 112a

Device: banner with the strange device 74a

Devil: cleft the Devil's foot 44a
  Devil always builds a chapel 42b
  devil is asleep 86a
  how then was the Devil dressed 105b
  match for the devil 21a

Devotion: justify this devotion by our behavior 90b

Dew: Dew not think we Dew 116a
  dew was on the lawn 107a
  into a sea of dew 50a

Dewey: Dewey was the Admiral 116a

Dial: finger that turns the dial 46b

Diamond: like a diamond in the sky 110a

Die: about to die salute you 14b, 109a
  after many a summer dies the swan 111b
  be ashamed to die 76a
  die is cast 31b
  die not, poor death 44a
  glad did I live and gladly die 108b
  if I should die 27a
  let us do or die 30a
  live or die by his orders 27a
  love her till I die 51a
  no man dies for love, but on the stage 46a
  poison us, do we not die? 100b
  seemly thing to die for one's country 62b
  theirs but to do and die 110b
  time to die 23b
  to die means that I 113a
  to die: to sleep 97b
  what an artist dies 83a
  whom the gods favor dies young 87a
  young person, who either marries or dies 16a
  youth . . . must fight and die 62a

Died: died like a Duke and a Duchess's daughter 18a
  would God I had died 22b

Diem: carpe diem 62b

Difference: that has made all the difference 52b

Diminishes: any man's death diminishes 44b

Dinner: conservatives after dinner 49a

Diplomat: diplomat is a man 52b

Dire: dire effects from civil discord 11b

Direction: rode madly off in all directions 70b

Disappoint: can't abide to disappoint myself 55a

Disapprove: disapprove of what you say 115b

Disaster: in disaster, calm 64b

Discipline: discipline must be maintained 43a

Discontent: winter of our discontent 101a

Discovered: plant whose virtues have not been discovered 49a

Discoverer: they are ill discoverers 16a

Discretion: better part of valour is discretion 98a

Disdainful: motionless, proud and disdainful 113a

Disease: desperate diseases 49b
  extreme remedies . . . for extreme diseases 60b
  poverty—that most deadly . . . of all diseases 84b

Disgruntled: if not disgruntled 120a

Dishonest: free from all dishonest deeds 32a

Disinterested: shopkeepers . . . so disinterested 11b

Dismemberment: dismemberment of America from this empire 53b

Distress: beauty in distress 29a

Distressed: mind distressed 40a

Ditch: distracted in the ditch 40a

Divided: if a house be divided 25a

Divine: to forgive, divine 88a

Dixie: look away, Dixie land 49a

Docility: sometimes marvel at the extraordinary docility 107b

Dodger: artful Dodger 43b

Dodo: Dodo never had a chance 40b

Dog: dog teaches a boy 19b
  dog will have his day 98a
  let dogs delight 116b
  mad dogs and Englishmen 39b
  problem of dog versus cat 107b
  they fought the dogs 28a
  when a dog bites a man 41a
  when the little toy dog was new 50a
  woman's preaching is like a dog's walking 66b

Doing: child is known by his doings 23b

Dominion: His Majesty's dominions 84a

Done: no sooner said than done 88b

Donkey: if I had a donkey 21b

Don't: don't give up the ship 70b

Doodah: oh, doodah day 51a

Door: Door to which I found no Key 69a
  exceed in interest a knock at the door 70b
  handle of the big front door 54a
  hard at death's door 23a
  make a beaten path to his door 49a

Dooryard: when lilacs last in the dooryard 118a

Double: double, double 99b

Dove: beside the springs of Dove 120b
  wings like a dove 23a

Down: coming down let me shift for myself 82a

he that is down 28b
when they were down 14a
Downstairs: I'll kick you downstairs 34a
known many kicked downstairs 29a
upstairs and downstairs 79b
Drab: drab and hopeless round of toil 52b
Dreadful: other people are quite dreadful 119a
Dream: arise from dreams of thee 103a
from a deep dream of peace 64a
life is but an empty dream 74b
love's young dream 82a
to sleep: perchance to dream 97b
Dreamed: dreamed that life was beauty 14a, 62a
Dreary: how dreary to be somebody 43b
Dressed: dressed up, with nowhere to go 118a
Drink: drink to me only with thine eyes 67a
nor any drop to drink 38a
Drinking: drinking largely sobers us again 88a
Drive: difficult to drive 27a
Drop: nor any drop to drink 38a
Drought: droghte of Marche 36b
Drum: beat the drums 82a
ruffle of drums 21b
Duck: angel-duck, winged and silly 70a
four ducks on a pond 12b
Duckling: Ugly Duckling 13a
Dueling: abhorring the practice of dueling 58a
Duke: died like a Duke and a Duchess's daughter
18a
noble Duke of York 14a
Dulce: dulce et decorum 62b
Dullness: relieved our dullness 52b
Dunghill: out of the dunghill 23a
Dust: dust thou art 22a, 74b
excuse my dust 85a
in the dust, in the cool tombs 93b
night is grandeur to our dust 48b
out of the dust 23a
richer dust concealed 27a
Duties: brace ourselves to our duties 37a
Duty: do your duty, and leave the rest 39b
duty of being happy 108b
duty of everyone to unite 71b
duty that lies nearest thee 32b
Duty whispers low, Thou must 38b
every man will do his duty 83a
life was duty 14a
what's a man's first duty 64a
when constabulary duty's to be done 54b
woke, and found that life was Duty 62a
Dwell: world, and they that dwell therein 23a
Dwelt: dwelt among the untrodden ways 120b
dwelt in the land of Nod 22a
Dying: dying . . . too many physicians 12b
insult dying majesty 12b
they are all dying 117b

E

Each: each for one another 71b
each man kills the thing he loves 119a
each to each by natural piety 120b
ech man for him-self 36b
from each according to his abilities 77b
Ear: ever penetrated into the ear of man 51a
lend me your ears 99a
Early: nobody who does not rise early 66b
Earn: set to earn their livings 55b
Earnest: I am in earnest 53b
life is earnest 74b
Earth: back to the nourishing earth 93b
earth is the Lord's 23a
firm spot . . . and I will move the earth 15a
flowers appear on the earth 23b
giants in the earth 22a
God created the heaven and the earth 22a
in that rich earth 27a
let me enjoy the earth no less 58b
man appears on earth 18b
more things in heaven and earth 97a
resting on the solidness of earth 73a
sad old earth must borrow its mirth 118b
salt of the earth 24a
Ease: ease after war 106a
with an age of ease 55a
East: Dawn . . . had lit the East 61b
East is East 69b
east of Eden 22a
Easy: bid me take love easy 121b
easy to marry a rich woman 111b
Eat: let them eat cake 76b
shall eat the fat of the land 22a
tell me what you eat 27a
whatever Miss T. eats 42b
Eaten: eaten me out of house and home 98a
Eating: all the eating and none of the work 73a
Economic: bottom of the economic pyramid 91a
Eden: east of Eden 22a
Education: education makes a people 27a
race between education and catastrophe 117a
Effigies: light of my own effigies 44b
Egg: roast their eggs 16b
Elaine: Elaine, the lily maid of Astolat 111b
Electricity: horrible suspicion that electricity was
dripping 113a
Elementary: "Elementary," said he 45a
Else: happening to somebody else 90b
Elsewhere: not to be elsewhere for thousands 83a
Embarrassment: embarrassment of riches 12b

Embattled: once the embattled farmers stood 48b

Emergency: in a perilous emergency 26a

Emotion: gamut of her emotions from A to B 85a

Emperor: dey makes you emperor 84b
　Emperor has nothing at all on! 13a
　Hail, Emperor 109a

Empire: British Empire and its Commonwealth 37a
　dismemberment of America from this empire 53b
　empire founded by war 81b

Emptiness: emptiness of ages in his face 76b

End: beginning and the end 25b
　ends its days in apple pie 61a
　sea—the beginning and the end 35b
　some say the world will end in fire 52a
　till you come to the end 34b
　way the world ends 48a

Endearing: those endearing young charms 82a

Endowed: endowed by their Creator 66a

Endure: government cannot endure . . . half slave and half free 73a

Enemies: keep our inimies 46b
　too careful in the choice of his enemies 119a

Enemy: areas occupied by the enemy 106a
　hardly a warm personal enemy 117b
　met the enemy and they are ours 86b
　to the enemy must not be left 106a

Energy: uranium . . . turned into . . . source of energy 47a

Enfants: allons, enfants de la patrie 93a

England: always be an England 85b
　as wooden as in England 68a
　England expects every man 83a
　England hath need of thee 120b
　England, home and beauty 15b
　nor, England! did I know 120a
　of a king of England too 48a
　oh, to be in England 28a
　or England breed again 45a
　stately homes of England 59b
　that is for ever England 27a
　this realm, this England 101a
　ye Mariners of England 32a

English: English winter—ending in July 31a
　when shall English men 45a

Englishman: to be an Englishman 83a

Englishmen: mad dogs and Englishmen 39b

Enjoy: after that, to enjoy it 105a
　let me enjoy the earth no less 58b

Ensign: tear her tattered ensign down 61b

Enslave: impossible to enslave 27a

Entangling: entangling alliances with none 66a

Enter: enter not into temptation 25a

Enthusiasm: nothing great . . . achieved without enthusiasm 48b

Envy: in envy of great Caesar 99a

Equal: all men are created equal 66a
　death makes equal the high and the low 60a
　equal and exact justice to all men 66a
　equal right . . . to the use of the land 53b
　more equal than others 84b
　proposition that all men are created equal 72a
　separate and equal station 65b

Equality: Equality of Man Before His Creator 107b
　Liberty! Equality! Fraternity! 15a

Equivocate: I will not equivocate 53b

Err: to err . . . is common to mankind 105a
　to err is human 88a

Error: error of opinion may be tolerated 66a
　popular error to imagine 29a

Esau: Esau selleth his birthright 22a

Escape: once a word has been allowed to escape 62b

Escaped: escaped with the skin of my teeth 22b

Eskimo: Eskimo had his own explanation 86a

Estate: fourth estate of the realm 75b
　Three Estates in Parliament 32a

Esteem: how he esteems your merit 39b

Estimate: thou know'st thy estimate 102b

État: L'État c'est moi 75a

Eternal: general and eternal source 113a
　know that we are eternal 106a
　our eternal home 116b

Eternity: mighty ages of eternity 32b

Ethiopian: Ethiopian change his skin 24a

Eton: playing fields of Eton 117a

Eureka: eureka! 15a

Europe: despots of Europe . . . are the savages 70a
　last territorial claim . . . in Europe 61a
　people of Western Europe 47b

European: dependencies of any European power 81a

Evacuated: rolling stock must be evacuated 106a

Evening: shadows of the evening 18a
　soup of the evening 34a

Event: in the Course of human events 65b

Eventide: fast falls the eventide 75b

Every: every day in every way 39b
　to every thing there is a season 23b

Everyone: everyone has, inside himself 21b

Everything: everything in its place 104b

Everywhere: everywhere that Mary went 58a

Evidence: some circumstantial evidence 113a

Evil: doing evil on the ground of expediency 92a
　don't let's make imaginary evils 55a
　evil that men do 99a
　evil thereof 24b

evils which never arrived 48b
expect new evils 16b
government . . . a necessary evil 85a
I will fear no evil 23a
less grievous of two evils 94a
resist not evil 24b
root of all evil 25b
Exaggeration: report of my death . . . exaggeration 114a
Excellent: "Excellent!" I cried 45a
Excelsior: Excelsior! 74a
Excess: nothing to excess 14b
Exchange: by just exchange one for another 104b
Exclusive: most exclusive club there is 83a
Excuse: excuse my dust 85a
   I will not excuse 53b
   ignorance . . . law excuses no man 95b
Executioner: mine own Executioner 44b
Exercise: 'tis their exercise 18b
   what exercise is to the body 106b
Exiled: exiled by Fate, to Italy 115a
Existence: struggle for existence 41a
Expediency: doing evil on the ground of expediency 92a
Expedient: pursue the expedient 55a
Experience: moment's insight . . . worth a life's experience 61b
Expert: expert is one who 30b
Extinct: sole purpose of becoming extinct 40b
Extreme: extreme remedies . . . for extreme diseases 60b
Eye: apple of his eye 22b
   burning in their eyes 21a
   drink to me only with thine eyes 67a
   eye for eye 22a
   had but one eye 43b
   in the eye of the beholder 64a
   lift up mine eyes 23a
   look at an infantryman's eyes 78b
   many an eye has danced to see 61b
   mine eyes have seen the glory 63a
   night has a thousand eyes 26b
   pearls that were his eyes 102a
   see the whites of their eyes 88b
   thine eye offend 24b
   through the eye of a needle 25a
   throws handfuls of sand in their eyes 61a
   to tear each other's eyes 116b
   twinkling of an eye 25b
   with such a wistful eye 119a
   with unshut eye 15b
Eyeless: eyeless in Gaza 80a
Eyelid: with eyelids heavy and red 62a

F

Face: everybody's face but their own 109a
   face that launched a thousand ships 76b
   his face shine upon thee 22a
   looks the whole world in the face 75a
   never face so pleased my mind 51a
   she has a lovely face 111a
Fade: cheek that doth not fade 67b
   nothing of him that doth fade 102a
Faded: companions are faded and gone 82a
Failure: half the failures in life 59a
   we are not a failure 115a
Fair: deserves the fair 46a
   fair as a star, when only one 120b
   my love, my fair one 23b
   she was good as she was fair 90b
Fairies: beginning of fairies 18a
Fairy: little fairy somewhere 18a
Faith: faith as a grain of mustard 24b
   faith, hope, charity 25b
   no tricks in plain and simple faith 99a
   only tell you my own faith 58b
   simple faith than Norman blood 111a
   World, you have kept faith with me 58b
Faithful: faithful to thee, Cynara 45a
Fall: hurry to get up when we fall down 46b
Fallen: how are the mighty fallen 22b
Falling: go, and catch a falling star 44a
False: beware of false prophets 24b
   canst not then be false 97a
   confess . . . false teeth 38a
   ring out the false 111a
Fame: Fame is the spur 80b
   puts you in de Hall o' Fame 84b
   which fame did not delay 45a
Families: only two families in the world 35b
Family: each unhappy family 113a
Fancy: in the spring a young man's fancy 111a
Far: far and few 71b
   far, far better thing 43b
   over the hills and far away 53b
   so near and yet so far 111a
Far East: those who brought war to the Far East 113b
Farce: farce is over 88b
Farewell: farewell! thou art too dear 102b
Farmer: once the embattled farmers stood 48b
Fashion: in my fashion 45a
Fast: run at least twice as fast as that 34b
Fat: butter will only make us fat 55a
   ever hears of fat men heading a riot 65a

shall eat the fat of the land 22a
Fate: architect of his own fate 15a
  cannot suspend their fate 42b
  exiled by Fate, to Italy 115a
  Fate chooses your relations 42b
  fate of unborn millions 116b
  hanging breathless on thy fate 74a
  jeers at Fate 11a
  master of my fate 59b
  when fate summons 46a
Father: child is father of the man 120b
  Father, forgive them 25a
  father of nations 64b
  fathers have eaten sour grapes 24b
  full fathom five thy father lies 102a
  in my Father's house 25a
  wise father that knows his own child 100a
  you are old, Father William 34a, 105b
Fathom: full fathom five thy father lies 102a
Fatling: young lion and the fatling 24a
Fault: fault ... not in our stars 98b
Fear: discreet without fear 64b
  fear lent wings to his feet 115a
  fear the Greeks 115a
  fears that I may cease to be 68a
  freedom from fear 91b
  I will fear no evil 23a
  only thing we have to fear 91a
  so ... robs the mind ... as fear 29a
  to him who is in fear 105a
Feather: fine feathers that make fine birds 12a
  stuck a feather in his cap 17b
February: February hath twenty-eight alone 55b
  excepting February alone 14b
Federal: our Federal Union 65a
Feeble: body of a weak and feeble woman 48a
Feel: hit feel lak sparrer-grass 59a
Feeling: as old as he's feeling 38b
Feet: fear lent wings to his feet 115a
  fog comes on little cat feet 93b
  lamp unto my feet 23a
  with little snow-white feet 121b
Fell: do not love thee, Doctor Fell 27b
Fellowship: such a fellowship of good knights 76a
Female: female of the species 69b
  male and female created he them 22a
Femme: cherchez la femme 46a
Fen: fen of stagnant waters 120b
Fence: good fences make good neighbors 52a
Fermi: recent work by E. Fermi 47a
Fern: sparkle out among the fern 110b
Few: far and few 71b
  most may err as grossly as the few 45a
  so much owed by so many to so few 37a
  we happy few 98a

Fiction: stranger than fiction 31b
Fidelity: fidelity, perseverance 19b
Field: lilies of the field 24b
  resumed work in the field 52b
  shall fight in the fields 37a
Fifteen: fifteen men on the Dead Man's Chest 108a
Fifth: fifth column 80b
Fifty: fifty million Frenchmen can't be wrong 57a
Fifty-four: fifty-four forty or fight 12b
Fig: fig for care 60a
Fight: bears and lions growl and fight 116b
  cannot fight against the future 54b
  fifty-four forty or fight 12b
  fight and not to heed the wounds 75b
  he that fights and runs away 13b
  must fight on to the end 58a
  not yet begun to fight 67a
  purpose to fight it out on this line 56a
  shall fight on the beaches 37a
  sleep before you fight 15b
  too proud to fight 120a
  youth ... must fight and die 62a
Filthy: not greedy of filthy lucre 25b
Fine: fine feathers that make fine birds 12a
Finest: this was their finest hour 37a
Finger: finger that turns the dial 46b
  Moving Finger writes 69a
  with fingers weary and worn 62a
Fire: bush burned with fire 22a
  don't fire unless fired upon 85b
  fire burn 99b
  fire when you are ready, Gridley 43a
  set an house on fire 16b
  set fire to forest, stores 106a
  some say the world will end in fire 52a
  when your neighbour's wall is on fire 62b
Firing: faced the firing squad 113a
First: first and the last 25b
  first in war 71b
  if at first you don't succeed 60b
  that loved not at first sight 76b
  we were the first owners 110b
Fish-ball: don't give bread with one fish-ball 70b
Fishes: were to make little fishes talk 55b
  where the flyin'-fishes play 69b
Fishing: love any discourse of ... fishing 115b
Fish-peddler: good shoemaker and a poor fish-peddler 115a
Fit: only the Fit survive 95b
Fittest: Survival of the Fittest 41a
Flag: flag is passing by 21b
  spare your country's flag 118b
  tonight, the American flag floats 106b
  whose flag has braved 32a

truth shall make you free 25a
Freedom: all who love freedom 47b
    battle for freedom and truth 64a
    four essential freedoms 91b
    freedom of religion 66a
    in giving freedom to the slave 72a
    let no man of peace and freedom despair 68b
    new birth of freedom 72a
Freely: nothing so freely as advice 90a
Freemen: whether Americans are to be freemen or slaves 116b
Frenchies: those Frenchies seek him everywhere 84b
Frenchmen: fifty million Frenchmen can't be wrong 57a
Friar: cannot all be friars 35b
Friday: takes my man Friday 42b
Friend: a friend is a person 48b
    angry with my friend 26a
    animals are such agreeable friends 48a
    don't tell your friends about your indigestion 57a
    friend of mankind 64b
    friends . . . compliment him about looking young 65a
    friends, Romans, countrymen 99a
    friends were poor but honest 95b
    golden friends 63a
    Huron and Iroquois forests . . . peopled with my friends 70a
    old friends are best 95b
    paint a portrait I lose a friend 94a
    save me, from the candid friend 32a
    very much his friend indeed 40a
    Win Friends and Influence People 32b
    you choose your friends 42b
Friendly: universe is not . . . friendly 61a
Friendship: two for friendship 112a
Frigate: no frigate like a book 43b
Fringe: lunatic fringe in all reform 92a
Frittered: life is frittered away by detail 112a
Frog: how public, like a frog 43b
    outjump any frog in Calaveras county 113b
Fullness: fulness thereof 23a
Funeral: at the funeral his mother 14a
Funny: everything is funny 90b
    funny peculiar 59a
Fur: make the fur fly 30b
Fury: fury of a patient man 45a
Future: cannot fight against the future 54b
    with all the hopes of future years 74a

G

Gaels: great Gaels of Ireland 37a
Gai: toujours gai, archy 77a
Gaining: something might be gaining 85a
Gallery: gallery in which the reporters sit 75b
Gallia: Gallia est omnis divisa 31b
Game: marks . . . how you played the game 89a
Gamut: gamut of her emotions from A to B 85a
Gang: gang aft a-gley 30b
Garden: down by the salley gardens 121b
    in the garden of Shut-Eye Town 50a
Gardener: law, say the gardeners 15b
Garland: green willow is my garland 60b
Gas: gas smells awful 85a
Gate: after we pass the gate 45a
    gates of hell 24b
    matters not how strait the gate 59b
Gather: gather ye rosebuds 60a
Gaul: Gaul is divided into three 31b
Gaza: eyeless in Gaza 80a
Gazed: too much gazed at 67b
Geese: geese are swans 15b
General Motors: what's good for General Motors 119b
Generalization: all generalizations are dangerous 46b
Generation: generation of vipers 24a
Genius: genius does what it must 79a
    genius is one per cent inspiration 47a
    nothing to declare except my genius 119a
    those of the great geniuses 114a
Gentle: as the gentle rain from heaven 100b
Gentleman: definition of a gentleman 84a
    king . . . cannot make a gentleman 29a
    prince of darkness is a gentleman 99b
Geography: geography is about maps 21b
George: George the Third may profit by their example 60a
    King George will be able to read that 58b
Germany: Nazi Germany had become a menace 84a
Get: get thee behind me, Satan 24b
Ghastly: made a ghastly writhe 43a
Giant: battle of giants 117a
    giants in the earth 22a
    not giants but windmills 35b
Gift: God's gifts 27b
    though they offer gifts 115a
Gift-horse: look a gift-horse in the mouth 30b
Gild: to gild refined gold 99b
Gills: man—who has no gills 26a

Gimble: gyre and gimble in the wave 34b
Girded: I girded up my Lions 116a
Girl: at girls who wear glasses 85a
    in little girls is slamming doors 19b
    of all the girls 32a
    "Old girl," says Mr. Bagnet 43a
    Poor Little Rich Girl 39b
    there was a little girl 74b
    with the girls be handy 17a
Girlish: filled to the brim with girlish glee 54a
Gitchee: by the shores of Gitchee Gumee 74b
Give: blesseth him that gives 100b
    give and not to count the cost 75a
    give me your tired, your poor 70b
    give us this day 24b
    more blessed to give 25b
Given: to whom much is given, much is required
    68a
Glad: glad did I live and gladly die 108b
    too soon made glad 28a
Gladness: gladness of her gladness 18a
Glass: gold-fish in a glass bowl 93b
Glasses: at girls who wear glasses 85a
Glee: filled to the brim with girlish glee 54a
    midst of his laughter and glee 34b
Glen: down the rushy glen 12b
Gloire: jour de gloire est arrivé 93a
Gloom: amid the encircling gloom 84a
Gloria: sic transit gloria mundi 68a
Glory: glory in the flower 120b
    glory of rulers or of races 21b
    glory of the world passes 68a
    glory that was Greece 87b
    glory to God in the highest 25a
    Here Rests in Honored Glory 64b
    it's glory is all moonshine 104b
    mine eyes have seen the glory 63a
Glove: glove upon that hand 101a
    too big for white-kid gloves 21a
Go: go, and catch a falling star 44a
    then go ahead 40b
Gobble-uns: gobble-uns 'll git you 89a
God: against stupidity the gods themselves 94a
    American Soldier Known But to God 64b
    as God gives us to see the right 73a
    best thing God invents 28a
    Cabots talk only to God 26b
    can worship God or love his neighbor 119b
    children of God 24a
    dear God who loveth us 38a
    doth God exact day-labour 80b
    forbid it, Almighty God 60a
    glory to God in the highest 25a
    God bears his chosen to heaven 35b
    God bless us every one 43a
    God created man in his own image 22a

God created the heaven and the earth 22a
God has made them so 116b
God hath given liberty 40b
God hath joined together 24b
God in his mercy lend her grace 111a
God is any respecter of persons 27a
God is our refuge 23a
God made the country 40a
God moves in a mysterious way 40a
God, our help in ages past 116b
God said, Let there be light 22a
God save the king 32a
God shed his grace on thee 18b
God's gifts 27b
gods help them 12a
God's in his heaven 28a
hand folks over to God's mercy 48a
if God did not exist 115b
leave the rest to the gods 39b
Lord God of Hosts 70a
Love is God 113a
my God, my God 23a, 25a
one, on God's side is a majority 86b
only God can make a tree 69a
presume not God to scan 88a
respect for God demands 110a
so near is God to man 48b
things that are God's 25a
this nation, under God 72a
thy God my God 22b
trust God 28a
wherever God erects 42b
whom God wishes to destroy 49b
whom the gods favor dies young 87a
with God all things 25a
Gold: all the gold that the goose 12a
    fringing the . . . road with harmless gold 75a
    gold and silver becks me 99b
    if gold rusts 36b
    upon a cross of gold 28a
Gold-fish: gold-fish in a glass bowl 93b
Gone: gone tomorrow 19a
Good: administer . . . for the good of the com-
    munity 32b
    any good thing I can do 57a
    as well to create good precedents 16b
    cucumber . . . good for nothing 67a
    good die early 42b
    good in everything 96a
    good is oft interred 99a
    good must associate 29a
    good name in man 100b
    good name is rather to be chosen 23b
    good of the people . . . chief law 37b
    good poet's made as well as born 67a
    good will toward us, the American people 119b

highest good 37b
I will be good 115a
music, the greatest good 11b
my religion is to do good 85a
never hear anything but good 90b
nothing can harm a good man 105a
nothing either good or bad 97a
only noble to be good 111a
peace, good will toward men 25a
piece of good news 21b
policy of the good neighbor 91a
she was good as she was fair 90b
so shines a good deed in a naughty world 100b
what is good for the country 119b
when she was good 74b
Good-by: good-by, Grover's Corners 119a
Good-night: good-night, good-night 101b
  good-night, sweet prince 98a
Goose: all the gold that the goose 12a
Gore: avenge the patriotic gore 89a
  gore no more 73b
Gossip: not in gossip with women 110a
Govern: easy to govern 27a
Governed: not so well governed as they ought
  to be 62a
Government: government . . . a necessary evil 85a
  government cannot endure . . . half slave and
    half free 73a
  government is itself an art 51b
  government of men and morning newspapers
    86b
  no Government can be long secure 44a
  object of government 21b
  thirteen states . . . able to support a national
    government 58a
  those who have joined the Government 37a
Grace: God in his mercy lend her grace 111a
  grow old with a good grace 106b
Gracious: be gracious unto thee 22a
  if a man be gracious 16b
Grain: faith as a grain of mustard 24b
Grandeur: grandeur that was Rome 87b
  night is grandeur to our dust 48b
Grape: fathers have eaten sour grapes 24b
  grapes are sour 12a
  grapes of wrath are stored 63a
Grasp: man's reach should exceed his grasp 27b
Grass: hit look lak sparrer-grass 59a
  hour of splendour in the grass 120b
  I am the grass 93b
  pigeons on the grass, alas 107a
  two blades of grass to grow 109a
Grasshopper: half a dozen grasshoppers 29a
Grave: a-moldering in the grave 58a
  grave is not its goal 74b
  grave, where is thy victory? 25b, 88a

see myself go into my grave 86a
  up the hill—to my grave 119a
Gray: this old gray head 118b
Great: fate of all great minds 94a
  great is to be misunderstood 49a
  great men are always bad men 11a
  great men have their poor relations 43a
  I don't say he's a great man 79a
  lives of great men all remind us 74b
  nothing great . . . achieved without enthusiasm
    48b
  rule of men entirely great 75b
  some men are born great 102a
  very great, very important character 21b
Greatest: greatest happiness of the greatest
    number 21b
  greatest men and women 118a
Greatness: be not afraid of greatness 102a
Greece: glory that was Greece 87b
  isles of Greece 31a
Greedy: not greedy of filthy lucre 25b
Greek: I fear the Greeks 115a
  it was Greek to me 98b
Green: green in judgement 95b
  green willow is my garland 60b
  lie down in green pastures 23a
Green-eyed: it is the green-eyed monster 101a
Greeting: "How are you!" is a greeting 57a
Gridley: fire when you are ready, Gridley 43a
Grief: no greater grief 41a
  torments of grief you endured 48b
  with a great bundle of grief 93b
Grin: ending with the grin 34a
Grizzly: Grizzly Bear is huge and wild 62b
Grove: seek the truth in the groves of Academus
    62b
Grow: grow old along with me 28a
  grow up with the country 57a
  I 'spect I growed 109a
  two blades of grass to grow 109a
Gruntled: far from being gruntled 120a
Guard: that guard our native seas 32a
Guerilla: foment guerilla warfare everywhere 106a
Guide: custom . . . great guide of human life 63b
Guilt: what art can wash her guilt away 55a
Guiltless: guiltless heart is free 32a
Guilty: better that ten guilty persons escape 26a
  not be guilty of innocent blood 47a
Gun: guns aren't lawful 85a
  guns will make us powerful 55a
Gunga: better man than I am, Gunga Din 69b
Gypsy: sets the gypsy blood astir 32b
Gyre: gyre and gimble in the wave 34b

H

Habeas corpus: freedom of person under . . .
    habeas corpus 66a
Habit: other habits are good 116a
Habitual: nothing is habitual but indecision 65b
Ha-ha: funny ha-ha 59a
Hail: hail fellow, well met 109a
    hail to the chief 94b
    hail to thee, blithe spirit 103b
    man that hails you Tom or Jack 39b
Hair: stars in her hair were seven 92b
    your hair has become very white 34a
Half: half slave and half free 73a
    space of half an hour 25b
Half-a-dozen: six of one and half-a-dozen of the
    other 77a
Halter: halters in the hanged man's house 35b
Hand: Dawn with her rose-tinted hands 61b
    glove upon that hand 101a
    hand for hand 22a
    hand that rocks the cradle 115b
    let not man have the upper hand 22b
    let not thy left hand know 24b
    pale hands I loved 62a
    Uriah, with his long hands 43a
    with mouths only and no hands 73a
Handle: polished up that handle so successfullee
    54a
Handy: with the girls be handy 17a
Hang: must, indeed, all hang together 52a
Hangar: toward the floodlights and hangars 73a
Hanged: halters in the hanged man's house 35b
Hanging: hanging is too good 28b
Hanner: lost our little Hanner 12a
Happiness: consume happiness without produc-
    ing it 103a
    foes of human happiness 94a
    great step towards happiness 107a
    greatest happiness of the greatest number 21b
    happiness of the common man 21b
    Life, Liberty and the pursuit of happiness 66a,
    70a
    secret of happiness 93b
    time of happiness when in misery 41a
    with reasonable happiness 51b
Happy: all happy families resemble 113a
    children aren't happy 83a
    duty of being happy 108b
    happy highways where I went 63a
    happy the man 46a
    happy the man whose wish 88a

    how happy he 55a
    let us be happy 116a
    perfectly happy till all are happy 105b
    this happy breed of men 101a
    we happy few 98a
    we should all be as happy as kings 108b
    who is the happy warrior? 120a
Hard: hard at death's door 23a
    "Hard," replied the Dodger 43b
    though hard be the task 35b
Hardship: many hardships on the high seas 61b
Hare: March Hare went on 34a
Hark: hark! hark! the lark 96b
Harmony: reestablishment of peace and harmony
    71b
Harp: harp that once through Tara's halls 82a
    wild harp slung behind him 82a
Harry: such a King Harry 45a
Harsh: harsh as truth 53b
Harvard: my Yale College and my Harvard 78b
Haste: haste to repay an obligation 90a
Hat: hats off 21b
    whose hat was in his hand 66b
    wid my hat caved in 51a
Hatchet: did it with my little hatchet 116a
Hate: hate of those ye guard 70a
    hate the man one has injured 110a
    I know enough of hate 52a
    love and desire and hate 45a
    sprung from my only hate 101a
    strong enough to keep hate out 114a
Hatred: hatred comes from the heart 94b
    stalled ox and hatred therewith 23b
Haughty: haughty spirit before a fall 23b
Haunt: haunts of coot and hern 110b
Have-not: *Haves* and the *Have-nots* 35b
Havoc: cry "Havoc!" 98b
Head: heart runs away with his head 38b
    if you can keep your head 69b
    incessantly stand on your head 34a
    off with her head 34a
    she has the head 43a
    shorter by a head 48a
    uneasy lies the head 98a
    which way the head lieth 89a
Heal: physician, heal thyself 25a
Health: health of nations 46b
Heard: ain't heard nothin' yet 67a
    I will be heard 53b
Heart: because my heart is pure 111b
    blessed are the pure in heart 24a
    come to pass in the heart of America 47b
    give . . . not your heart away 62b
    heart and stomach of a king 48a
    heart—how shall I say? 28a
    heart is a lonely hunter 76a

heart is like a singing bird 92a
heart runs away with his head 38b
humble and a contrite heart 70a
Indian Summer of the heart 118b
kind hearts are more than coronets 111a
maketh the heart sick 23b
man after his own heart 22b
meditation of my heart 23a
merry heart 23b
my heart is turning ebber 51a
my heart leaps up 120b
my heart's in the Highlands 30a, 94b
now cracks a noble heart 98a
our heart is not quiet 15b
so the heart be right 89a
somewhere hearts are light 112a
strings . . . in the human heart 43a
though the heart be still as loving 31b
true love hath my heart 104b
upon the hearts of men 94a
way to a man's heart 119b
wear my heart upon my sleeve 100b
Heather: know I how the heather looks 43b
Heaven: all Heaven in a rage 26a
  all of heaven 11b
  all this and heaven too 59b
  every purpose under the heaven 23b
  fair and open face of heaven 68a
  flowerless fields of heaven 109b
  God bears his chosen to heaven 35b
  God created the heaven and the earth 22a
  help yourself, and heaven will help you 70a
  is he in heaven? 84b
  kingdom of heaven 25a
  leave her to heaven 97a
  more things in heaven and earth 97a
  pray Heaven to bestow 11a
  silence in heaven 25b
  starry heavens above me 67b
  what's a heaven for 27b
Heavy: are heavy laden 24b
Heed: lesson you should heed 60b
Height: at that far height 28b
Held: must be held to the last man 58a
Helen: Helen, thy beauty is to me 87a
  sweet Helen 76b
Hell: gates of hell 24b
  Hell is murky 100a
  is he in hell? 84b
  war is hell 104b
Hellespont: Leander swam the Hellespont 61a
Hello: hello, sucker! 57a
Help: God, our help in ages past 116b
  gods help them 12a
  help of the helpless 75b
  help yourself, and heaven will help you 70a

people must help one another 70a
very present help in trouble 23a
whence cometh my help 23a
Helper: antagonist is our helper 29a
Hemisphere: extend their system to any portion
    of this hemisphere 81a
Hence: hence loathed Melancholy 80a
Herb: dinner of herbs where love is 23b
Hercules: let Hercules himself 98a
Herd: lowing herd winds slowly o'er the lea 56a
Here: here lies my wife 46a
  here today 19a
  neither here nor there 101a
Heretic: heretic, rebel, a thing to flout 76b
Hero: conquering hero comes 82a
Hessian: yonder are the Hessians 106b
Hickory: tough as a hickory rail 21a
Hidden: half hidden from the eye! 120b
High: death makes equal the high and the low
    60a
  up above the world so high 110a
Highest: glory to God in the highest 25a
Highland: my heart's in the Highlands 94b
  sweet Highland Mary 29b
  yon solitary Highland lass 121a
Hill: hunter home from the hill 108b
  if the hill will not come to Mahomet 16b
  little hills like lambs 23a
  over the hills and far away 53b
  shall fight in the hills 37a
  unto the hills 23a
Himself: answer's brief: To be himself 64a
  hear a man talk about himself 90b
Hippopotamus: shoot the Hippopotamus 19b
Hiroshima: one bomb on Hiroshima 113a
History: epoch in the history of America 11a
  higher value than history 15a
  history is bunk 50b
  history is the essence 32a
  human history becomes more 117a
  read no history 44a
Hitch: hitch your wagon to a star 49a
Hither: fetch them water from hither and thither
    61a
Hoe: leans upon his hoe 76b
Hold: first cries, "Hold, enough!" 100a
  hold the fort 104b
  we hold these truths . . . self-evident 66a
Hollow: we are the hollow men 48a
Hollyhock: like . . . the hollyhock 18b
Home: aggress upon our rights and homes 41b
  are there any more at home like you 58a
  eaten me out of house and home 98a
  England, home and beauty 15b
  father and mother say at home 110a
  home is the place where 52a

home is the sailor 108b
home life ceases to be free 64a
home of the brave 68b
I am far from home 84a
Oh give me a home 60b
stately homes of England 59b
stay peacefully at home 35b
struggles to . . . bring his comrades home 61b
there's no place like home 85b
Homely: homely as a plowed 21a
Honest: few honest men 40b
   friends were poor but honest 95b
   none but honest and wise men 11b
Honey: gather honey all the day 116b
   land flowing with milk and honey 22a
   tiggers don't like honey 79b
   took some honey, and plenty of money 71b
Honor: considerations which men of the world
      denominate honor 58a
   louder he talked of his honor 48b
   peace with honor 36a
   prophet is not without honour 24b
Honored: Here Rests in Honored Glory 64b
Hoof-mark: many hoof-marks going in 12a
Hook: silken lines, and silver hooks 44a
Hope: all hope abandon 41a
   faith, hope, charity 25b
   hope deferred 23b
   hope for years to come 116b
   hope is a good breakfast 16b
   hope springs eternal 88a
   with all the hopes of future years 74a
Hopeful: more hopeful than to be forty years old
      61b
Horde: one polished horde 31a
Horn: hounds and his horn in the morning 56a
Horribly: who was horribly bored by a bee 70b
Horrid: horrid, hideous notes of woe 31a
   when she was bad she was horrid 74b
Horse: carriages without horses 104b
   dark horse 44a
   difference of opinion that makes horse races
      113b
   flung himself upon his horse 70b
   fly . . . may sting a stately horse 66b
   horse was lost 51b
   king of France's horses are better housed 58b
   more careful of the breed of their horses 86a
   my kingdom for a horse! 101a
   pulling in one's horse as he is leaping 59a
   swap horses when crossing a stream 72b
   where the wild horses fed 52b
Host: crowd, a host, of golden diaffodils 120a
   Lord God of Hosts 70a
Hostile: universe is not hostile 61a
Hot: hot and cold with the same breath 12a

Hound: hounds and his horn in the morning 56a
   hounds of spring are on winter's traces 110a
Hour: gold hours on angel wings 29b
   improve each shining hour 116b
   shorter hours and better pay 13b
   this was their finest hour 37a
House: blessings on this house 11b
   eaten me out of house and home 98a
   house where I was born 61b
   I would say to the House 37a
   if a house be divided 25a
   in my Father's house 25a
   we two kept house 58b
Housed: king of France's horses are better housed
      58b
How: "How are you!" is a greeting 57a
Human: characteristic of the human mind 110a
   custom . . . great guide of human life 63b
   do any human beings ever realize life 119a
   he's a human being 79a
   human history becomes more 117a
   human mind can invent peace 39b
   human nature is so well disposed 16a
   human race, to which so many 37a
   human species . . . composed of two . . . races
      70b
   human things are subject to decay 46a
   in the Course of human events 65b
   members of the human community 91b
   never in the field of human conflict 37a
   no more miserable human being 65b
   same way with the human race 77a
   to err is human 88a
Humanity: humanity with all its fears 74a
   won some victory for humanity 76a
Humble: be it ever so humble 85b
   so very 'umble 43a
Humbly: walk humbly with thy God 24a
Humor: in all thy humours 11b
   own up to a lack of humor 38a
Hundred: live to be only about a hundred 47a
   ran a hundred years to a day 61a
Hunger: hunger is the best sauce 35b
Hungry: lean, hungry men . . . continually worry-
      ing society 65a
   she makes hungry where most she satisfies 96a
Hunter: heart is a lonely hunter 76a
   hunter home from the hill 108b
Huron: Huron and Iroquois forests . . . peopled
      with my friends 70a
Hurt: hurts you have cured 48b
   lie that . . . doth the hurt 16b
   who shall hurt the little wren 26a

I

I: I am the state 75a
I shall return 75b
I think, therefore I am 43a
I took the one less travelled by 52b
Past and I 58b
youth replies, I can 48b
Ice: some say in ice 52a
Icumen: sumer is icumen in 13a
Idea: long on ideas 47a
only country deliberately founded on a good idea 57a
Ides: beware the Ides of March 98b
Idiot: tale told by an idiot 100a
If: if you can keep your head 69b
Ignorance: ignorance of the law 95b
where ignorance is bliss 56b
Ignorant: everybody is ignorant 90b
ignorant armies clash by night 15b
learned fool is more foolish than an ignorant fool 90b
Ilium: burnt the topless towers of Ilium 76b
Ill: will . . . looking ill prevail? 109a
Illinois: from Kansas to Illinois 21a
Illusion: illusion that times that were are better 57a
Image: God created man in his own image 22a
Imaginary: don't let's make imaginary evils 55a
Imagination: imagination is more important than knowledge 47a
Imaginative: brief season of imaginative life 52b
Imagine: popular error to imagine 29a
Immortal: immortal hand or eye 26a
make me immortal with a kiss 76b
Immortality: in the hope of religion, immortality 64b
Impossible: in two words; im-possible 55a
Impressed: too easily impressed 28a
Improve: improve each shining hour 116b
In: they have to take you in 52a
Inalienable: as much an inalienable right 70a
Income: in which a good income is of no avail 105a
Incroachment: incroachment, injustice and wrong 55b
Indecision: nothing is habitual but indecision 65b
Independence: governments who have declared their independence 81a
Indian: give the country back to the Indians 21a
Indian Summer of the heart 118b

only good Indian 104a
Indictment: indictment against a whole people 29a
Indifferent: universe . . . is simply indifferent 61a
worst sin . . . to be indifferent 103a
Indigestion: don't tell your friends about your indigestion 57a
Indispensable: no longer indispensable 31a
Individual: worth of the individuals composing it 79a
Individualism: American system of rugged individualism 62a
Industrial: modern societary and industrial conditions 55b
Inevitable: no good in arguing with the inevitable 75a
Infamy: date that will live in infamy 91b
Infantryman: look at an infantryman's eyes 78b
Infinite: her infinite variety 96a
Infirmity: last infirmity of noble mind 80b
Influence: Win Friends and Influence People 32b
Influenza: call it influenza if ye like 21a
Information: woman of . . . little information 16a
Ingratitude: as man's ingratitude 96b
kind of ingratitude 90a
Inhumanity: essence of inhumanity 103a
man's inhumanity to man 30a
Injured: hate the man one has injured 110a
Injuries: adding insult to injuries 82a
Injury: injury is much sooner forgotten 37a
Injustice: incroachment, injustice and wrong 55b
Ink: all the sea were ink 13b
Inn: no room . . . in the inn 25a
Innocency: by my own innocency 47a
Innocent: source of innocent merriment 54a
than one innocent suffer 26a
Innovator: time is the greatest innovator 16b
Inscrutable: inscrutable to the last 113a
Insect: one is but an insect 66b
Inseparable: one and inseparable 117a
Insight: moment's insight 61b
Inspiration: genius is one per cent inspiration 47a
Insult: adding insult to injuries 82a
only cowards insult 12b
sooner forgotten than an insult 37a
Intelligent: intelligent Mr. Toad 56a
Intent: truth that's told with bad intent 26a
Intercourse: intercourse with foreign nations 42b
Interested: not interested in the possibilities of defeat 115a
Interesting: obligation . . . novel . . . that it be interesting 65b
International: order into its international affairs 47a

Internationally: why we cannot do that internationally 113b

Interpose: those who in quarrels interpose 53b

Interposition: could not view any interposition 81a

Intoxicate: shallow draughts intoxicate the brain 88a

Invent: necessary to invent Him 115b

Invention: all one's inventions are true 50a
necessity . . . the mother of invention 86b

Ireland: great Gaels of Ireland 37a

Iron: iron curtain 37a
what shal iren do 36b

Iroquois: Huron and Iroquois forests . . . peopled with my friends 70a

Ishmael: call me Ishmael 78b

Island: defend our island 37a
no man is an Island 44b

Italy: exiled by Fate, to Italy 115a

Itching: itching palm 99a

pure and complete joy 113b
there is no joy in Mudville 112a
thing of beauty is a joy for ever 67b

Jubjub: beware the jubjub bird 34b

Judge: sober as a judge 50a

Judgment: green in judgement 95b
nor . . . people's judgment always true 45a

Juliet: Juliet is the sun 101a

July: second day of July, 1776 11a

Jumblies: lands where the Jumblies 71b

June: what is so rare as a day in June 75a

Jungle: cutting through the jungle 73b
this is the Law of the Jungle 69b

Juno: sweeter than the lids of Juno's eyes 102b

Juries: trial by juries impartially selected 66a

Just: rain it raineth on the just 26b
strong are just 68b
that hath his quarrel just 103a

Justice: believing in the justice 58a
equal and exact justice to all men 66a
let justice be done 49b
temper so justice with mercy 80a
uncompromising as justice 53b

Justly: do justly 24a

J

Jabberwock: beware the Jabberwock 34b

Jackson: Jackson standing like a stone wall 18b

James: James James Morrison Morrison 79b
Jesse James was a two-gun man 21a

Jane: Jane, Jane 104b

Japan: forces of the Empire of Japan 91b

Jay: poor Jim Jay 42b

Jealousy: beware, my lord, of jealousy 101a

Jenny: Jenny kissed me 64a

Jest: he jests at scars 101a

Jesus: with the Cross of Jesus 18a

Jewel: immediate jewel of their souls 100b
wears yet a precious jewel 96a

Jo: John Anderson my jo 29b

Joe: Old Black Joe 51b

John: speak for yourself, John 74a

Johnson: you are a philosopher, Dr. Johnson 47a

Joined: God hath joined together 24b

Joke: furnished us with jokes 52b

Journalist: journalists 21a

Joy: homely joys and destiny obscure 56b

K

Kansas: from Kansas to Illinois 21a

Kate: kiss me, Kate 101b

Keener: sharp tongue . . . grows keener 65a

Keep: if you can keep your head 69b
Lord . . . keep thee 22a

Keeper: my brother's keeper 22a

Ken: d'ye ken John Peel 56a

Kentucky: old Kentucky Home 51a

Kept: he kept him 22b

Kew: down to Kew in lilac-time 84b

Key: Door to which I found no Key 69a

Kid: I kid you not 121a
lie down with the kid 24a

Kill: bullet that is to kill me 82b
each man kills the thing he loves 119a

Killed: Woman Killed with Kindness 60b

Killing: more ways of killing a cat 69b

Kin: little less than "kin" 18a
little more than kin 97a

Kind: lady sweet and kind 51a
less than kind 97a
rather more than "kind" 18a

too kind—too kind 84a
Kindly: Lead, Kindly Light 84a
Kindness: any kindness I can show 57a
  kill a wife with kindness 101b
  Woman Killed with Kindness 60b
King: all kings is mostly rapscallions 114a
  catch the conscience of the king 97a
  chief defect of Henry King 19b
  God save the king 32a
  heart and stomach of a king 48a
  keep even kings in awe 41a
  king is dead 15a
  King of China's daughter 104b
  king of France's horses are better housed 58b
  king may make a nobleman 29a
  kings must murder still 73b
  levels the shepherd with the king 36a
  necessary things to . . . ruin kings 45a
  of cabbages—and kings 34b
  Ozymandias, king of kings 103b
  sad stories of the death of kings 101a
Kingdom: enter into the kingdom of God 25a
  in a kingdom by the sea 87a
  kingdom of heaven 25a
  my kingdom for a horse! 101a
Kiss: coward does it with a kiss 119a
  for to kiss his dear 61a
  kiss and tell 38b
  kiss me, Kate 101b
  leave a kiss but in the cup 67a
  make me immortal with a kiss 76b
  only to kiss that air 60a
Kissed: Jenny kissed me 64a
  said when she kissed her cow 109b
Kisses: you have forgotten my kisses 110a
Kite: this kite is to be raised 52a
Knavery: knavery seems . . . striking feature 53b
Knell: curfew tolls the knell of parting day 56a
Knight: Knight of the Sad Countenance 35b
  such a fellowship of good knights 76a
  verray parfit gentil knight 36b
Knit: knits up the ravelled sleeve 99b
Knock: exceed in interest a knock at the door 70b
Know: all I know 90b
  He Won't Know 83a
  know all that there is to be knowed 56a
  know her was to love her 90b
  know then thyself 88a
  know thyself 14b
  thinks he knows everything 103a
Knowledge: all knowledge to be my province 16b
  imagination is more important than knowledge 47a
Known: American Soldier Known But to God 64b
Kubla: in Xanadu did Kubla Khan 38a

L

Labor: all ye that labour 24b
  labor and not ask for any reward 75b
  upon the brow of labor 28a
  youth of labour 55a
Laborer: settest the weary labourer free 31b
Laborious: scorn delights, and live laborious days 80b
Lad: many a lightfoot lad 63a
  when I was a lad 54a
Ladder: climbed the dusty ladder 113a
Lady: Colonel's Lady an' Judy O'Grady 69b
  here lies a most beautiful lady 42b
  lady doth protest too much 97b
  Lady of Shalott 111a
  lady sweet and kind 51a
  lady that's known as Lou 95b
  weep no more, my lady 51a
  young lady of Riga 14a
Lafayette: Lafayette, we are here 106b
Lama: when the High Lama asked him 60b
Lamb: dwell with the lamb 24a
  little hills like lambs 23a
  little Lamb, who made thee 26b
  Mary had a little lamb 58a
  white in the blood of the Lamb 25b
Lamp: lamp burns low and dim 11a
  lamp unto my feet 23a
  lift my lamp beside the golden door 70b
Land: and the pleasant land 32b
  equal right . . . to the use of the land 53b
  land flowing with milk and honey 22a
  land of lost content 62b
  my own, my native land 94b
  o'er the land of the free 68b
  shall eat the fat of the land 22a
  these lands are ours 110b
  think there is no land 16a
  wary to the welcome land 28b
Landing: landing . . . on the coast of France 47b
Language: fine command of language 19b
  language all nations understand 19a
  speaking one language 37b
Lark: hark! hark! the lark 96b
  lark's on the wing 28a
  the bisy larke 36b
Lass: yon solitary Highland lass 121a
Lasses: then she made the lasses O 29b
Last: first and the last 25b
  Last of the Mohicans 39b
  must be held to the last man 58a

Laugh: deserves paradise who makes his companions laugh 80b
  laugh and the world laughs 118b
  nothing sillier than a silly laugh 35b
  tickle us, do we not laugh? 100b
  to laugh is proper to a man 88b
Laughed: first baby laughed 18a
  no man who has once . . . laughed 32b
Laughing: cannot be always laughing at a man
16a
  somewhere men are laughing 112a
Laughter: better . . . laughter than . . . tears 88b
  died of laughter 19a
  midst of his laughter and glee 34b
  weeping and the laughter 45a
Launched: face that launched a thousand ships
76b
Laundry-list: laundry-list and I'll set it to music
92b
Law: custom, that unwritten law 41a
  each a law to himself 111b
  good of the people . . . chief law 37b
  ignorance of the law 95b
  Law of the Yukon 95b
  law, say the gardeners 15b
  laws . . . made to be broken 84a
  Laws of Nature and of Nature's God 65b
  moral law within me 67b
  nature's law 70a
  no force in law 38a
  obey the law 44b
  one with the law is a majority 39a
  this is the Law of the Jungle 69b
  when laws have been written down 15a
Lea: lowing herd winds slowly o'er the lea 56a
Lead: easy to lead 27a
  Lead, Kindly Light 84a
  little child shall lead them 24a
Leadeth: leadeth me beside the still waters 23a
League: half a league onward 110b
Lean: grew lean while he assailed 90a
  lean and hungry look 98b
  lean, hungry men . . . continually worrying so-
ciety 65a
Leander: Leander swam the Hellespont 61a
Leap-year: twenty-nine in each leap-year 14b
Learn: never too old to learn 89a
Learning: little learning is a dang'rous thing 88a
Leave: leave a kiss but in the cup 67a
  leave her to heaven 97a
Leaves: men . . . like the leaves of the trees 61b
Left: let not thy left hand know 24b
Leg: thinks with his legs 26a
  which leg goes after which 40a
Legislation: attempt to resolve it by legislation
107b

foundation of morals and legislation 21b
Lend: men who borrow and the men who lend
70b
Lender: neither a borrower nor a lender 97a
Leopard: leopard his spots 24b
  leopard shall lie down 24a
Less: less than kind 97a
  little less between me and the sun 44a
Lesson: lesson you should heed 60b
  three lessons I would write 94a
Library: don't be afraid to go to your library 47b
Liberté: Liberté! Égalité! Fraternité! 15a
Liberty: give me liberty or give me death 60a
  Liberty and Union 117a
  Liberty! Equality! Fraternity! 15a
  liberty of the country 31b
  liberty . . . plant of rapid growth 116b
  liberty to man 40b
  liberty's in every blow 30a
  life, liberty and the pursuit of happiness 66a,
70a
  new nation, conceived in liberty 72a
  proclaim liberty throughout the land 64b
  sweet land of liberty 105a
  tree of liberty must be refreshed 66a
  what then is the spirit of liberty 58b
Lie: all the lies you can invent 26a
  lie down in green pastures 23a
  lie that passeth through the mind 16b
  I cannot tell a lie 116a
  never venture to lie 81a
Life: all the voyage of their life 99a
  and this our life 96a
  average cabin of a life 28a
  bear a charmed life 100a
  biography . . . life without theory 44a
  death after life 106a
  do any human beings ever realize life 119a
  doest every act of thy life 16a
  dreamed that life was beauty 14a
  is life so dear 60a
  life is but an empty dream 74b
  life is frittered away by detail 112a
  life is made up of marble and mud 59a
  life is real 74b
  Life, Liberty and the pursuit of happiness 66a,
70a
  life so short 60b
  life'd not be worth livin' 46b
  life's but a walking shadow 100a
  one life to lose for my country 58a
  only end of life 108a
  present life of man 18b
  resurrection, and the life 25a
  slept, and dreamed that life was Beauty 62a
  two things to aim at in life 105a

value of life 81a
variety's the very spice of life 40a
well-written Life is almost as rare 32a
what is this life 41b
when life's path is steep 62b
young life's before us 14b
Lifteth: lifteth the needy 23a
Light: consider how my light is spent 80a
    it gives a lovely light 79a
    Lead, Kindly Light 84a
    light of the bright world 26b
    light unto my path 23a
    more light 55a
    speed was far faster than light 28b
    what light through yonder window 101a
Like: every one as they like 109b
    never met a man I didn't like 90b
Lilac: when lilacs last in the dooryard 118a
Lilac-time: down to Kew in lilac-time 84b
Lilies: lilies of the field 24b
    most useless, peacocks and lilies 93a
    three lilies in her hand 92b
Lily: Elaine, the lily maid of Astolat 111b
    pouring a watering-pot over a lily 70a
    to paint the lily 99b
Limit: limits of his own field of vision 94b
Lincoln: Lincoln, six feet one 21a
    memory of Abraham Lincoln is enshrined 65a
    when Abraham Lincoln was shovelled 93b
Line: silken lines, and silver hooks 44a
Lion: beard the lion in his den 94b
    bears and lions growl and fight 116b
    calf and the young lion 24a
    fox . . . answered the sick lion 62b
    I girded up my Lions 116a
    lion is in the streets 23b
Lip: good words for the lips 43a
    stiff upper lip 35b
    up and up, her white lips saying 113a
Liquefaction: that liquefaction of her clothes 60a
List: I've got a little list 54a
Listen: I didn't listen to him 107a
    listen, my children, and you shall hear 74b
    stop; look; listen 114a
Little: blessings on thee, little man 118b
    fear of little men 12b
    little child shall lead them 24a
    little Lamb, who made thee 26b
    little lower than the angels 22b
    little more than kin 97a
    our Little Boy Blue 50a
    sleep, my little one, sleep 111b
    tall oaks from little acorns 49b
    there was a little girl 74b
Live: come live with me 44a, 76b
    glad did I live and gladly die 108b

let us live then 14b
live as the Romans 12b
live to be only about a hundred 47a
long live the king 15a
might as well live 85a
read in order to live 50a
we live in such an age 46a
Lived: might have lived out my life 115a
Lives: we can make our lives sublime 74b
Living: no living with thee 12a
    set to earn their livings 55b
Livingstone: Dr. Livingstone, I presume 106b
Lizzie: Lizzie Borden took an axe 14a
Loaf: loaf and invite my soul 118a
Lochinvar: young Lochinvar is come 94b
Locomotive: ranged where the locomotives sing 73b
Lodgest: where thou lodgest 22b
Logical: built in such a logical way 61a
Lollipop: on the shore of the Lollipop sea 50a
Loman: Willy Loman never made a lot of money 79a
London: anything . . . to be found out of London 59b
    one road leads to London 77b
Lonely: heart is a lonely hunter 76a
    to the lonely sea and the sky 77b
    wandered lonely as a cloud 120a
Lonesome: I'm lonesome 117b
Long: craft so long to learn 60b
    so you love me long 60a
Look: don't look back 85a
    hit look lak sparrer-grass 59a
    I'll not look for wine 67a
    lean and hungry look 98b
    look away, look away 49a
    some do it with a bitter look 119a
    stop; look; listen 114a
    woman as old as she looks 38b
Lord: earth is the Lord's 23a
    I pray the Lord 14a
    Lord bless thee 22a
    Lord is my shepherd 23a
    Lord prefers common-looking people 73a
    Lord require of thee 24a
    praise the Lord 51a
    see the works of the Lord 23a
Lore: volume of forgotten lore 87a
Lose: no man can lose 115b
Losers: in war . . . all are losers 36a
Lost: all will be lost 31b
    better to have loved and lost 111a
    little lost pup with his tail tucked in 57a
Lou: lady that's known as Lou 95b
Louder: louder he talked of his honor 48b
Loudest: often and in the loudest voice 92a

Love: absence from whom we love 40a
  all for love 106a
  all mankind loves a lover 48b
  and be my love 44a, 76b
  and hold love in 114a
  bid me take love easy 121b
  can worship God or love his neighbor 119b
  course of true love 100b
  dinner of herbs where love is 23b
  each man kills the thing he loves 119a
  gotta love for Angela 40b
  how do I love thee 27b
  I do not love thee 27b
  if music be the food of love 102a
  if thou must love me 27b
  if you speak love 100b
  know her was to love her 90b
  lightly turns to thoughts of love 111a
  love and desire and hate 45a
  Love and I had the wit to win 76b
  love and unquestioned loyalty 90b
  love begins to sicken 99a
  love her till I die 51a
  love is blind 100a
  Love is God 113a
  Love is not love 102b
  love itself shall slumber on 103b
  love thy neighbour as thyself 22a, 24b
  love's young dream 82a
  my love and I did meet 121b
  my love is come to me 92a
  my Luve's like a red red rose 30a
  my only love 101a
  no man dies for love, but on the stage 46a
  one that loves his fellowmen 64a
  pray love me little 60a
  rise up, my love 23b
  she never would love me 104b
  talk of tides of love 40b
  true love hath my heart 104b
  understand only because I love 113a
  very few to love 120b
Loved: better to have loved and lost 111a
  if I loved you Wednesday 79a
  one that loved not wisely 101a
  that loved not at first sight 76b
Lovely: lovely apparition, sent 120b
  more lovely and more temperate 102b
  she has a lovely face 111a
  when lovely woman stoops to folly 55a
Lover: all mankind loves a lover 48b
  pair of star-crossed lovers 101a
  pale and wan, fond lover 109a
Lovesick: winds were lovesick with them 95b
Low: death makes equal the high and the low 60a

sweet and low 111b
Lowells: Lowells talk to the Cabots 26b
Lower: little lower than the angels 22b
Loyalty: love and unquestioned loyalty 90b
Luck: and watching his luck 95b
Lucre: not greedy of filthy lucre 25b
Lunatic: lunatic fringe in all reform 92a
Luxurious: are most luxurious 49a

M

Macaroni: and called it Macaroni 17b
Macbeth: Macbeth does murder sleep 99b
Macduff: lay on, Macduff 100a
Mad: he first makes mad 49b
  mad dogs and Englishmen 39b
  men that God made mad 37a
Made: good poet's made as well as born 67a
Madness: anger is a brief madness 62b
  though this be madness 97a
Mahomet: if the hill will not come to Mahomet 16b
Maiden: archly the maiden smiled 74a
  many a rose-lipt maiden 63a
  tell me, pretty maiden 58a
Mail: future as a carrier of mail 121a
Main: part of the main 44b
Maine: as Maine goes 49b
Majesty: His Majesty's dominions 84a
Majority: one, on God's side is a majority 86b
  one with the law is a majority 39a
Maker: our Great Maker is preparing the world 37b
Male: male and female created he them 22a
  more deadly than the male 69b
Malice: malice toward none 73a
  set down aught in malice 101a
Man: a man's a man for a' that 29b
  century of the common man 115b
  child is father of the man 120b
  each man kills the thing he loves 119a
  each man the architect 15a
  Equality of Man Before His Creator 107b
  every man meets his Waterloo 86b
  every man paddle his own canoe 77a
  fury of a patient man 45a
  God created man in his own image 22a
  happiness of the common man 21b
  happy the man 46a

if a man be gracious 16b
if man . . . solution for world peace 77b
is man an ape 44a
let any man speak long enough 108b
let no man of peace and freedom despair 68b
let not man put asunder 24b
love not man the less 31a
liberty to man 40b
man . . . a political animal 15a
man after his own heart 22b
man doth not live by bread only 22b
man errs so long as he strives 55a
man has his will 61b
man is a social animal 106a
man is a tool-making animal 52a
man is born unto trouble 22b
man is something . . . to be surpassed 84a
man made the town 40a
man marks the earth 31a
man may build himself a throne of bayonets 64b
man may live long, yet live very little 81a
man . . . measure of all things 88a
man must be a non-conformist 49a
man that studieth revenge 16b
man was born free 93a
man—who has no gills 26a
man who shaves and takes a train 118a
man write a better book 49a
man's bewilderment 59a
man's house is his castle 38a
man's inhumanity to man 30a
man's love is of man's life 31a
man's reach should exceed his grasp 27b
man's to keep unmarried 103a
most married man I ever saw 116a
near is God to man 48b
no man can lose 115b
no man can serve two masters 24b
no man is an island 44b
no man is born an artist 115b
no man who has once . . . laughed 32b
none is more wonderful than man 105a
nothing can harm a good man 105a
nothing happens to any man 16a
one man in his time 96b
one man that can stand prosperity 32b
present life of man 18b
reasonable man adapts himself 103a
strange what a man may do 111b
way to a man's heart 119b
what's a man's first duty 64a
when a man should marry 16b
who's master, who's man 109a
wicked man that comes after children 61a
Mandalay: on the road to Mandalay 69b

Mandrake: get with child a mandrake root 44a
Manila: down in Manila Bay 116a
Mankind: all mankind loves a lover 48b
  I am involved in Mankind 44b
  our countrymen are all mankind 53b
  proper study of mankind is man 88a
  shall not crucify mankind 28a
  to err . . . is common to mankind 105a
Manner: to the manner born 97a
Mansion: are many mansions 25a
  build thee more stately mansions 61b
Manure: its natural manure 66a
Many: so much owed by so many to so few 37a
Map: geography is about maps 21b
Marble: life is made up of marble and mud 59a
March: beware the ides of March 98b
  in the night . . . the people march 93b
  March Hare went on 34a
  winds of March 102b
Marched: marched them up 14a
Marine: marines have landed 41b
Mariner: it is an ancient mariner 38a
  ye Mariners of England 32a
Mark: marks . . . how you played the game 89a
Marksmen: you are all marksmen 88b
Marriage: marriage of true minds 102b
Married: most married man I ever saw 116a
  what delight we married people have 86a
  woman's business to get married 103a
Marries: young person, who either marries or dies 16a
Marry: easy to marry a rich woman 111b
  no can marry both o' dem 40b
  when a man should marry 16b
Marvel: sometimes marvel at the extraordinary docility 107b
Mary: Mary had a little lamb 58a
Maryland: Maryland! My Maryland! 89a
Masses: back the masses against the classes 54b
  huddled masses, yearning to breathe free 70b
  masses of the people . . . fall victims to a great lie 60b
Master: master of my fate 59b
  masters of their fates 98b
  no man can serve two masters 24b
  who's master, who's man 109a
Materialist: materialists have pestered the world 107b
Mathematics: mathematics possesses not only truth 93a
Matilda: come a-waltzing, Matilda 85b
  Matilda told such dreadful lies 19b
May: fresh as is the month of May 36b
  gathering nuts in May 14a
  I'm to be Queen o' the May 111a
Mayflower: burying ground . . . of the passengers

N

to tell your name the livelong day 43b
what's in a name 101b
Nap: world should . . . take an age-long nap 59a
Nation: become one nation 37b
  fierce contending nations 11b
  friendship with all nations 66a
  health of nations 46b
  nation is not governed 29a
  nation of shopkeepers 11b
  new nation, conceived in liberty 72a
  one-third of a nation 91b
  this nation, under God 72a
  well-being of other nations 91b
National: thirteen states . . . able to support a
    national government 58a
Native: content to breathe his native air 88a
  my own, my native land 94b
  native warrior of North America 39b
Natural: term of Natural Selection 41a
Nature: all Nature was degraded 26a
  auld nature swears 29b
  human nature is so well disposed 16a
  in nature . . . neither rewards nor punishments
    64b
  love . . . Nature more 31a
  nature abhors a vacuum 106a
  nature made him 15a
  nature's law 70a
  progress . . . a part of nature 105b
  'tis their nature to 116b
Naughty: there was a naughty Boy 68a
Nazi: Nazi Germany had become a menace 84a
Near: so near and yet so far 111a
Necessity: necessity . . . the mother of invention
    86b
  peculiar necessity not to decline the call 58b
Need: to each according to his needs 77b
Needle: plying her needle and thread 62a
  through the eye of a needle 25a
Needy: lifteth the needy 23a
Neglect: let me not defer it or neglect it 57a
  little neglect may breed mischief 51b
Neighbor: good fences make good neighbors 52a
  love thy neighbour as thyself 22a, 24b
  policy of the good neighbor 91a
  when your neighbour's wall is on fire 62b
Nest: all built their nests in my beard 71b
Neutrality: armed neutrality 120a
Never: I never saw a moor 43b
  never in the field of human conflict 37a
  never saw a man who looked 119a
  never too old to learn 89a
Nevermore: quoth the Raven, "Nevermore" 87a
New: new deal for the American people 91a
  ring in the new 111a

New Hampshiremen: if two New Hampshire-
    men 21a
New York: anywhere but in little old New York
    60a
  New York City . . . meets the most severe test
    57a
News: man bites a dog that is news 41a
  piece of good news 21b
Newspaper: government of men and morning
    newspapers 86b
Nicest: they are the nicest 79a
Nicholas: hopes that St. Nicholas 81b
Night: dark night is near 28b
  forests of the night 26a
  metropolis—it stays up all night 57a
  must follow as the night the day 97a
  night before Christmas 81b
  night has a thousand eyes 26b
  night is beginning to lower 74a
  night is dark 84a
  night is drawing nigh 18a
  night is grandeur to our dust 48b
  night of cloudless climes 31b
  night with her train of stars 59b
  shades of night were falling fast 74a
  so late into the night 31b
  watch that ends the night 116b
  when Daniel Boone goes by at night 21a
Nile: pour the waters of the Nile 34a
Noble: last infirmity of noble mind 80b
  only noble to be good 111a
Nobleman: king may make a nobleman 29a
Noblesse: noblesse oblige 72a
Noblest: noblest Roman of them all 99a
Nobody: more space where nobody is 107a
Nod: dwelt in the land of Nod 22a
  Wynken, Blynken and Nod 50a
Noise: most sublime noise 51a
Non-conformist: man must be a non-conformist
    49a
None: none but the brave 46a
Noon: been lying till noon 66b
Norman: simple faith than Norman blood 111a
  while the Norman Baron lay 13b
North America: native warrior of North America
    39b
Nose: did not see further than his own nose 70a
  must often wipe a bloody nose 53b
Not: he was not of an age 67a
  I kid you not 121a
Nothing: do nothing upon myself 44b
  Emperor has nothing at all on! 13a
  I have nothing 88b
  I said nothing 19b
  nothing can be said to be certain 51b
  nothing can stop it now 121b

nothing for reward 106a

nothing . . . half so much worth doing 55b

nothing happens to any man 16a

nothing to say, say nothing 38b

our lives—our pains—nothing! 115a

we brought nothing into this world 25b

Nothingness: never pass into nothingness 67b

Noticed: we never noticed 119a

Notion: come from the wrong notions we have 107a

Novel: more entertaining than half the novels 78a

obligation . . . novel . . . that it be interesting 65b

November: thirty days hath November 55b

Now: now, and where you stand 108b

now he belongs to the ages 106b

now is the time 117a

Nowhere: dressed up, with nowhere to go 118a

Number: better than numbers 40b

Nut: Brazil, where the nuts come from 112a

gathering nuts in May 14a

Nutmeg: upon her nutmeg tree 104b

Nuts: nuts! 76a

Nymph: haste thee, nymph 80a

O

Oak: bend a knotted oak 38b

tall oaks from little acorns 49b

Oat: Oats. A grain 66b

Obey: monarchs must obey 46a

Obligation: without the accompanying obligation 90b

Oblige: *noblesse oblige* 72a

oblige you, if my passes were respected 73a

Obscure: homely joys, and destiny obscure 56b

Obstacle: biggest obstacle to professional writing 19b

Occupation: absence of occupation 40a

Occupied: areas occupied by the enemy 106a

Ocean: deep and dark blue Ocean 31a

make the mighty ocean 32b

ocean, n. 26a

ocean of this world 28a

October: something in October 32b

Odd: very odd thing 42b

Odour: odours, when sweet violets sicken 103b

Off: off with her head 34a

Offend: thine eye offend 24b

Office-boy: as office-boy to an Attorney's firm 54a

O'Grady: Colonel's Lady an' Judy O'Grady 69b

Old: as old as he's feeling 38b

auld lang syne 29a

grow old along with me 28a

grow old with a good grace 106b

I grow old . . . I grow old 48a

more hopeful than to be forty years old 61b

never too old to learn 89a

ring out the old 111a

there was an Old Man in a tree 70b

think he is growing old 65a

when he is old 23b

you are old, Father William 34a, 105b

Omega: Alpha and Omega 25b

One: all for one 46b

become one nation 37b

one and inseparable 117a

one, on God's side is a majority 86b

one with the law is a majority 39a

One-and-twenty: when I was one-and-twenty 62b

One-horse: poor little one-horse town 114a

One-hoss: wonderful one-hoss shay 61a

Oneself: only possible society is oneself 119a

One-third: One-third of a nation 91b

Only: drink to me only with thine eyes 67a

understand only because I love 113a

Onward: half a league onward 110b

onward, Christian soldiers 18a

Oozing: I feel it oozing out 104a

Opinion: as many opinions as there are men 111b

decent respect to the opinions of mankind 65b

difference of opinion that makes horse races 113b

error of opinion may be tolerated 66a

give him my opinion 43a

new opinions are always suspected 74a

Opposition: secure without . . . Opposition 44a

Optimism: just as agreeable as optimism 21a

Orchard: before the cherry orchard was sold 36b

Organ: seated one day at the organ 88a

Ornament: to be a moment's ornament 120b

Other: hear the other side 15b

other people are quite dreadful 119a

Otherwise: some are otherwise 51b

Out: out, damned spot! 100a

out of the cradle endlessly rocking 118a

Outlaw: chief of an outlaw clan 21a

Outrageous: slings and arrows of outrageous fortune 97a

Over: over the hills and far away 53b

Owe: I owe much 88b

if I can't pay, why I can owe 60a

owes not any man 75a

Owl: Owl and the Pussy Cat 71b

Own: can call to-day his own 46a

Ox: stalled ox and hatred therewith 23b
Oxford: reminds me very slightly of Oxford 60b
Oyster: bold man who first swallowed an oyster 65b
    world's mine oyster 100b
Ozymandias: Ozymandias, king of kings 103b

P

Paddle: every man paddle his own canoe 77a
Pain: one who never inflicts pain 84a
    pain and boredom 94a
Painful: very painful manner 12a
Paint: paint a portrait I lose a friend 94a
    sucked the paint all off 12a
    to paint the lily 99b
Palace: 'mid pleasures and palaces 85b
Pale: pale hands I loved 62a
    why so pale 109a
Palm: itching palm 99a
Paper: all the world were paper 13b
    what I see in the papers 90b
Paradise: deserves paradise who makes his companions laugh 80b
Pardon: to pardon or to bear it 40a
Parent: what parents were created for 83a
Parish: all the world as my parish 117a
Parliament: Three Estates in Parliament 32a
Parodies: parodies and caricatures . . . most penetrating of criticism 64a
Parrot: parrots, and tropical trees 75a
Parting: parting is such sweet sorrow 101b
Party: come to the aid of the party 117a
Pass: I shall not pass this way again 57a
    pass the ammunition 51a
    they shall not pass 15a
Passes: men seldom make passes 85a
    oblige you, if my passes were respected 73a
Passing: but see her passing by 51a
Passion: no passion so effectually robs 29a
Past: Past and I 58b
    past, at least is secure 117a
    remembrance of things past 102b
Pasture: lie down in green pastures 23a
Patches: thing of shreds and patches 54a
Path: light unto my path 23a
    make a beaten path to his door 49a
Pathless: pleasure in the pathless woods 31a
Patience: patience, to prevent that murmur 80b

Patient: fury of a patient man 45a
Patriot: blood of patriots and tyrants 66a
    sunshine patriot 85a
Patriotic: avenge the patriotic gore 89a
Patriotism: patriotism . . . last refuge of a scoundrel 66b
Pawnee: with the Pawnees lying low 73b
Pay: shorter hours and better pay 13b
Peace: cannot live alone, in peace 91b
    human mind can invent peace 39b
    if man . . . solution for world peace 77b
    in peace, just, generous 39b
    is . . . peace so sweet 60a
    men live together in peace 51b
    never . . . a good war or a bad peace 51b
    not to send peace, but a sword 24b
    peace for our time 36a
    peace, good will toward men 25a
    reestablishment of peace and harmony 71b
    who will bring white peace 73b
Peacemaker: blessed are the peacemakers 24a
Peacock: most useless, peacocks and lilies 93a
Pearl: pearls before swine 24b
    pearls that were his eyes 102a
Peasant: no peasant in my kingdom so poor 59b
    rogue and peasant slave am I 97a
Peculiar: funny peculiar 59a
    peculiar necessity not to decline the call 58b
Peel: d'ye ken John Peel 56a
Pen: before my pen has gleaned my teeming brain 68a
    pen is mightier than the sword 75b
    with such acts fill a pen 45a
People: fool all the people some of the time 73a
    good of the people . . . chief law 37b
    has such people in't 102a
    in the night . . . the people march 93b
    indictment against a whole people 29a
    Lord prefers common-looking people 73a
    masses of the people . . . fall victims to a great lie 60b
    nor . . . people's judgment always true 45a
    of the people, by the people 72a
    people all exulting 118a
    people have always some champion 87a
    people must help one another 70a
    people will live on 93b
    saw the cities of many peoples 61b
    thy people shall be my people 22b
    two things only the people . . . desire 67b
Perfect: then . . . come perfect days 75a
Perform: his wonders to perform 40a
Perilous: in a perilous emergency 26a
Perish: if I had to perish twice 52a
    shall not perish from the earth 72a
    though the world perish 49b

Permanent: steer clear of permanent alliance 116b

Perpetual: perpetual struggle for room and food 76a

Person: freedom of person under . . . habeas corpus 66a

God is any respecter of persons 27a

Perspiration: genius . . . ninety-nine per cent perspiration 47a

Persuade: goeth about to persuade a multitude 62a

Pessimism: pessimism when you get used to it 21a

Peter: thou art Peter 24b

Phantom: phantom of delight 120b

Philosopher: some philosopher has not said it 37b

you are a philosopher, Dr. Johnson 47a

Philosophy: advantage . . . philosophy . . . substantially true 94a

dreamt of in your philosophy 97a

Phone: why did you answer the phone 113a

Physician: dying . . . too many physicians 12b

physician can bury his mistakes 121a

physician, heal thyself 25a

Picture: all his pictures faded 26a

reader look not on his picture 67a

Pie: ends its days in apple pie 61a

Pie-crust: promises and pie-crust 109b

Piety: each to each by natural piety 120b

nor all your Piety nor Wit 69a

Pig: whether pigs have wings 34b

Pigeon: pigeons on the grass 107a

Pimpernel: demmed, elusive Pimpernel 84b

Pink: very pink of perfection 55a

Pioneer: pioneers! O pioneers! 118a

Pioneering: days of pioneering . . . deader now than Camelot 72a

Pipe: ye soft pipes, play on 67b

Pistol: have you your pistols? 118a

Place: place for everything 104b

Plague: plague o' both your houses 101b

of all plagues 32a

Plant: liberty . . . plant of rapid growth 116b

plant whose virtues have not been discovered 49a

time to plant 23b

Plantation: longing for de old plantation 51a

Platinum: bullets made of platinum 19b

Play: play's the thing 97a

Playboy: playboy of the Western World 110a

Played: marks . . . how you played the game 89a

Player: men and women merely players 96b

poor player that struts and frets 100a

Playing: playing fields of Eton 117a

Pleased: never face so pleased my mind 51a

Pleasure: all the pleasures prove 76b

pleasure in the pathless woods 31a

pleasures with youth pass away 105b

some new pleasures prove 44a

soul of pleasure 19a

understand the pleasures of the other 16a

Pleasure-dome: stately pleasure-dome decree 38a

Pledge: I will pledge with mine 67a

Plot: plots, true or false 45a

Ploughman: ploughman homeward plods his weary way 56a

Plowshare: beat their swords into plowshares 24a

Pluck: pluck it out 24b

time to pluck up 23b

Plymouth: monument marks the first burying ground in Plymouth 64b

Pocket: traveller with empty pockets 67b

wid a pocket full of tin 51a

Poem: poems are made by fools like me 69a

Poet: good poet's made as well as born 67a

perhaps no person can be a poet 75b

to have great poets 118a

Poetry: page of prancing poetry 43b

poetry is as exact a science 50a

poetry is more philosophical 15a

Poison: food to one man is bitter poison to others 75b

Policeman: policeman's lot is not a happy one 54b

Policy: it is our true policy 116b

policy of the good neighbor 91a

Polished: polished up the handle so successfullee 54a

Political: man . . . a political animal 15a

necessary . . . to dissolve the political bands 65b

points clearly to a political career 103a

Politician: I'm not a politician 116a

most successful politician 92a

whole race of politicians 109a

Politics: politics makes strange bedfellows 116a

politics . . . only profession . . . no preparation 108a

Pony: riding on a pony 17b

Poor: blessed are the poor 24a

friends were poor but honest 95b

give me your tired, your poor 70b

great men have their poor relations 43a

no peasant in my kingdom so poor 59b

Poor Little Rich Girl 39b

raiseth up the poor 23a

rest I leave to the poor 88b

short and simple annals of the poor 56b

Pop: pop goes the weasel 76a

Poppies: in Flanders fields the poppies blow 76a

Popular: dear ar-re always pop'lar 46b

Port: port after stormy seas 106a

in nature . . . neither rewards nor punishments 64b
let the punishment fit the crime 54a
Pup: little lost pup with his tail tucked in 57a
Pure: as pure in thought as angels 90b
because my heart is pure 111b
blessed are the pure in heart 24a
truth is never pure 119a
Purest: purest and most thoughtful minds 93a
Purple: never saw a Purple Cow 28b
Willie had a purple monkey 12a
Purpose: every purpose under the heaven 23b
Purse: put money in thy purse 100b
who steals my purse 100b
Pussy-Cat: Owl and the Pussy-Cat 71b
Pyramid: from the summit of these pyramids 82b

Q

Quarrel: hath his quarrel just 103a
those who in quarrels interpose 53b
when Kansas and Colorado have a quarrel 113b
Quarreling: when chickens quit quarrelling 77a
Queen: every lass a queen 69b
I'm to be Queen o' the May 111a
queens I might have enough 76a
Queer: all the world is queer 85a
Question: ask no questions 48a
that is the question 97a
Quiet: all quiet along the Potomac 76a
All Quiet on the Western Front 89a
men lead lives of quiet desperation 112a
our heart is not quiet 15b
Quote: kill you if you quote it 28b

R

Race: glory of rulers or of races 21b
Other Cemeteries Limited as to Race 107b
race is not to the swift 23b
slow and steady wins the race 73b
Rag: woman sat in unwomanly rags 62a

Rage: all Heaven in a rage 26a
Rail: some folks rail 50a
Rain: as the gentle rain from heaven 100b
becomes a small town when it rains 57a
lisp of leaves and ripple of rain 110a
rain is over and gone 23b
rain it raineth on the just 26b
Rainbow: rainbow in the sky 120b
Raiseth: raiseth up the poor 23a
Ram: mountains skipped like rams 23a
Rapscallion: all kings is mostly rapscallions 114a
Rapture: rapture on the lonely shore 31a
Rare: what is so rare as a day in June 75a
Rat: rats! They fought the dogs 28a
Rattle: spoiled his nice new rattle 34b
Raven: quoth the Raven, "Nevermore" 87a
Reach: man's reach should exceed his grasp 27b
Read: King George will be able to read that 58b
nobody wants to read 114a
read in order to live 50a
read just as inclination leads him 66b
sooner read a time-table or a catalogue 78a
Reader: reader look not on his picture 67a
Reading: reading is to the mind 106b
Ready: fire when you are ready, Gridley 43a
Real: life is real 74b
Reason: if it be against reason 38a
tell me the reason, I pray 105b
theirs not to reason why 110b
where reason is left free to combat it 66a
Reasonable: reasonable man adapts himself 103a
Reasoning: powers of acting and reasoning 29a
Rebel: heretic, rebel, a thing to flout 76b
Rebellion: a little rebellion now and then 66a
Recent: recent work by E. Fermi 47a
Redbreast: robin redbreast in a cage 26a
Refinement: toward refinement 19a
Reform: lunatic fringe in all reform 92a
Reformation: age of revolution and reformation 66a
Refuge: God is our refuge 23a
Regent: Dewey were the Regent's eyes 116a
Regret: I only regret 58a
Rejoice: all the vales rejoice 26b
Relation: Fate chooses your relations 42b
great men have their poor relations 43a
Relief: thou wilt give thyself relief 16a
Religion: freedom of religion 66a
in the hope of religion, immortality 64b
men will wrangle for religion 38b
my religion is to do good 85a
Remain: here we will remain 110b
Remedies: desperate remedies 49b
will not apply new remedies 16b
Remedy: remedy for everything except death 35b
remedy is worse than the disease 16b

Remember: always remember a woman's birth-
     day 52b
   I remember, I remember 61b
   remember and be sad 92b
   remember with tears 12b
Remembrance: remembrance of things past 102b
   that's for remembrance 97b
Remind: reminds me very slightly of Oxford 60b
Remove: remove hence 24b
Render: render therefore unto Caesar 25a
Rendezvous: I have a rendezvous with Death 94b
   rendezvous with destiny 91a
Reply: theirs not to make reply 110b
Reporter: gallery in which the reporters sit 75b
Repose: Repose in This Quiet and Secluded
     107b
Representation: taxation without representation
     is tyranny 84b
Require: Lord require of thee 24a
Required: to whom much is given, much is re-
     quired 68a
Resist: can resist everything except temptation
     119a
   resist not evil 24b
Respect: respect for God demands 110a
Respecter: God is any respecter of persons 27a
Rest: be at rest 23a
   far, far better rest 43b
   Here Rests in Honored Glory 64b
   I will give you rest 24b
   lie there and rest 46b
   mourning figure walks, and will not rest 73b
   now she's at rest 46a
   rest is silence 98a
   toil and not to seek for rest 75b
Resurrection: resurrection, and the life 25a
Retirement: must be no retirement 58a
Retreat: forced retreat of Red Army units 106a
   I will not retreat 53b
   my right is in retreat 50a
Return: I shall return 75b
Revenge: man that studieth revenge 16b
   wrong us, shall we not revenge? 100b
Revere: midnight ride of Paul Revere 74b
Revolting: they're pretty revolting 83a
Revolution: age of revolution and reformation
     66a
Revolutionary: most revolutionary reversal of his
     record 77b
Reward: in nature . . . neither rewards nor punish-
     ments 64b
   nothing for reward 106a
   reap his old reward 70a
Reynolds: when Sir Joshua Reynolds died 26a
Rich: easy to marry a rich woman 111b
   Poor Little Rich Girl 39b

rich man to enter 25a
   rich man has his motor car 11a
Riches: embarrassment of riches 12b
   rather to be chosen than great riches 23b
   riches are . . . from a contented mind 80b
Richmond: to go to Richmond 73a
Rid: would have rid the earth 90a
Rider: rider was lost 51b
Right: agress upon our rights and homes 41b
   as God gives us to see the right 73a
   be always sure you're right 40b
   certain unalienable Rights 66a
   defend . . . your right to say it 115b
   equal right of all men 53b
   has a right to remove us 110b
   not too sure that it is right 58b
   our country, right or wrong 42b, 94b
   rather be right than be President 37b
   right, by chance 39b
   right to food, shelter, and clothing 70a
   thy right hand doeth 24b
   too fond of the right 55a
Ring: ring down the curtain 88b
   ring out the old 111a
   ring out, wild bells 111a
Riot: ever hears of fat men heading a riot 65a
Rise: nobody who does not rise early 66b
   rise up, my love 23b
River: Alph, the sacred river, ran 38a
   love any discourse of rivers 115b
   time is like a river 16a
Road: doubtless there are other roads 40a
   one road leads to London 77b
   road to Mandalay 69b
   two roads diverged in a wood 52b
Roam: where the buffalo roam 60b
Robe: washed their robes 25b
Robin: robin redbreast in a cage 26a
Rock: charms . . . to soften rocks 38b
   hand that rocks the cradle 115b
   rock underlies all America 86b
   upon this rock 24b
Rocking: million cradles now rocking 114a
   out of the cradle endlessly rocking 118b
Rod: he that spareth his rod 23b
   rod and thy staff 23a
Rode: rode madly off in all directions 70b
Rogue: rogue and peasant slave am I 97a
Roll: roll on, thou deep and dark 31a
Roman: friends, Romans, countrymen 98b
   live as the Romans 12b
   noblest Roman of them all 99a
Rome: at Rome, all things . . . at a price 67b
   grandeur that was Rome 87b
   when in Rome 12b
Romeo: Romeo! wherefore art thou 101b

S

all the sea were ink 13b
by the deep sea 31a
can see nothing but sea 16a
down to a sunless sea 38a
down to the sea in ships 23a
hardships on the high seas 61b
home from sea 108b
I must down to the seas again 77b
I never saw the sea 43b
kingdom by the sea 87a
plants his footsteps in the sea 40a
sea folds away from you 94a
stomach behave itself, the first day at sea 114a
when I put out to sea 110b
why the sea is boiling hot 34b
wind of the western sea 111b
Sea-change: doth suffer a sea-change 102a
Seal: seventh seal 25b
Sealing-wax: of shoes—and ships—and sealing-
     wax 34b
Season: as the swift seasons roll 61b
     in vain the envious seasons roll 61a
     to every thing there is a season 23b
Seated: seated one day at the organ 88a
Seawards: my road leads me seawards 77b
Second: happens to be a second entry 11b
Secret: secret, for it's whispered 38b
     secret of happiness 93b
Secure: past, at least is secure 117a
     secure within, can say 46a
See: come up and see me 117a
     did not see further than his own nose 70a
     to see oursels 30a
Seek: seek him here, we seek him there 84b
Seem: things are not what they seem 74b
Seen: woman should be seen, not heard 105a
Self-evident: we hold these truths . . . self-evident
     66a
Self-indulgence: favourite form of self-indul-
     gence 78a
Self-lover: nature of extreme self-lovers 16b
Self-sufficient: know how to be self-sufficient 81a
Selling: lives by selling something 107b
Semper: sic semper tyrannis 26b
Sense: live within the sense they quicken 103b
     money speaks sense 19a
Sentiment: sentimentality is only sentiment 78a
     them's my sentiments 111b
Sentimentality: sentimentality is only sentiment
     78a
Separation: causes which impel them to the sep-
     aration 65b
     wedded to him . . . through separation 78a
September: thirty days hath September 14a
Series: beginning of the World Series 90a
Sermon: preach a better sermon 49a

sermons in stones 96a
Serpent: sharper than a serpent's tooth 99b
Serve: also serve who only stand and wait 80b
     no man can serve two masters 24b
Service: more essential service to his country 109a
Session: sessions of sweet silent thought 102b
Set: children's teeth are set on edge 24a
Seventh: seventh seal 25b
Seventy: to be seventy years young 61b
Shadow: fills the shadows and windy places 110a
     grasping at the shadow 12a
     I have a little shadow 108b
     shadows of the evening 18a
     valley of the shadow of death 23a
Shaken: to be well shaken 38b
Shakespeare: Shakespeare made use of it first 104a
Shalimar: beside the Shalimar 62a
Shalott: Lady of Shalott 111a
Shangri-la: Shangri-la was not unique 60b
Sharper: sharper than a serpent's tooth 99b
Shave: then rides back to shave again 118a
Shay: wonderful one-hoss shay 61a
Sheep: come to you in sheep's clothing 24b
     wolf in sheep's clothing 12b
Shell: heart is like a rainbow shell 92a
     Sea Shell, Sea Shell 75a
Shelter: right to food, shelter, and clothing 70a
     shelter from the stormy blast 116b
Shepherd: levels the shepherd with the king 36a
     Lord is my shepherd 23a
Sheridan: Sheridan twenty miles away 89a
Shift: coming down let me shift for myself 82a
Shine: his face shine upon thee 22a
Ship: all I ask is a tall ship 77b
     don't give up the ship 70b
     down to the sea in ships 23a
     face that launched a thousand ships 76b
     of shoes—and ships—and sealing-wax 34b
     sail on, O Ship of Fate 74a
     ship is always referred to 84a
     ship has weathered every rack 118a
     ships that pass in the night 74b
     song of ships, and sailormen 75a
Shoe: call for his old shoes 95b
     sailed off in a wooden shoe 50a
     shoe was lost 51b
     shoes—and ships—and sealing-wax 34b
     stood in his shoes and he wondered 68a
Shoemaker: good shoemaker and a poor fish-ped-
     dler 115a
Shoot: shoot, if you must 118b
     shoot the Hippopotamus 19b
Shopkeeper: nation of shopkeepers 11b
Shore: by the shores of Gitchee Gumee 74b
     rapture on the lonely shore 31a
Shorter: shorter by a head 48a

Shot: shot heard round the world 48b
Shout: somewhere children shout 112a
Shouting: timult and the shouting dies 70a
Shut-Eye: in the garden of Shut-Eye Town 50a
Sick: fox . . . answered the sick lion 62b
   made him deathly sick 12a
   nearly all his comrades are sick 114a
Sieve: went to sea in a sieve 71b
Sight: acceptable in thy sight 23a
   first she gleamed upon my sight 120a
Signifying: signifying nothing 100a
Silence: rest is silence 98a
   silence in heaven 25b
Silent: silent church before the service 49a
Silently: as silently steal away 74a
Silk: in silks my Julia goes 60a
Silly: nothing sillier than a silly laugh 35b
Silver: gold and silver becks me 99b
Silvia: who is Silvia? 102b
Simple: levels . . . the simple with the wise 36a
   on the stage, he was . . . simple 55a
   simple as all truly great swindles 60a
   simple faith than Norman blood 111a
   truth is . . . rarely simple 119a
Simplify: Simplify, Simplify 112a
Sin: his sins were scarlet 19b
   saddest sights in a world of sin 57a
   wages of sin is death 25b
   without sin among you 25a
   worst sin towards our fellow creatures 103a
Sincere: with whom I may be sincere 48b
Sing: angels sing thee to thy rest 98a
   he didn't sing to me 107a
   I sing of arms 115a
   I . . . sing myself 118a
   of thee I sing 105a
   sing in the thief's face 67b
   sing me a song, O please 75a
   sing no sad songs for me 92b
   we will sing one song 51a
Singing: I hear America singing 118a
   singing in the Wilderness 68b
   time of the singing of birds 23b
Single: single in the field 121a
   single man in possession of a good fortune 16a
Singularity: singularity . . . invariably a clue 45a
Sinning: more sinned against than sinning 99b
Sister: sisters, and his cousins, and his aunts 54a
   sisters under their skins 69b
Situation: situation is well in hand 41b
Six: six of one and half-a-dozen of the other 77a
Six hundred: rode the six hundred 110b
Skies: skies are not cloudy all day 60b
Skillful: all that was skillful 52b
Skin: escaped with the skin of my teeth 22b
   Ethiopian change his skin 24b

sisters under their skins 69b
Skipped: mountains skipped like rams 23a
Skugg: Skugg lies snug 51b
Sky: as true as the sky 69b
   lay waste the sky 113a
   rainbow in the sky 120b
   that banner in the sky 61b
   to the wild sky 111a
   which prisoners call the sky 119a
Slain: Saul hath slain his thousands 22b
Slave: at the mill with slaves 80a
   Britons never will be slaves 112a
   design . . . to free the slaves 27a
   government cannot endure . . . half slave and
     half free 73a
   in giving freedom to the slave 72a
   slave for livelihood 11a
   whether Americans are to be freemen or slaves
     116b
Slavery: at the price of chains and slavery 60a
Sleep: cannot sleep upon his hillside now 73b
   down to sleep 14a
   first sweet sleep of night 103a
   great want . . . at this present moment is sleep
     59a
   her great gift of sleep 59b
   inventor of sleep 35b
   sleep after toil 106a
   sleep, my little one, sleep 111b
   sleep that knits up 99b
   sleep with their windows open 79a
   talks in some one else's sleep 15b
   time enough for sleep 62b
   to sleep: perchance to dream 97b
Sleeve: wear my heart upon my sleeve 100b
Slept: slept, and dreamed that life was Beauty
   62a
Slide: let the world slide 60a
Slothful: slothful man saith 23b
Slow: slow and steady wins the race 73b
Smile: nods, and becks, and wreathed smiles 80a
   rode with a smile on a tiger 14a
   smiles, tears, of all my life 27b
   when you call me that, smile 120a
   you should forget and smile 92b
Smiling: smiling through her tears 61b
Smite: whosoever shall smite thee 24b
Smith: smith, a mighty man is he 75a
Smoke: smokes a fifty-cent cigar 11a
Smooth: love never did run smooth 100b
Snail: snail's on the thorn 28a
Snark: Snark was a Boojum 34b
Sneeze: beat him when he sneezes 34a
Sneezed: not to be sneezed at 38b
Snow: fleece was white as snow 58a

mourn with ever-returning spring 118a
when the spring comes round 61b
year's at the spring 28a
Spur: Fame is the spur 80b
Staff: rod and thy staff 23a
Stage: all the world's a stage 96b
  frets his hour upon the stage 100a
  no man does for love, but on the stage 46a
  on the stage he was natural 55a
Stair: as I was going up the stair 78b
Stand: now, and where you stand 108b
  stand your ground 85b
Star: bright star, would I were steadfast 68a
  fault . . . not in our stars 98b
  go, and catch a falling star 44a
  great star early dropped 118a
  hitch your wagon to a star 49a
  mistress of the months and stars 109b
  night with her train of stars 59b
  pair of star-crossed lovers 101a
  star that bringest home the bee 31b
  star to steer her by 77b
  stars are shining bright 103b
  stars in her hair were seven 92b
  star-spangled banner 68b
  twinkle, twinkle, little star 110a
Stark: Molly Stark sleeps a widow 106b
Starry: cloudless climes and starry skies 31b
  starry heavens above me 67b
Start: breathe deep, and start 73b
State: I am the state 75a
  idea that a State . . . commits crimes is a fiction 65a
  portentous, and a thing of state 73b
  sail on, O Ship of State 74a
  thirteen states . . . able to support a national government 58a
  within sight of State Street 11a
  worth of a State 79a
Stately: stately homes of England 59b
Stay: stay longer in an hour than others can in a week 63a
Steadfast: bright star, would I were steadfast 68a
Steady: slow and steady wins the race 73b
Steal: who steals my purse 100b
Stealing: for de little stealin' 84b
Steed: his steed was the best 94b
Steel: when the foeman bares his steel 54b
Steep: when life's path is steep 62b
Step: mind the music and the step 17a
Stick: climbing on a yellow stick 12a
  speak softly and carry a big stick 92a
Stiff: stiff upper lip 35b
Still: leadeth me beside the still waters 23a
Sting: fly . . . may sting a stately horse 66b
Stitch: stitch! stitch! stitch! 62a

Stocking: six feet one, in his stocking feet 21a
Stolen: he that has stolen the treasure 38b
Stomach: army marches on its stomach 82b
  heart and stomach of a king 48a
  stomach behave itself, the first day at sea 114a
  through his stomach 119b
  worship God on an empty stomach 119b
Stood: should of stood in bed 65b
Stoop: when lovely woman stoops to folly 55a
Stop: first cries out stop thief 38b
  stop; look; listen 114a
Stories: sad stories of the death of kings 101a
Storm: rides upon the storm 40a
Stormy: port after stormy seas 106a
  shelter from the stormy blast 116b
Story-book: read it in the story-book 61a
Storyteller: good storyteller 37b
Strait: matters not how strait the gate 59b
Strand: I walked into the Strand 66b
Strange: into something rich and strange 102a
  strange what a man may do 111b
Stranger: courteous to strangers 16b
Stray: if with me you'll fondly stray 53b
Stream: large streams from little fountains 49b
  swap horses when crossing a stream 72b
Street: lion is in the streets 23b
  shall fight . . . in the streets 37a
  talking on street corners to scorning men 115a
Strength: as the strength of ten 111b
  hast thou ordained strength 22b
  refuge and strength 23a
  so shall thy strength be 22b
  strength to bear other people's troubles 90a
Stretched: things which he stretched 114a
Strife: madding crowd's ignoble strife 56b
String: chewing little bits of string 19b
  ". . . strings," said Mr. Tappertit 43a
Strive: man errs so long as he strives 55a
Strong: nor the battle to the strong 23b
  only the Strong shall thrive 95b
  strong are just 68b
Struggle: alarms of struggle 15b
  in a contemptible struggle 29a
  struggle for existence 41a
Stuck: stuck fast in Yesterday 42b
Student: student to the end of my days 36b
Study: proper study of mankind is man 88a
Stuffed: we are the stuffed men 48a
Stupidity: against stupidity the gods themselves 94a
Subject: only on different subjects 90b
Sublime: most sublime noise 51a
  my object all sublime 54a
  we can make our lives sublime 74b
Submarine: sighted sub. Sank same 78a
Substance: do not lose the substance 12a

Substitute: in war . . . no substitute for victory 75b
Succeed: if at first you don't succeed 60b
Success: in success, moderate 64b
    success four flights Thursday 121a
Sucker: hello, sucker! 57a
    sucker born every minute 18a
Suckling: mouth of babes and sucklings 22b, 25a
Suffer: suffer the little children 25a
Suffered: folks who ain't suffered much 63b
Sufficient: sufficient unto the day 24b
Sugar-Plum: have you ever heard of the Sugar-Plum Tree? 50a
Summer: after many a summer dies the swan 111b
    bears eternal summer in his soul 61a
    compare thee to a summer's day 102b
    fight . . . if it takes all summer 56a
    in summer quite the other way 108b
    Indian Summer of the heart 118b
    last rose of summer 82a
    made glorious summer 101a
    sumer is icumen in 13a
    summer soldier 85a
Summum: summum bonum 37b
Sun: before the rising sun 116b
    cock who thought the sun had risen 47b
    dies with the dying sun 26b
    force from which the sun 113b
    go out in the midday sun 39b
    Juliet is the sun 101a
    law . . . is the sun 15b
    little less between me and the sun 44a
    little window where the sun 61b
    on which the sun never sets 84a
    Sun and Moon should doubt 26a
    sun is shining bright 112a
Sunday: chicken in his pot every Sunday 59b
    he was in his Sunday best 105b
    Sunday clears away 12a
Sunflower: broad-faced sunflower 18b
Superman: I teach you the superman 84a
Supper: hope is a . . . bad supper 16b
Sure: be always sure you're right 40b
Surpassed: man is something . . . to be surpassed 84a
Surplus: surplus wealth is a sacred trust 33b
Surrender: shall never surrender 37a
    unconditional and immediate surrender 56a
Survival: Survival of the Fittest 41a
Susanna: O, Susanna! 51a
Suspicion: horrible suspicion that electricity was dripping 113a
    must be above suspicion 31b
Swagman: once a jolly swagman 85b
Swain: all our swains commend her 102b

Swallow: come before the swallow dares 102b
Swan: after many a summer dies the swan 111b
    every goose a swan, lad 69b
    swans are geese 15a
Swanee: down upon de Swanee Ribber 51a
Swap: swap horses when crossing a stream 73a
Swear: swear not by the moon 101b
Sweat: blood, toil, tears and sweat 37a
Sweet: lady sweet and kind 51a
    love to get sweets into your list 64a
    nothing half so sweet 82a
    sweet and low 111b
    sweet are the uses of adversity 96a
    sweet will be the flower 40a
    sweets to the sweet 97b
Swift: race is not to the swift 23b
Swim: I will swim this here 61a
Swimmin'-hole: old swimmin'-hole! where the crick 90a
Swindle: simple as all truly great swindles 60a
Swine: pearls before swine 24b
Sword: beat their swords into plowshares 24a
    brave man with a sword 119a
    father's sword he has girded on 82a
    not to send peace, but a sword 24b
    pen is mightier than the sword 75b
Symmetry: fearful symmetry 26a
    spoilers of the symmetry of shelves 70b
Symphony: Beethoven's Fifth Symphony 51a
Szilard: recent work by . . . L. Szilard 47a

T

T: whatever Miss T. eats 42b
Table: buy some flowers for your table 61a
    not your trade to make tables 66b
Tact: tact consists in knowing 38a
Tail: beginning with the end of the tail 34a
    hole where his tail came through 105b
    little lost pup with his tail tucked in 57a
Taken: when taken 38b
Talcum: bit of talcum 83a
Tale: tale told by an idiot 100a
    thereby hangs a tale 96b
Talent: one talent which is death to hide 80a
    Talent does what it can 79a
Talk: hear a man talk about himself 90b
    talk of many things 34b
    women should talk an hour 18b
    would talk like whales 55a

Tall: tall as a crane 104b
  tall oaks from little acorns 49b
Tangled: what a tangled web 94b
Tappertit: ". . . strings," said Mr. Tappertit 43a
Tapping: suddenly there came a tapping 87a
Tara: harp that once through Tara's halls 82a
Tar-Baby: contrapshun what he call a Tar-Baby 59a
Tarry: longer will tarry 45a
Task: though hard be the task 35b
Taste: arbiter of taste 110a
  bud may have a bitter taste 40a
Tattered: tear her tattered ensign down 61b
Taxation: taxation without representation is tyranny 84b
Taxes: death and taxes 51b
Teach: I teach you the superman 84a
Teaches: he who cannot, teaches 103a
Tear: better . . . laughter than . . . tears 88b
  blood, toil, tears and sweat 37a
  nor all your Tears wash out a Word 69a
  remember with tears 12b
  smiles, tears, of all my life 27b
  though our tears thaw not 103a
Tease: because he knows it teases 34a
Tea-tray: like a tea-tray in the sky 34a
Teeth: children's teeth are set on edge 24b
  escaped with the skin of my teeth 22b
Tell: child tells in the street 110a
  kiss and tell 38b
Telling: I am telling you 117b
Temper: woman of . . . uncertain temper 16a
Temperate: more lovely and more temperate 102b
Tempora: O tempora, O mores 37b
Temptation: can resist everything except temptation 119a
  enter not into temptation 25a
Ten: as the strength of ten 111b
Ten thousand: David his ten thousands 22b
Tent: fold their tents, like the Arabs 74a
Territorial: last territorial claim . . . in Europe 61a
Thankless: to have a thankless child 99b
Thanks: what thanks do you get 61a
Thaw: thaw not the frost 103a
Their: theirs but to do and die 110b
Them: them's my sentiments 111b
Theme: choose a mighty theme 78b
Theory: biography . . . life without theory 44a
There: neither here nor there 101a
Thereby: thereby hangs a tale 96b
Thief: first cries out stop thief 38b
  sing in the thief's face 67b
  time, you thief 64a
Thing: things that are God's 25a

with God all things 25a
Think: before him I may think aloud 48b
  he thinks too much 98b
  I think, therefore I am 43a
  thinks with his legs 26a
Thinking: says what everybody is thinking 92a
  thinking makes it so 97a
Thirteen: thirteen states . . . able to support a national government 58a
Thirty: thirty days hath November 55b
  thirty days hath September 14a
This: this above all 97a
Thorn: crown of thorns 28a
  thorns that in her bosom lodge 97a
Thou: Thou Beside me 68b
Thought: comforting thought in time of trouble 77a
  covers all men's thoughts 35b
  happened to hit on the same thought 104a
  no thought for the morrow 24b
  sessions of sweet silent thought 102b
  thoughts of youth are long, long thoughts 74a
  thoughts shall fly 104b
  thoughts, when thou art gone 103b
Thousand: face that launched a thousand ships 76b
  night has a thousand eyes 26b
  Saul hath slain his thousands 22b
  thousand ages in Thy sight 116b
  wind had a thousand words 52b
Thread: plying her needle and thread 62a
Three: stoppeth one of three 38a
  though he was only three 79b
  three lessons I would write 94a
  three little maids from school 54a
Thrice: thrice is he armed 103a
Throat: scuttled ship or cut a throat 31a
Throne: throne of bayonets 64b
Thump: thumps upon your back 39b
Thunder-cloud: any of the thunder-clouds 52a
Thursday: I do not love you Thursday 79a
Thusness: reason of this thusness 116a
Thyself: love thy neighbour as thyself 22a
Tiddely: Tiddely pom 79b
Tide: tide in the affairs of men 99a
  talk of tides of love 40b
Tiger: rode with a smile on a tiger 14a
  Tiger! Tiger! 26a
Tigger: tiggers don't like honey 79b
Time: don't have time to look 119a
  footprints on the sands of time 74b
  he was for all time 67a
  in the time of your life 94a
  it is time to start the flight 73a
  last syllable of recorded time 100a
  no time to stand and stare 41b

old times dar am not forgotten 49a
short on time 47a
"time has come," the Walrus said 34b
time is but the stream 112a
time is like a river 16a
time is money 51b
time is on our side 54b
Time is still a-flying 60a
time is the greatest innovator 16b
time of the singing of birds 23b
time of which we have no knowledge 18b
Time, the subtle thief of youth 80a
time to be born 23b
time, you thief 64a
times that try men's souls 85a
Time-table: sooner read a time-table or a cata-
    logue 78a
Timid: poor little timid furry man 92b
Tiny Tim: Tiny Tim, the last of all 43a
Titwillow: willow, titwillow, titwillow 54b
Toad: intelligent Mr. Toad 56a
    until the Toad in fun 40a
Today: I have lived to-day 46a
    seize today 62b
    which you can do to-day 51b
    woman of to-day 15a
Toe: how cold my toes 79b
Together: must, indeed, all hang together 52a
Toil: blood, toil, tears and sweat 37a
    drab and hopeless round of toil 52b
    let not ambition mock their useful toil 56b
    sleep after toil 106a
    they toil not 24b
    toil and not to seek for rest 75b
Told: I told you so 31a
Toll: curfew tolls the knell of parting day 56a
    for whom the bell tolls 44b
Tom: Tom's no more 31a
Tomb: in the dust, in the cool tombs 93b
Tomorrow: gone tomorrow 19a
    never leave that till to-morrow 51b
    to-morrow, and to-morrow 100a
    to-morrow do thy worst 46a
Tongue: finds tongues in trees 96a
    sharp tongue . . . grows keener 65a
    speak with the tongues of men 25b
Tool: man is a tool-making animal 52a
Tooth: sharper than a serpent's tooth 99b
    tooth for tooth 22a
Top: always room at the top 117a
    looking at the men at the top 38a
Topsy: "Never was born," persisted Topsy 109a
Torment: torments of grief you endured 48b
Torpedo: damn the torpedoes 49b
Toujours: toujours gai, archy 77a
Toves: slithy toves 34b

Tower: burnt the topless towers of Ilium 76b
Town: becomes a small town when it rains 57a
    man made the town 40a
    poor little one-horse town 114a
Toy: when the little toy dog was new 50a
Track: with a golden track 73b
Trade: not your trade to make tables 66b
    two of a trade can ne'er agree 53b
Tragedy: tragedy to those that feel 115b
Train: man who shaves and takes a train 118a
    train up a child 23b
Tramped: frequently tramped . . . through the
    deepest snow 112a
Trampling: trampling out the vintage 63a
Transgressor: way of transgressors 23b
Transit: sic transit gloria mundi 68a
Transportation: surplant surface transportation
    121a
Travel: travel for travel's sake 108a
    travel from Boston to Chicago 44b
    travel . . . to find the beautiful 48b
    travels fastest who travels alone 70a
Traveled: I took the one less travelled by 52b
    travelled among unknown men 120a
Traveler: traveller with empty pockets 67b
Traveling: traveling is almost like talking 43a
Treason: confess to treason 38a
    if this be treason, make the most of it 60a
Treasure: he that has stolen the treasure 38b
Tree: all the trees are green 69b
    all the trees were bread and cheese 13b
    billboard lovely as a tree 83a
    fool sees not the same tree 26b
    have you ever heard of the Sugar-Plum Tree?
        50a
    men . . . like the leaves of the trees 61b
    my apple trees will never get across 52a
    on a tree by a river 54b
    only God can make a tree 69a
    there was an Old Man in a tree 70b
    under the spreading chestnut tree 75a
    when the trees bow down 92b
    woodman, spare that tree 82b
Trial: trial by juries impartially selected 66a
Tribulation: out of great tribulation 25b
Trick: a trick that everyone abhors 19b
Triumph: agony is our triumph 115a
Trojan: ever approved of was the Trojan War 86b
Tropical: parrots, and tropical trees 75a
Trouble: against a sea of troubles 97a
    comforting thought in time of trouble 77a
    has trouble enough of its own 118b
    man is born unto trouble 22b
    strength to bear other people's troubles 90a
    very present help in trouble 23a
Trousers: bottoms of my trousers rolled 48a

never put on one's best trousers 64a
Trout: when you find a trout in the milk 113a
Troy: came from the shores of Troy 115a
True: advantage . . . philosophy . . . substantially
    true 94a
  I hold it true 111a
  ring in the true 111a
  thing that they know isn't true 21a
  to thine own self be true 97a
Trump: last trump 25b
Trumpet: sound the trumpets 82a
Trust: put . . . little trust . . . in the morrow 62b
  surplus wealth is a sacred trust 32b
  trust God 28a
Truth: battle for freedom and truth 64a
  beauty is truth, truth beauty 68a
  mainly he told the truth 114a
  melancholy truth 43a
  pathway to truth 40a
  seek the truth in the groves of Academus 62b
  strict regard for truth 19b
  takes two to speak the truth 112a
  trouthe is the hyeste thing 36b
  truth crushed to earth 28b
  truth is always strange 31b
  truth is never pure 119a
  truth is on the march 121b
  truth shall make you free 25a
  truth that's told with bad intent 26a
  truth universally acknowledged 16a
  truth will conquer 121b
  we hold these truths . . . self-evident 66a
  what is truth? said jesting Pilate 16b
Try: times that try men's souls 85a
  try, try again 60b
Tumult: tumult and the shouting dies 70a
Turn: turn to him the other 24b
Turtle: voice of the turtle 23b
Twain: never the twain shall meet 69b
Tweedledee: Tweedledum and Tweedledee 34b
Tweedledum: Tweedledum and Tweedledee 34b
Twenty: Sheridan twenty miles away 89a
Twenty-four: twenty-four hour day 19a
Twin: one of us was born a twin 71b
Twinkle: twinkle, twinkle, little bat 34a
  twinkle, twinkle, little star 110a
Twinkling: twinkling of an eye 25b
Two: in two words: im-possible 55b
  takes two to speak the truth 112a
  two of a trade can ne'er agree 53b
Typewriter: changing a typewriter ribbon 19b
Tyrannis: sic semper tyrannis 26b
Tyrant: blood of patriots and tyrants 66a
  root from which a tyrant springs 87a

U

Ugly: Ugly Duckling 13a
Umbrella: unjust steals the just's umbrella 26b
Unalienable: certain unalienable Rights 66a
Unborn: fate of unborn millions 116b
Unbowed: my head is bloody, but unbowed 59b
Uncompromising: uncompromising as justice 53b
Unconditional: unconditional and immediate
    surrender 56a
Understand: understand all is to forgive all 106a
  understand only because I love 113a
  understand the minds of other men and
    women 58b
Uneasy: uneasy lies the head 98a
Unhappy: each unhappy family 113a
Union: Liberty and Union 117a
  our Federal Union 65a
  people for whom he saved the Union 65a
  sail on, O Union 74a
  trade unions are the legitimate outgrowth 55b
  Union, sir, is my country 37b
Unique: Shangri-la was not unique 60b
Unite: duty of everyone to unite 71b
  workers of the world, unite 77b
United States: amicable relations . . . between the
    United States and those powers 81a
  United States . . . deliberately attacked 91b
Universe: universe is not hostile 61a
Unjust: unjust steals the just's umbrella 26b
Unknown: travelled among unknown men 120a
Unlucky: so unlucky that he runs into accidents
    77a
  these unlucky deeds relate 101a
Unpopular: society . . . safe to be unpopular 107b
Unsatisfied: keep me still unsatisfied 114a
Untrodden: dwelt among the untrodden ways
    120b
Unwashed: great Unwashed 27a
Unwritten: custom, that unwritten law 41a
Up: up and up, her white lips saying 113a
  up, lad, when the journey's over 62b
  up, Lord 22b
  when they were up 14a
Upper: let not man have the upper hand 22b
Upright: man of life upright 32a
Upstairs: never knew any kicked upstairs 29a
  upstairs and downstairs 79b
  upstairs into the world 38b
Uranium: uranium . . . turned into . . . source of
    energy 47a

Uriah: Uriah, with his long hands 43a
Useless: most useless, peacocks and lilies 93a

V

Vacuum: nature abhors a vacuum 106a
Valiant: valiant never taste of death 98b
Valley: all in the valley of Death 110a
  bicker down a valley 110b
  valley of decision 24a
  valley of the shadow of death 23a
Valor: better part of valour is discretion 98a
  my valour is certainly going 104a
Value: value of life 81a
Vanished: it . . . vanished quite slowly 34a
  softly and suddenly vanished away 34b
Vanity: free from . . . thought of vanity 32a
  name of Vanity Fair 28b
Variation: each slight variation, if useful 41a
Variety: her infinite variety 96a
  variety is the soul 19a
  variety's the very spice of life 40a
Veil: Veil through which I might not see 69a
Veni: *veni, vidi, vici* 31b
Vermont: so goes Vermont 49b
Verse: Book of Verses underneath the Bough
  68b
Vice: boredom, vice and poverty 115b
  no distinction between virtue and vice 66b
  pride the . . . vice of fools 88a
Victim: victim must be found 54a
Victor: to the victors belong the spoils 76b
Victory: grave! where is thy victory 88a
  in war . . . no substitute for victory 75b
  we shall achieve victory 47b
  won some victory for humanity 76a
Vigilance: eternal vigilance 40b
Vigorous: are least vigorous 49a
Village: village smithy stands 75a
Vine: advise his client to plant vines 121a
  little foxes that spoil the vines 24a
Violet: violet by a mossy stone 120b
  violets dim 102b
Viper: generation of vipers 24a
Virginia: crow that flies over the Valley of Virginia 104a
  gentleman speak of Virginia 37b
Virtue: greater virtues to bear good fortune 90a

no distinction between virtue and vice 66b
plant whose virtues have not been discovered 49a
ready way to virtue 27b
Vision: limits of his own field of vision 94b
Vita: *vita brevis* 60b
Voice: her voice was ever soft 99b
  voice of the turtle 23b
Void: without form and void 22a

W

Wag: give them something to wag against 90b
Wage: wages of sin is death 25b
Wagon: hitch your wagon to a star 49a
Wait: also serve who only stand and wait 80b
Waiter: waiter roars it through the hall 70b
Waiting: policy of watchful waiting 120a
Wales: one road runs to Wales 77b
Walk: as men do walk a mile 18b
  mourning figure walks, and will not rest 73b
  she walks in beauty 31b
  yea, though I walk 23a
Wall: shattering walls are thin 114a
  stone walls do not a prison make 75a
  when your neighbour's wall is on fire 62b
Wallop: d'ye think I'd wollop him 21b
Walrus: Walrus and the Carpenter 34b
Wan: pale and wan, fond lover 109a
Wandered: wandered lonely as a cloud 120a
Wandering: wandering minstrel 54a
Want: for want of a nail 51b
  freedom from want 91b
  great want . . . at this present moment is sleep 59a
  I shall not want 23a
War: accursed be he that first invented war 76b
  all their wars are merry 37a
  be a factor in war 121a
  ease after war 106a
  empire founded by war 81b
  if they mean to have a war 85b
  in war, he is daring 39b
  in war . . . no substitute for victory 75b
  in war . . . there are no winners 36a
  let slip the dogs of war 98b
  marching as to war 18a
  midst of a cold war 18a
  Minstrel Boy to the war is gone 82a

neither . . . learn war any more 24a
never . . . a good war or a bad peace 51b
no discharge in the war 69b
older men declare war 62a
only war I ever approved 86b
they don't . . . go to war over it 113b
those who brought war to the Far East 113b
war being at an end 71b
war is an invention 39b
war is hell 104b
you can tell how much war he has seen 78b
Warm: it is warm work 83a
Warrior: who is the happy warrior? 120a
Wary: wary fox in the fable 62b
  wary to the welcome land 28b
Washed: hands and the feet be washed once a
  day 110a
  washed their robes 25b
Washington: Washington, the brave, the wise
  64b
Wasn't: he wasn't there again today 78b
Waste: lay waste our powers 120a
Watch: ef you don't watch out 89a
  watch and pray 25a
  watch that ends the night 116b
Watchful: policy of watchful waiting 120a
Water: bread upon the waters 23b
  do business in great waters 23a
  everybody drinks water 114a
  fetch them water from hither and thither 61a
  leadeth me beside the still waters 23a
  little drops of water 32b
  under water men shall walk 104b
  water, water everywhere 38a
Waterfall: from the waterfall he named her 74b
Watering-pot: pouring a watering-pot over a lily
  70a
Waterloo: at Austerlitz and Waterloo 93b
  battle of Waterloo was won 117a
  every man meets his Waterloo 86b
Watery: see the watery part of the world 78b
Watson: Mr. Watson come here 19a
Wave: what a wave must be 43b
Way: Great White Way 85a
  woman has her way 61b
Weak: body of a weak and feeble woman 48a
  flesh is weak 25a
  weak secure and the peace preserved 68b
  surely the Weak shall perish 95b
Weakness: cannot run away from a weakness
  108b
Wealth: consume wealth without producing it
  103a
  increasing wealth of our times 19a
  surplus wealth is a sacred trust 32b
  wealth of nations 46b

Weary: ploughman homeward plods his weary
  way 56a
  with fingers weary and worn 62a
Weasel: pop goes the weasel 76a
Weather: kind of weather we are having 26a
  some are weather-wise 51b
Web: what a tangled web 94b
Wedded: wedded to him . . . through separa-
  tion 78a
Wedding: bought her wedding clothes 12a
Wednesday: if I loved you Wednesday 79a
Wee: Wee Willie Winkie 79b
Weed: thickly grown with weeds 40a
  what is a weed 49a
Week: all the days that's in the week 32a
  rust of the whole week 12a
  stay longer in an hour than others can in a
  week 63a
Weep: weep, and you weep alone 118b
  weep for Adonais—he is dead 103a
  weep no more, my lady 51a
Weeping: weeping and the laughter 45a
Welcome: advice is seldom welcome 37a
Welfare: anxious for its welfare 29a
Well: it is not done well 66b
West: ever was in the West Country 42b
  go West, young man 57a, 105b
  out of the west 94b
  West is West 69b
Western: playboy of the Western World 110a
Whale: great whales come sailing by 15b
  whale ship was my Yale 78b
What: what's mine is yours 100a
What-is-it: certain what-is-it in his voice 120a
Wheat: better bread than is made of wheat 35b
Where: where are you now 62a
Wherefore: he had a wherefore 30b
Whimper: not with a bang but a whimper 48a
Whispered: secret, for it's whispered 38b
Whistling: whistling to keep . . . from being
  afraid 46a
White: fleece was white as snow 58a
  Great White Way 85a
  see the whites of their eyes
  take up the White Man's burden 70a
  white in the blood of the Lamb 25b
  who will bring white peace 73b
Whither: whither thou goest 22b
Whole: any number less than the whole 58a
Whooping: cure the whooping cough 14a
Why: for every why 30b
  why is this thus? 116a
Wicked: I's wicked—I is 109a
  wicked man that comes after children 61a
Wickedness: depths of wickedness 67b
Wife: Caesar's wife must be 31b

devil . . . having trouble with his wife 86a
here lies my wife 46a
in want of a wife 16a
kill a wife with kindness 101b
not even his own wife 110a
Wig: confess to a . . . wig 38a
Wigwam: stood the wigwam of Nokomis 74b
Wild: and all lost, wild America 21a
   to the wild sky 111a
   where the wild horses fed 52b
Wilderness: singing in the Wilderness 68b
Will: boy's will is the wind's will 74a
   good will toward us, the American people 119b
   knowing that we do Thy will 75b
   man has his will 61b
William: you are old, Father William 34a, 105b
Willie: Wee Willie Winkie 79b
Willing: Barkis is willin' 43a
   spirit indeed is willing 25a
Willow: green willow is my garland 60b
Wind: boy's will is the wind's will 74a
   fair stood the wind for France 45a
   only argument available with an east wind 75a
   thy winds, thy wide gray skies 79a
   who has seen the wind 92b
   wind blows and one year's leaves 61b
   wind had a thousand words 52b
   wind of the western sea 111b
   wind was on the lea 107a
   winds were lovesick with them 95b
Windmill: not giants but windmills 35b
Window: what light through yonder window
   101a
Wine: I'll not look for wine 67a
   Jug of Wine, a Loaf of Bread 68b
Wing: fear lent wings to his feet 115a
   on wings of song 59b
   wings have fanned 28b
   wings like a dove 23a
Winter: English winter—ending in July 31a
   hounds of spring are on winter's traces 110a
   in winter I get up at night 108b
   winter is past 23b
   winter of our discontent 101a
Wisdom: begin to attain wisdom 31a
   measure of his wisdom 59a
Wise: be wise with speed 121b
   I heard a wise man say 62b
   levels . . . the simple with the wise 36a
   none but honest and wise men 11b
   reputed one of the wise man 16b
   same tree that a wise man sees 26b
   'tis folly to be wise 56b
   wise father that knows his own child 100a
   wise man indulges himself not in gossip 110a
Wisely: one that loved not wisely 101a

Wiser: be wiser than other people 36b
   sadder and a wiser man 38a
Wisest: only the wisest of mankind 105a
Wishes: sober wishes never learned to stray 56b
Wistful: with such a wistful eye 119a
Wit: brevity is the soul of wit 97a
   Love and I had the wit to win 76b
   men of wit 109a
   nor all your Piety nor Wit 69a
   so much wit, and mirth, and spleen 11b
Witchcraft: detecting of witchcraft and witches
   47a
Witches: detecting of witchcraft and witches
   47a
   there are witches 27b
Wither: age cannot wither her 96a
   they wither 61a
Witty: stumbling on something witty 16a
Woe: accidents fill the world with woe 104b
   hideous notes of woe 31a
   fig for woe 60a
Woke: woke, and found that life was Duty 62a
Wolf: boy cried, 'Wolf, wolf!' 12b
   wolf also shall dwell with the lamb 24a
   wolf in sheep's clothing 12b
Wolves: ravening wolves 24b
Woman: always remembers a woman's birthday
   52b
   body of a weak and feeble woman 48a
   different woman from her grandmother 15a
   easy to marry a rich woman 111b
   excellent thing in woman 99b
   look for the woman 46a
   sort of woman now 43a
   war . . . fought over a woman 86b
   when lovely woman stoops to folly 55a
   woman as old as she looks 38b
   woman has her way 61b
   woman is only a woman 69b
   Woman Killed with Kindness 60b
   woman of mean understanding 16a
   woman sat in unwomanly rags 62a
   woman seldom asks advice 12a
   woman should be seen, not heard 105a
   woman will always sacrifice herself 78a
   woman yet think him an angel 111b
   woman's business to get married 103a
   woman's preaching is like a dog's walking 66b
   woman's whole existence 31a
Women: not in gossip with women 110a
   other women cloy 96a
   understand the minds of other men and
      women 58b
   women are not so young 19a
   women should talk an hour 18b

Wonder: fill my mind with . . . wonder and awe 67b

  his wonders to perform 40a

  how I wonder what you are 110a

  wonders are many 105a

  wonders in the deep 23a

Wondered: stood in his shoes and he wondered 68a

Wonderful: earth, you're too wonderful 119a

Wood: pleasure in the pathless woods 31a

  two roads diverged in a wood 52b

  woods, or steepy mountain yields 76b

Wooden: sailed off in a wooden shoe 50a

Woodman: woodman, spare that tree 82b

Wool: many go for wool 35b

Word: by every word that proceedeth 22b

  good words for the lips 43a

  live on good soup, not on fine words 80b

  once a word has been allowed to escape 62b

  seldom is heard a discouraging word 60b

  some with a flattering word 119a

  thy word is a lamp 23a

  words of my mouth 23a

Work: all the eating and none of the work 73a

  see the works of the Lord 23a

  work banishes those three 115b

Worker: necessity of workers to protect and defend themselves 55b

  workers of the world, unite 77b

World: all the world as my parish 117a

  all the world is queer 85a

  all the world were paper 13b

  all the world's a stage 96b

  best of all possible worlds 115b

  brave new world 102a

  citizen of the world 16b

  citizens of the world 91b

  from this world to another 87a

  glory of the world passes 68a

  good-by, world 119a

  hand that rules the world 115b

  I am a citizen . . . of the world 105a

  let the world slide 60a

  looks the whole world in the face 75a

  my country is the world 85a

  one half of the world 16a

  our country is the world 53b

  our Great Maker is preparing the world 37b

  pass through this world but once 57a

  shot heard round the world 48b

  some say the world will end in fire 52a

  though the world perish 49b

  way the world ends 48a

  we brought nothing into this world 25b

  when all the world is young, lad 69b

  workers of the world, unite 77b

  world, and they that dwell therein 23a

  world, I cannot hold thee close enough 79a

  world is so full of a number of things 108b

  world is too much with us 120a

  world should . . . take an age-long nap 59a

  World, you have kept faith with me 58b

  world's mine oyster 100b

Worm: why should a worm turn 37b

Worship: can worship God or love his neighbor 119b

  worship God in his own way 91b

Worst: best and the worst of this is 110a

  his worst is better 59b

  worst is yet to come 66b

Worth: acts your man of worth 88b

  never knew the worth of him 90a

  worth of the individuals composing it 79a

Wound: keeps his own wounds green 16b

  that never felt a wound 101a

Wrath: I told my wrath 26a

  wrath to come 24a

Wren: Sir Christopher Wren 21b

  who shall hurt the little wren 26a

Wrestle: he that wrestles with us 29a

Wrigley: all Wrigley had was an idea 90a

Write: Moving Finger writes 69a

Writhe: made a ghastly writhe 43a

Writing: biggest obstacle to professional writing 19b

Written: well-written Life is almost as rare 32a

Wrong: fifty million Frenchmen can't be wrong 57a

  from the wrong notions we have 107a

  I always feel that I must be wrong 119a

  if I called the wrong number 113a

  Incroachment, injustice and wrong 55b

  our country, right or wrong 42b, 94b

Wynken: Wynken, Blynken and Nod 50a

Xanadu: in Xanadu did Kubla Khan 38a

Y

Yale: my Yale College and my Harvard 78b
Yankee: Yankee Doodle came to town 17b
Year: ran a hundred years to a day 61a
Yell: yell like furies when you charge 65b
Yesterday: and all our yesterdays 100a
    stuck fast in Yesterday 42b
Yesteryear: where are the snows of yesteryear?
    115a
Yet: yet it does move 52b
Yo-ho-ho: Yo-ho-ho, and a bottle of rum 108a
Yorick: alas! Poor Yorick 97b
Young: friends . . . compliment him about look-
    ing young 65a

I, being young and foolish 121b
in the spring a young man's fancy 111a
to be seventy years young 61b
too young to understand 27a
when all the world is young, lad 69b
whom the gods favor dies young 87a
young life's before us 14b
young man not yet 16b
young person, who either marries or dies 16a
Yours: what is yours is mine 100a
Youth: pleasures with youth pass away 105b
    thoughts of youth are long, long thoughts 74a
    Time, the subtle thief of youth 80a
    youth . . . must fight and die 62a
    youth of labour 55a
    youth replies, I can 48b
    youth shows but half 28a
    youth, who bore, 'mid snow and ice 74a
Yukon: Law of the Yukon 95b

LIST OF AUTHORS